Albert Schweitzer's Ethical Vision

A Sourcebook

Albert Schweitzer's Ethical Vision

A Sourcebook

EDITED BY
PREDRAG CICOVACKI

UNIVERSITY PRESS

2009

OXFORD
UNIVERSITY PRESS

Oxford University Press, Inc., publishes works that further
Oxford University's objective of excellence
in research, scholarship, and education.

Oxford   New York
Auckland   Cape Town   Dar es Salaam   Hong Kong   Karachi
Kuala Lumpur   Madrid   Melbourne   Mexico City   Nairobi
New Delhi   Shanghai   Taipei   Toronto

With offices in
Argentina   Austria   Brazil   Chile   Czech Republic   France   Greece
Guatemala   Hungary   Italy   Japan   Poland   Portugal   Singapore
South Korea   Switzerland   Thailand   Turkey   Ukraine   Vietnam

Published by Oxford University Press, Inc.
198 Madison Avenue, New York, New York 10016

www.oup.com

Oxford is a registered trademark of Oxford University Press

Library of Congress Cataloging-in-Publication Data
Schweitzer, Albert, 1875–1965.
[Essays. English. Selections]
Albert Schweitzer's ethical vision : a sourcebook / edited by Predrag Cicovacki.
    p. cm.
Includes bibliographical references and index.
ISBN 978-0-19-537788-0; 978-0-19-537789-7 (pbk.)
1. Ethics.   I. Cicovacki, Predrag.   II. Title.
B2430.S374A25 2009
170—dc22   2008025761

9 8 7 6 5 4 3 2 1

Printed in the United States of America
on acid-free paper

Contents

Part III "My Life Is My Argument": The Application of the Ethics of Reverence for Life

Albert Schweitzer's Ethical Vision

A Sourcebook

Introduction

I have given up the ambition to become a great scholar, I want to be more—*simply a human.*

—Albert Schweitzer

I. Schweitzer's Life

A narrow path leads uphill from the village of Gunsbach, into the thick woods. After a five-minute climb, one comes to a clearing with a huge rock and a beautiful view of the Munster valley beneath. This place was Albert Schweitzer's favorite spot. Since 1969, next to the rock, there rises a monument in honor of Schweitzer. Built out of Alsatian sandstone, the monument is the work of Fritz Behn, a disciple of Auguste Rodin. The monument is located at this hidden spot, rather than in front of Schweitzer's house, because he wanted it that way: "It is there I should like to remain in stone, so that my friends could pay me a visit, devote a thought to me, and could listen to the murmur of the river, the music that accompanied the flux of my thoughts. It is on this rock that civilization and ethics was born and the Jesus in his epoch emerged to me. There I feel completely at home."[1]

1. Quoted from the Web site of the Albert Schweitzer Museum in Gunsbach, France: www. schweit zer.org/english/assoc/asegun.htm.

Schweitzer enjoyed the solemnity of this place many times during his long life. He was born in Kaysersberg, Alsace, on January 14, 1875. He grew up in nearby Gunsbach, which was then part of Germany but nowadays belongs to France. Schweitzer was raised bilingual (or trilingual, if one also counts the Alsatian dialect of German, spoken at home). He grew up in a tight community in which the local Protestants and Catholics sometimes had their church services together. Schweitzer's father was a Protestant pastor, a gentle and generous man. His mother was more practical, more knowledgeable of world affairs, perhaps also more intelligent. At an early age Schweitzer learned to play piano and soon afterward organ as well. In 1893 Schweitzer went to Strasbourg to study theology and philosophy but also made frequent visits to Paris, where he studied organ with the famous organist and composer Charles-Marie Widor. After graduating from the University of Strasbourg in 1898, Schweitzer made a firm decision to dedicate his life to humanity when he turned thirty. Without a concrete plan for pursuing this calling, he decided, for the time being, to continue his studies of philosophy, theology, and music in Strasbourg, Paris, and Berlin. In 1889 he obtained his PhD, having written a thesis on Kant's religious philosophy (published in English as *The Religious Philosophy of Kant*) and began preaching at St. Nicholas Church in Strasbourg. A year later, he received his licentiate in theology, with a thesis on the Last Supper and the messianic consciousness of Jesus (published in English as *The Mystery of the Kingdom of God*). In 1905 he published a monumental book on Johann Sebastian Bach (*J. S. Bach*), and a year after his most controversial and still influential book on the life and mission of Jesus (published in English as *The Quest of the Historical Jesus*).

Having already written major books in three different fields, and having been appointed the chair of the Protestant Theological Seminary in Strasbourg, Schweitzer decided to abandon his academic and musical career at the age of thirty in order to study medicine; he wanted to devote the rest of his life to being a physician to the natives of Africa.

Schweitzer's plan encountered powerful resistance. Among his family and friends there was only one person who fully supported Schweitzer's decision: Hélène Bresslau. Inspired by him, she qualified as a nurse and decided to tie her fate to that of Schweitzer. They were married in 1912 and left together for Africa on Good Friday, March 26, 1913. They settled in Lambaréné, in Equatorial Africa, which presently belongs to Gabon. The medical situation in this part of Africa was desperate:

At the time he arrived there, he was the only medical doctor in a thousand-square-mile area between the Congo and the Gold Coast, in malaria-infested West Equatorial Africa, serving a few miles south of the equator in the world's most uncomfortable tropical climate. It was from this area in West Africa that most of the slaves sold into bondage in the New World had been shipped. Libreville, in the Gulf of Guinea, was named after those liberated slaves returned by the English and French men-of-war. Unfortunately, their campaign was a losing battle against slave traders in the early nineteenth century. Schweitzer knew this local history, and it reinforced his commitments to devote himself . . . to Africa and the reparations he felt the white man owed the black.[2]

Schweitzer was overwhelmed by work in the hospital but, by the sheer determination of his powerful will, he managed to dedicate an hour or two to practicing music and to his intellectual work almost every evening.[3] The plan for his most important philosophical work, *The Philosophy of Civilization*, was conceived on his rock above Gunsbach in 1900 but matured only during his stay in Africa. In fact, what in 1923 finally appeared under the title *The Philosophy of Civilization* is only the first two parts of the conceived four-volume work. The first part, *The Decay and the Restoration of Civilization*, is relatively short, and it deals more with the destructive shift toward the material aspect of civilization and away from its spiritual counterpart rather than with any detailed vision for its restoration. The second and much longer part, *Civilization and Ethics*, outlines Schweitzer's understanding of the history of Western ethics and then develops his antidote to the decay of civilization: the ethics of reverence for life. The third part was to deal in detail with the ideology of reverence for life, and the fourth with the state. These volumes would have analyzed a history of European social and political movements and the life of society from the standpoint of reverence for life. Despite writing hundreds of pages of notes, Schweitzer never completed the last two parts.[4] Instead, he offered numerous popular expositions of the ethics of reverence for life (e.g., *The Primeval Forest, Christianity and the Religions of the World, African Notebook, Out of My Life and Thought: An Autobiography, The Story of My Pelican,* and *The Teaching of Reverence for Life*).

2. Quoted from George Marshall and David Poling, *Schweitzer: A Biography* (New York: Albert Schweitzer Fellowship and Pillar Books, 1975), 292.

3. For valuable descriptions of the daily life in Schweitzer's hospital, see, for instance, Clara Urquhart, *With Dr. Schweitzer in Lambaréné* (London: George C. Harrap, 1957); Frederick S. Franck, *Days with Albert Schweitzer: A Lambaréné Landscape* (New York: Holt, Rinehart and Winston, 1959); and Edgar Berman, *In Africa with Schweitzer* (Far Hills, NJ: New Horizon, 1986).

4. Schweitzer's writings and notes for the third part of his project—approximately one thousand pages—have been recently published in two volumes as Albert Schweitzer, *Die Weltanschauung der Ehrfurcht vor dem Leben,* ed. Claus Günzler and Johann Zürcher (München: C. H. Beck, 1999–2000).

6   INTRODUCTION

When he needed rest and more funding for the hospital, Schweitzer would return to his beloved Gunsbach. From there, he made trips to various parts of Europe to give concerts and lecture tours. In 1949, he also came to the United States, where he enjoyed enormous popularity and financial support. In 1950, opinion polls revealed that Americans believed him to be the greatest non-American who had ever lived, and countless magazine articles about him were published, with astonishing titles such as: "Man of Our Century," "The Greatest Man in the World," "The Great Men's Greatest Man," "Man of God," "God's Own Man," "The Greatest Christian," and "The Thirteenth Disciple."[5] Throughout the 1950s honorary degrees and awards were pouring in from all parts of Europe: election to the French Academy of Moral and Political Sciences, King Gustav Adolf's Prince Charles Medal for his great humanitarian achievements, the Nobel Peace Prize, the British Empire's Order of Merit, and the West German order *Pour le Mérite*. Schweitzer was perturbed by all this publicity, for when he first went to Africa he had nothing else in mind but to alleviate pain in some place where no medical help was previously available.

What disturbed Schweitzer even more than his sudden prominence were the flocks of journalists who started chasing him not only through Europe but even when he was in Lambaréné. They all wanted to know what Schweitzer was thinking about current political problems, such as the nuclear arms race and the decolonization of Africa. When Schweitzer accepted the challenge, the audience did not like what he had to say. He accused the governments of the nuclear powers of an irresponsible arms race, not only because of their cover-up of the danger of radioactive fallout but, more importantly, because of the potential destruction of all human life. With Jean Rostand, Schweitzer argued that the continuation of nuclear testing is "the crime projected into the future."[6] In the West, his insistence that the superpowers renounce nuclear testing and his calls to the U.S. government to do so unilaterally were perceived as signs of sympathizing with the Communists. He provoked even more outrage with his views on the future of Africa. Schweitzer warned that most African nations are tribally divided and are not yet ready for full independence. He predicted that, without further economic and cultural development, many newly formed countries would end up entangled in vicious civil wars. Several government and public figures in Africa accused him of "white-hat imperialism" and demanded

5. See, for instance, "Reverence for Life," *Time*, July 11, 1949. For detailed discussion of this fascination with Schweitzer, see James Brabazon, *Albert Schweitzer: A Biography*, 2nd ed. (Syracuse, NY: Syracuse University Press, 2000), 396–416.

6. Quoted from Marshall and Poling, *Schweitzer*, 282.

that he leave Africa for good.[7] These sentiments were soon echoed in the North-ern Hemisphere. In 1963 *Time* magazine published the most derogatory article to date, full of inaccurate information about Schweitzer's hospital and his opin-ions. Under the title, "Albert Schweitzer: An Anachronism," the author of the article concluded that Schweitzer "lives in the Africa of 1913, hardly knowing or caring that a continent and a century have passed him by."[8]

Since Schweitzer was not interested in fame but in alleviating the pain of those around him, he continued to live according to the same principles—simplicity in personal lifestyle, passion for truth, and reverence for all life—that he had followed long before he became "the greatest man in the world" and then "the worst public enemy of progress and democracy." The last sev-eral years of his life, Schweitzer did not travel. He lived in the seclusion of the African jungle, working during the day and playing music and writing at night. On January 14, 1965, Schweitzer celebrated his ninetieth birthday in Lambaréné, and stopped working in the hospital only a month before he died, on September 4. He was buried near his hospital, at a place similar to his favorite spot above Gunsbach.

II. Schweitzer's Conception of Philosophy

Schweitzer may be better known as a theologian, or as a humanist, or even as a musician, but he considered himself primarily a philosopher. Yet he was not a philosopher of a usual theoretical bent. Schweitzer summed up his conception of philosophy by declaring: "My life is my argument."[9] This connection between life and argument, practice and theory, was important to him in both direc-tions. First, the occasions for arguments and reflections are not mere abstract ideas but life in its numerous manifestations. Second, arguments and reflec-tions are significant only insofar as they can be practiced and lived. Schweitzer did not think of philosophy as a primarily academic discipline but believed it

7. See Manuel M. Davenport, "The Moral Paternalism of Albert Schweitzer," *Ethics* 84 (1973–1974): 116–27. Schweitzer wrote about his attitude toward the natives of Africa and the malaise of colonialism in all of his autobiographical writings. For his most explicit statements regarding these issues, see "The Relations of the White and Coloured Races," *Contemporary Review* 133 (1928): 65–70; and *Primeval Forest*, trans. C. T. Champion (New York: Pyramid Books, 1963). For further discussion, see Brabazon, *A Biography*, 427–42; George N. Mar-shall, *An Understanding of Albert Schweitzer* (New York: Philosophical Library, 1966), 115–46.

8. "Albert Schweitzer: An Anachronism," *Time*, June 21, 1963. Very damaging for Schweitzer's reputation were James Cameron's three articles for the *News Chronicle*, later reprinted in his autobiographical book *Point of Departure* (London: Arthur Barker, 1967). Also very critical was Gerald McKnight's book *Verdict on Schweitzer: The Man behind the Legend of Lambaréné* (New York: John Day, 1964).

9. For the emergence and explanation of this phrase, see Norman Cousins, *Dr. Schweitzer of Lambaréné* (New York: Harper and Brothers, 1960), 195. See also Marshall and Poling, *Schweitzer*, 260.

is important for every human being. Jesus and Paul, or Bach and Goethe, were for him philosophers as much as Socrates and Kant. He looked at them as philosophers because of their non-dogmatic and insightful thinking, and their outstanding actions and personalities. Their search for truth and their dedication to the highest ideals of humanity are central not only for philosophy in a narrow sense but for every aspect of life.

For most of us, Bach is a composer and Goethe is a poet; they are artists, not philosophers. Schweitzer did not see things in terms of such dividing categories. He held that we apply them in order to classify people and their works according to the artistic form they use. Yet a closer look at the great works of art unmistakably displays what they have in common: art is the medium for the transmission of ideas. The art of Bach, like the art of Goethe, does not exist for the sake of entertainment, or for the sake of art itself. Like Jesus and Paul, and like Socrates and Kant, Bach and Goethe were concerned with the ideas regarding the spiritual aspect of human existence. Together with rationality, spirituality was for Schweitzer an essential aspect of philosophy.

Schweitzer was often criticized for not separating philosophy from religion (referring primarily to Christianity), but for him they had a common core and served complementary functions. In his view, religion does not deal with life after death but with a spiritual way of life here and now. The most original and significant contribution of Jesus, according to Schweitzer, was the ethics of love, or the ethics of altruism. Schweitzer argued that ethics is the core of religion and treated Jesus as an ethical exemplar, not as a supernatural being. Religion is based on ethics, not the other way around. Yet religion and philosophy contribute different, although equally indispensable and complementary, elements to ethics. Religion focuses on love, which is the highest manifestation of spirituality, while philosophy contributes critical, non-dogmatic thinking, which is the highest manifestation of rationality. Unlike his contemporary, the famous theologian Karl Barth, who insisted that religion has nothing to do with thinking, Schweitzer believed (to paraphrase Kant) that philosophy without religious concerns is empty, and religion without philosophical thought is blind.[10] For Schweitzer, the central concern that brings together religion and philosophy was the following one: can Jesus' ethics of love, the ethics of altruism, be grounded in thought? Put differently: can there be a rational philosophy that compels adherence to the ethics of altruism? Schweitzer hoped for an affirmative answer to both questions, and his entire philosophical project can be seen as an elaborate defense of this affirmation.

10. Jackson Lee Ice similarly pointed out this Kantian rendering of the complementary functions of religion and philosophy; see Ice, *Schweitzer: Prophet of Radical Theology* (Philadelphia: Westminster, 1971), 20. Kant's original statement was that "thoughts without content are empty, intuitions without concepts are blind"; *Critique of Pure Reason*, trans. P. Guyer and A. W. Wood (New York: Cambridge University Press, 1998), 193–94 (A51/B75).

Despite his admiration for religion and philosophy, Schweitzer was critical of the ways in which they were practiced. He was critical of contemporary religion not only because it stubbornly followed the path of dogma but also because it abandoned its role as a moral guide. What was even worse, in times of war institutionalized religion put itself in the service of short-term political and economic interests. Schweitzer's criticism of modern philosophy developed along similar lines but was more detailed. He examined the role of philosophy in the context of the decline of civilization. "Civilization" (*Kultur*) means continued cultivation, and since the ultimate aim of civilization is the moral and spiritual perfecting of individuals and of humanity as a whole, the central role of philosophy must be normative: philosophy should articulate how we can live meaningful and fulfilled lives. Schweitzer was convinced that, in the last few centuries, philosophy had abandoned this fundamental orientation in two ways. First, philosophy had drifted away from considering the most elementary and fundamental problems of human existence. Instead, philosophers had become preoccupied with a number of complex issues of secondary importance or, even worse, with pseudo-problems that emerged from their obsession with ideas detached from real life (Can we refute an evil demon argument? Can we prove that the external world exists? Are mind and body two separate substances, or two properties of the same substance?). Second, impressed by the advancement of natural science and in the attempt to turn philosophy into one such science, philosophers had shifted their focus toward making quantifiable and tangible achievements, rather than perfecting individuals and humanity as a whole. This misdirection of philosophy had an enormous impact on the disorientation of civilization:

> The disastrous feature of our civilization is that it is far more developed materially than spiritually. . . . [A] civilization which develops only on its material side, and not in corresponding measure in the sphere of the spirit, is like a ship with defective steering gear which gets out of control at a constantly accelerating pace, and thereby heads for catastrophe.[11]

In order to explain in more detail how philosophy contributed to this predicament, Schweitzer borrowed from Goethe three criteria of a plausible philosophical orientation:

1. Does it approach nature without preconceived theories?
2. Does it include a profound ethical idea?

---

11. Schweitzer, *The Philosophy of Civilization*, trans. C. T. Campion (Amherst, NY: Prometheus Books, 1987), 86.

3. Does it have the courage, when it arrives at the ultimate problems raised by research and thought, to admit that there are mysteries that cannot be fathomed, or does it rather presume to offer a system which explains everything?[12]

The very first criterion put Schweitzer at odds with most modern philosophers, from Descartes and Leibniz, to Kant and Hegel. While ancient Greek philosophers found the inspiration for their philosophical thinking in wonder at the complexity and beauty of nature, which they then tried to explain in their theories, modern philosophers reversed this approach. What they took for granted was mind, not nature. Even when the existence of the external world was not doubted, nature was treated as something of secondary importance: as a dead mechanism, or as a material for the satisfaction of human needs and desires. Schweitzer believed that this *contemptus mundi* of modern philosophers had done considerable damage to our understanding of nature and our place and role in it. In their analytical zeal, modern philosophers had separated God from nature, humanity from the world, body from soul, intellect from will, and reason from emotion. Not surprisingly, then, they had experienced enormous difficulty in trying to explicate how these various aspects constantly interact with each other.

Schweitzer's own approach was decidedly synthetic, not analytic. In his theological writings, Schweitzer realized that we need to bring together emotions and reasoning, heart and mind. From his medical practice Schweitzer learned that, although he must attend to bodily suffering first, he must treat body and soul as one. His philosophical approach was similarly characterized by a conscious attempt to bring together seemingly opposed elements into harmony with each other. Just as he insisted that the truths of emotion and the truths of reason belong together, Schweitzer argued in favor of the essential interconnectedness of thought and action. His approach was centered on trying to heal the deepest wound of modern philosophy, the seemingly irreconcilable mind–body dualism, which significantly contributed to the unbalanced position of the material and the spiritual aspects of civilization.[13]

The second criterion of a plausible philosophical approach is important because "the ethical is the highest truth and the highest practicality."[14] Schweitzer

12. Schweitzer, "Goethe the Philosopher," in Schweitzer, *Goethe: Five Studies*, trans. C. R. Joy (Boston: Beacon, 1961), 102 [reprinted in this volume, p. 194].

13. Martin Buber emphasized this aspect of Schweitzer's contribution to philosophy, together with Schweitzer's attempt to overcome another deep wound of Western philosophy, that of the gap between nature and God, which was the central project of Buber's own religious philosophy; see Buber's short essay on Schweitzer, "A Realist of Spirit," in *To Dr. Albert Schweitzer: A Festschrift Commemorating His 80th Birthday*, ed. Friends of Albert Schweitzer (New York: Profile, 1955), 11–13. For further discussion of the similarities between Buber and Schweitzer, see J. L. Ice, *Prophet of Radical Theology*, 124–25.

14. Schweitzer, *Philosophy of Civilization*, 84 [reprinted in this volume, p. 113].

did not think that he thereby changed the common understanding of civilization, for at least European civilization has always had a positive attitude toward the world and life ("the world- and life-affirmation"). One of the fundamental mistakes of Western philosophy, however, was that it took for granted that the view of life—and with it an ethical ideal, and its conception of meaning of life—must be derived from its view of the world. In other words, knowledge has to be the foundation for ethics and for our conception of what makes life worth living. Schweitzer argued against this "cognitivistic optimism" and maintained that the opposite is true: science and knowledge cannot discover anything in reality that would demonstrate that the world is essentially good or that life has a predetermined meaning. Life is a riddle that reason can never fully penetrate: "But what life is, no science can tell us."[15]

Schweitzer warned that there are two fundamental dangers for every civilization: endorsing the ideals that do not correspond to reality, and endorsing no ideals at all. Since they have no grounding in reality, the first kind of ideals can be sustained only by means of stubborn dogmatism or fanaticism. Schweitzer thought that it is no less dangerous not to have any ideals at all. Our appropriately critical reaction to unfounded dogmatism and fanaticism should not lead to the relativization of all moral values and principles. Relativism is dangerous not only because it lowers our standards but also because it often leads to indifference and apathy, to a complete decline of a civilization's ethical and spiritual aspects. The attitude of world- and life-affirmation, usually taken for granted in the West, turns then into its opposite: optimism deflates into pessimism.

When he complained against an exaggerated development of the material aspect of civilization, Schweitzer did not argue against further development of science and technology. As a physician, he appreciated the discovery of new medications, medical instruments, and procedures, and applied them readily in his practice. What worried him was the insufficient presence of the ethical and spiritual ideals that would guide the development of science and technology toward serving the highest interest of humanity. In the absence of such ideals, science and technology may end up poisoning the environment and developing powerful weapons that can destroy all life on this planet.

Philosophy should not be, or even attempt to be, value neutral, but must serve as the moral and conscientious guide for the entire human race. Yet, through knowledge, philosophy can accomplish neither this leading role, nor the ethical ideal it has to pursue. Schweitzer thought that most modern philosophers refused to accept this conclusion and failed the third criterion of a plausible

15. Schweitzer, *Philosophy of Civilization*, 308 [reprinted in this volume, p. 136].

philosophical approach; instead of finding courage to admit the insurmountable boundaries of human reason, they insisted on advancing rationality beyond its natural limits. Philosophers then introduced various ad hoc arguments, more for the sake of the coherence of their systems than because they were convinced of the correspondence of their thoughts to reality.

Schweitzer believed that the highest credo of all critical thinking—"reverence for truth"—demands that we acknowledge when and where we have reached the limits of rationality. When rational thinking is pursued to its logical end, it arrives at something non-rational that, nevertheless, may be a necessity of thought. When philosophers try to eliminate this non-rational element, their thoughts lead to views of the world and life that lack both vitality and validity. The acceptance of the necessary limits of reason forces us to recognize that "the last fact which knowledge can discover is that the world is a manifestation, and in every way a puzzling manifestation, of the universal will to live."[16] This realization of the limits of knowledge also compels us to recognize the indispensability of mysticism. Schweitzer distinguished his own understanding of mysticism from what went by the same name in earlier European thought (e.g., Master Eckhart) and in India. While those types of mysticism were cognitive—they affirmed an intuitive grasp of the unity and the identity of all beings ("the world-spirit and the spirit of man"), Schweitzer's own brand of mysticism was agnostic and ethical: whether the world-spirit and the spirit in man are identical, we can never know; we are led to believe in the fundamental unity of all beings only by loving self-devotion to all life. What ultimately connects human beings with all other forms of life is not intelligence and knowledge but the inwardly experienced will.[17]

III. The Ethics of Reverence for Life

While contemporary analytic philosophers are reluctant to admit the existence of insurmountable limits to human rationality, their continental counterparts accept such limits as a postulate. They believe that the acceptance of such limits does not lead to a deterioration of philosophy but rather to its synthetic integration with other aspects of human experience. In their views, in exhibiting its own limitations, rational thinking opens up onto other aspects of society,

16. Schweitzer, *Philosophy of Civilization*, 76 [reprinted in this volume, p. 107].

17. Schweitzer offered a most detailed discussion of mysticism in *The Mysticism of Paul the Apostle*, trans. William Montgomery (Baltimore: Johns Hopkins University Press, 1998). For further elaboration of the distinction made in the text, see Schweitzer, *Indian Thought and Its Development*, trans. Mrs. Charles E. B. Russell (Boston: Beacon, 1936), chapters 1 [reprinted in this volume, pp. 33–43] and 16, pp. 1–18 and 250–265. For further discussion, see Henry Clark, *The Ethical Mysticism of Albert Schweitzer* (Boston: Beacon, 1962).

world, and life. For contemporary philosophers like Levinas, that other aspect is religion. For Habermas and Horkheimer, it is sociology. For Hannah Arendt, Adorno, Derrida, or Foucault, it is politics. For Heidegger and Benjamin, it is aesthetics. For Schweitzer, the recognition of the limitations of rational thought led primarily to a renewed focus on ethics. His novel approach consisted in recognizing that life was the central philosophical and ethical category. Despite our scientific and philosophical advances, life remains a mystery. Our best and perhaps only path toward experiencing this mystery is not through knowledge but through will. Schweitzer did not understand will in a way usually done by Descartes and the early British empiricists, that is, as a faculty of choice. Rather, his conception was closer to that of Schopenhauer and Nietzsche. Will was for him primarily a drive to continue and develop life, an urge to live life to its full potential.[18] For this reason, Schweitzer usually referred to will as "will to live."

According to Schweitzer, ethics consists in the affirmation of all life and the devotion to it, independent of our knowledge of the world. Put differently, ethics consists in the transformation of the will to live into the will to behave responsively toward all living beings, which Schweitzer called "reverence for life." His description of how he came upon this conception is quite illuminating:

> For months on end I lived in a continual state of mental agitation. Without the least success I concentrated—even during my daily work at the hospital—on the real nature of the affirmation of life and of ethics and on the question of what they have in common. I was wandering about in a thicket where no path was to be found. I was pushing against an iron door that would not yield.
>
> All that I had learned from philosophy about ethics left me dangling in midair. The notions of the Good that it had offered were all so lifeless, so unelemental, so narrow, and so lacking in content that it was impossible to relate them to an affirmative attitude.
>
> Moreover, philosophy never, or only rarely, concerned itself with the problem of the connection between civilization and concepts of the worldview. The affirmation of life in modern times seemed so natural that no need was felt to explore its meaning.

---

18. J. L. Ice compares Schweitzer's will to live to a psychoanalytic rendering of this issue: "While Freud introduced into psychology what is called the pleasure principle, or the will to pleasure; and Adler made us conversant with the role of the will to power as a main factor in human behavior; and while, more recently, Victor Frankl, a one-time Freudian psychiatrist now a psychotherapist, stresses the will to meaning, Schweitzer speaks of the will to live, which includes all of the above and several other important factors that he believes more adequately account for man's nature"; *Prophet of Radical Theology*, 101.

To my surprise I recognized that the central province of philosophy into which my reflections on civilization and the worldview had led me was virtually unexplored territory. Now from this point, now from that, I tried to penetrate to its interior, but again and again I had to give up the attempt. I saw before me the concept that I wanted, but I could not catch hold of it. I could not formulate it.

While in this mental state I had to take a long journey on the [Ogowe] river. I was staying with my wife on the coast at Cape Lopez for the sake of her health—it was in September 1915—when I was called out to visit Madame Pelot, the ailing wife of a missionary, at N'Gômô, about 160 miles upstream. The only transportation I could find was a small steamer, which was about to leave, towing two overloaded barges. In addition to myself, only Africans were on board, among them my friend Emil Ogouma from Lambaréné. Since I had been in too much of a hurry to arrange for enough provisions for the journey, they invited me to share their food.

Slowly we crept upstream, laboriously navigating—it was the dry season—between the sandbanks. Lost in thought I sat on the deck of the barge, struggling to find the elementary and universal concept of the ethical that I had not discovered in any philosophy. I covered sheet after sheet with disconnected sentences merely to concentrate on the problem. Two days passed. Late on the third day, at the very moment when, at sunset, we were making our way through a herd of hippopotamuses, there flashed upon my mind, unforeseen and unsought, the phrase "*Ehrfurcht vor dem Leben*" ("reverence for life"). The iron door had yielded. The path in the thicket had become visible. Now I had found my way to the principle in which affirmation of the world and ethics are joined together![19]

Schweitzer came to believe that ethics consists in the transformation of the natural drive to live, or the will to live, into the will to behave responsively toward all living beings, which he called "reverence for life." In its original German form, this phrase, *Ehrfurcht vor dem Leben*, contains a sense of awe, which we cannot translate into a suitable English expression. The word *Ehrfurcht* means literally "fear before an overwhelming force." This word suggests respect carried to an ultimate degree, and the acknowledgment of immensity

---

19. Schweitzer, *Out of My Life and Thought: An Autobiography*, trans. A. B. Lemke (Baltimore: Johns Hopkins University Press, 1998), 154–55.

and awesome power. The whole phrase, *Ehrfurcht vor dem Leben*, thus means respect for life, which is understood as being far more than sheer existence. Religious, ethical, and mystical elements are already implied in this attitude, in this bow before the sublime and inexplicable mystery that we call life.[20]

Schweitzer drew attention to the fact that the phrase "reverence for life" was never used before. When he was less intent on emphasizing the novelty of his approach, Schweitzer turned toward the connectedness of reverence for life with past religious and philosophical traditions. In his various writings, he mentioned six sources of his inspiration: (1) the spiritual aspect of reverence for life, as derived from Jesus' ethics of love; (2) the development of the ideal of self-perfection, as derived from the virtue ethics of Socrates, Plato, and Aristotle; (3) the ideal of brotherhood of all human beings, as developed by the Stoics; (4) the view that no life should be destroyed or harmed, as postulated by Jainism; (5) the idea of the essential interconnectedness of all beings, as developed by Buddhism; and (6) the monistic and pantheistic affirmation of the natural world, as advocated by Lao-tse, Chwang-tse, and the philosophy of Taoism. All these sources are integrated into Schweitzer's most detailed philosophical argument in favor of the ethics of reverence for life, as presented in his book *The Philosophy of Civilization*.[21]

Schweitzer introduced the ethics of reverence for life in three steps. He first prepared the ground by arguing against Descartes' "cogito" argument, which served as the foundation of modern philosophy. The primary concept may well be "I am." But what am I? The subject demands the predicate. Descartes concluded that he is a thinking being and a thinking substance, and from there went on to derive the existence of God, the existence of his body, and the rest of the world. Schweitzer rejected this line of thought. What I am aware of, first of all, is that I am life that wills to live. But that is not all. It is equally clear that I do not exist in isolation. The corollary is, therefore, that I am life that wills to live surrounded by other lives that will to live.[22] In Schweitzer's words,

20. For further discussion of the meaning of "reverence for life," see Brabazon, *A Biography*, 268–87; J. L. Ice, *Prophet of Radical Theology*, 99–125; Werner Picht, *The Life and Thought of Albert Schweitzer*, trans. Edward Fitzgerald (New York: Harper and Row, 1964), 88–127; and Robert Payne, *The Three Worlds of Albert Schweitzer* (New York: Thomas Nelson and Sons, 1957), 128–31.

21. For Schweitzer's own best account of these sources, see his essay "The Problem of Ethics in the Evolution of Human Thought," in Jacques Feschotte, *Albert Schweitzer: An Introduction*, trans. John Russell (Boston: Beacon, 1955), Appendix 2, 114–30 [reprinted in this volume, pp. 163–75]. For a valuable discussion, see Picht, *Life and Thought*, 108–10; Ara Paul Barsam, "Albert Schweitzer, Jainism, and Reverence for Life," in *Reverence for Life: The Ethics of Albert Schweitzer for the Twenty-First Century*, ed. Marvin Meyer and Kurt Bergel (Syracuse, NY: University of Syracuse Press, 2002), 207–45; and Ara Paul Barsam, *Reverence for Life: Albert Schweitzer's Great Contribution to Ethical Thought* (New York: Oxford University Press, 2008), 55–73.

22. My reconstruction of Schweitzer's argument relies here on George Seaver, *Albert Schweitzer: The Man and His Mind* (New York: Harper and Brothers, 1947), 284.

With Descartes, philosophy starts from the dogma: "I think, therefore I exist." With this paltry, arbitrarily chosen beginning, it is landed irretrievably on the road to the abstract. It never finds the right approach to ethics, and remains entangled in a dead world- and life-view. True philosophy must start from the most immediate and comprehensive fact of consciousness, which says: "I am life, which wills to live, in the midst of life, which wills to live." This is not an ingenious dogmatic formula. Day by day, hour by hour, I live and move in it.[23]

Schweitzer considered will as more elementary than knowledge, reason, or consciousness: will to live is the metaphysical center of every living individual and stands behind all manifestations of life. The initial awareness of that will is the awareness of its urge to live. From "I am life, which wills to live," we must advance to an anti-solipsistic realization that "I am life, which wills to live, in the midst of life, which wills to live." This important expansion of the horizon of the most elementary consciousness advances us toward the reverence for life proper:

Ethics consists . . . in my experiencing the compulsion to show to all will to live the same reverence as I do to my own. There we have given us that basic principle of the moral, which is a necessity of thought. It is good to maintain and to encourage life; it is bad to destroy life or to obstruct it.[24]

This understanding of good and evil implies that life is intrinsically valuable or, as Schweitzer would say, that all life is sacred. The ethics of reverence for life derives from an inner necessity, or an inner compulsion: ethics is the devotion to all life inspired by reverence for life. The key point here is that, despite an appearance to the contrary, reverence for life is a complex attitude. It can be neither reduced to Christian caring, compassion, and love for other human beings nor identified with the Buddhist sense of the unity with all beings. Schweitzer correctly called attention to the positive and active side of this attitude, for which he found inspiration in ancient Greek philosophy: reverence for life involves a drive toward a full development of one's human potential and a drive toward individual perfection. In this context Schweitzer often mentioned the relevance of sincerity and an uncompromising dedication to truth. Ethics carries within itself the impulse of life to realize its highest ideal.

---

23. Schweitzer, *Philosophy of Civilization*, 309 [reprinted in this volume, p. 137].
24. Schweitzer, *Philosophy of Civilization*, 309 [reprinted in this volume, pp. 137–38].

In his essay, "The Ethics of Reverence for Life," Schweitzer enumerated six defining characteristics of the ethics of reverence for life. First, this ethics is rational because it is developed as a result of thinking about life. Thinking was, for Schweitzer, significantly broader than knowledge and rationality: "Thinking is the argument between willing and knowing that goes on within me"[25] and that performs two essential functions: it "must lead us from the naïve to a deepened world- and life-affirmation, and must let us go on from mere ethical impulses to an ethics that is a necessity of thought."[26] Second, this ethics is absolute, not merely in terms of being opposed to what is relative but also in terms of being contrasted to that which is practicable and achievable. The ethics of reverence for life aspires toward the highest and ultimate ideals, without accepting compromises. Third, the ethics of reverence for life is universal insofar as it applies to all living beings: "It says of no instance of life, 'This has no value.'"[27] Fourth, the ethics of reverence for life promises no external reward— no virtue and happiness—but only the ennoblement of spirit. This ethics has spiritual significance insofar as it seeks to attain harmony with the mysterious Spirit of the universe. Such a harmony is accomplished by the community of life, not by the community of thought, that is, by reverentially serving this Spirit rather than by understanding it. Only in loving self-devotion to life do we realize our spiritual union with an infinite Being. Fifth, the ethics of reverence for life is natural in the sense in which Hume claims that sympathy is natural. Sixth, Schweitzer argued that this sympathy, which lies at the bottom of reverence for life, is part of our psychological makeup. By using several examples, Schweitzer tried to show that even animals display the rudiments of such sympathy. Yet, although necessary for morality, this natural sympathy is far from being sufficient. We need to develop it in the direction of highest spirituality.

The obvious opposites to the attitude of reverence for life are not only (1) killing, harming, and coercing other living beings but also (2) attitudes of contempt, insensitivity, and indifference. More subtle opposites to the attitude of reverence for life include (3) our attempts to master the world, as manifested through manipulating, intervening, controlling, using, abusing, and exploiting various fragments of the world. This Hegelian "master–slave" dialectic is totally foreign to the attitude of reverence for life, which calls for our participating in and appreciating the world. Reverence for life is about accepting, adjusting, caring, and responding to all living beings as sacred.

---

25. Schweitzer, *Philosophy of Civilization*, 308 [reprinted in this volume, p. 136].

26. Schweitzer, *Philosophy of Civilization*, 278. In his first sermon on "Reverence for Life," Schweitzer emphasizes that reason and heart must work together; see Schweitzer, *Reverence for Life: Sermons 1900–1919*, trans. Reginald H. Fuller (New York: Irvington Publishers, 1980), 108–17.

27. Schweitzer, "The Ethics of Reverence for Life," 188 [reprinted in this volume, p. 159].

Schweitzer furthermore contrasted the ethics of reverence for life to (4) thoughtlessness, egotistical self-assertion, and the ethics of society. Reverence for life demands constant thoughtfulness because it cannot be expressed in terms of moral precepts valid for all situations; it necessitates that we adjust our attitudes to the problems at hand. Reverence for life also calls for a restriction of egotistical self-assertiveness because it requires that we dedicate ourselves to the service of others. Nonetheless, to serve others does not mean to lose one's own personality. As the greatest "enemy" of the ethics of reverence for life, Schweitzer listed the "ethics of society," which he believed had dominated our civilization for at least a few centuries. The ethics of society imposes certain "supra-personal" obligations on individuals (e.g., patriotism, the common good, happiness of the largest possible number of people); it demands that, whenever such supra-personal obligations clash with our personal recognition of what we ought to do, the preference should be given to supra-personal obligations. Schweitzer argued that the ethics of society is pseudo-ethics, for we must serve society without abandoning ourselves to it. The only valid test of morality is whether or not our actions and attitudes promote humanity and life in general. In Schweitzer's words: "The conceptions of good and evil that are put in circulation by society are paper-money. . . . The collapse of civilization has come about through ethics being left to society. . . . Previous generations have made the terrible mistake of idealizing society as ethical."[28]

IV. Critical Examination of Schweitzer's Ethics

Schweitzer's ethical approach is quite original, and not easy to classify. Although his ethical theory is normative, strictly speaking it is neither deontological nor teleological. In Schweitzer's theory, concepts such as justice, rights, utility, and happiness play a secondary role. His criticism of the ethics of society indicates that he was never a supporter of consequentialism. Schweitzer considered Kant's categorical imperative to be superior to any utilitarian calculus yet emphasized that, for the exalted character of the moral law, Kant paid the price of having it devoid of all content; Kant gained profundity at the cost of vitality.

Schweitzer's ethical approach appears closer to the ancient ethics of virtue than to the modern ethics of conduct, for he was more interested in how one should live than in what one should do. Nonetheless, reverence for life should not be identified with virtue in its original sense of excellence (*arete*), but is primarily an attitude of responsiveness to other living beings. Schweitzer

---

28. Schweitzer, *Philosophy of Civilization*, 327–28 [reprinted in this volume, pp. 151–52].

believed that the central problem of any ethics is "the problem of a basic principle of morality founded on thought."[29] Reverence for life does not offer specific instructions with regard to our behavior in the world, but it provides us
with such a principle and encourages a healthier and more reverential attitude
toward all living beings.

Any radical position invites a number of objections and criticisms. Schweitzer's ethics of reverence for life is no exception, and we will consider several
of them. One of the most obvious criticisms deals with the universality of this
ethical approach. Schweitzer claimed that all life is sacred, but it is difficult to
accept this position. Why would the lives of invisible microbes or dangerous
animals be sacred? Why should we have any reverence for the lives of annoying
animals, such as flies and mosquitoes? What is so sacred about a number of
plants that are not used for food or medications and that do not seem to serve
any useful purpose?

This criticism can be answered from a holistic point of view: all life is inter-
connected and creates one biosphere. Even the organisms that appear useless
and harmful contribute to a delicate balance that, if disturbed, could endanger
the lives of the beings considered valuable and useful.

This point of view is nowadays defended by the advocates of environmental ethics, and this is why reverence for life plays an important role in their
discussions.[30] Schweitzer was very sympathetic to this approach, and the tes-
timonies of many doctors and nurses who worked in Schweitzer's hospital
community confirm that Lambaréné was a model of ecological responsibility.
Yet Schweitzer's reasoning put an even stronger emphasis on the view that,
ethically speaking, we cannot make any justified distinction in the value of living beings. We do make such distinctions on pragmatic and instrumentalist
grounds, but they are different from purely ethical considerations. According
to Schweitzer, each life is driven by the same urge, the same will to live, and
each one of them has an ethically equal right to life. Once we recognize that
our own will to live is one among infinitely many, we can but acknowledge not
only the interdependence of all life, as in the approach presented above, but the

29. Schweitzer, *Philosophy of Civilization*, 105.

30. See, for instance, John A. Passmore, *Man's Responsibility for Nature* (New York: Charles Scribner's Sons,
1974), 121–24; J. Baird Callicott, "Non-Anthropocentric Value Theory and Environmental Ethics," *American Philosophical Quarterly* 21 (1984): 299–309; J. Baird Callicott, "On the Intrinsic Value of Nonhuman Species," in *The
Preservation of Species: The Value of Biological Diversity*, ed. Bryan G. Norton (Princeton, NJ: Princeton University
Press, 1991), 47–56; Lawrence E. Johnson, *A Morally Deep World* (New York: Cambridge University Press, 1991),
134–41; Joseph R. DesJardins, *Environmental Ethics: An Introduction to Environmental Philosophy* (Belmont, CA:
Wadsworth, 1993), 147–51. See also Lois K. Daly, "Ecofeminism, Reverence for Life, and Feminist Theological Eth-
ics," in *Liberating Life: Contemporary Approaches in Ecological Theology*, ed. Charles Birch, William Eaken, and Jay
B. McDaniel (Maryknoll, NY: Orbis Books, 1990), 86–110.

entitlement of every organism to sustain and promote its existence. Even if the recognition that "I am life which wills to live, in the midst of life which wills to live" is not a sufficient condition for the proper ethical attitude and the recognition of sacredness of all life, it is a necessary condition of reverence for life.

A more difficult objection deals with Schweitzer's claim that the ethics of reverence for life is absolute. In this point he followed Kant, who maintained that absolute ethics is not concerned with whether it can be achieved. Kant developed the absoluteness of his ethics in terms of our respect for the moral law, but his approach left open the issue of content: "to justify the name, absolute ethics must be so not only in authority, but in matter of content as well."[31]

Schweitzer argued that this content is provided by reverence for life that treats every life as sacred. Yet he himself was fully aware of the paradox that life can exist only at the cost of other life. We kill in order to get food and to protect ourselves from dangerous diseases. If killing is inevitable, does that not show that life has no intrinsic value? More generally, does not the inevitability of killing demonstrate that there is something internally inconsistent with Schweitzer's ethics of reverence for life?

Schweitzer recognized the problem and offered a solution that he thought only strengthened his position further. Ordinarily, we accept that compromises and sacrifices must be made. Our mistake consists in making virtue out of necessity, and then accepting the relativity of ethical values. My killing of another life in order to survive is accepted as morally justified, but Schweitzer maintained that it is not: "All destruction of and injury to life, under whatever circumstances they take place, [the ethics of reverence for life] condemns as evil."[32] The practicality and usefulness of our decisions to destroy another life in order to survive do not make such acts moral, nor do they absolve us of moral responsibility toward the life destroyed. A lesser of two evils is still an evil.

Schweitzer's critics proposed that he resolve this issue of necessary killing by moderating some of his central claims. He could hold, for example, that reverence for life does not imply the sacredness of life, and certainly not the sacredness of all life. Schweitzer was emphatically opposed to such suggestions. He instead proposed that we should make a distinction between necessary and unnecessary killing, and also that we must accept an overwhelming sense of responsibility and guilt.

Both proposals are highly controversial. Consider first the distinction between necessary and unnecessary killing. According to Schweitzer, "Whenever I injure life of any sort, I must be quite clear whether it is necessary.

31. Schweitzer, "The Ethics of Reverence for Life," 187 [reprinted in this volume, p. 159].
32. Schweitzer, Philosophy of Civilization, 317 [reprinted in this volume, p. 143].

Beyond the unavoidable, I must never go, not even with what seems insignificant."[33] There are plenty of cases in which the distinction between necessary and unnecessary killing is clear enough. If I am walking through the woods, I can be careful and sidestep the insects on the path in front of me (as Jains do). Or I can avoid all killing of animals for the sake of pleasure (in the form of recreational hunting and fishing). There are, however, many examples when it is far from obvious what is necessary and what is not. The obscurity arises not only because of the complexity of those situations but also because the very concept of necessity is not easily definable. In order to preserve one life, we need to kill another; but why give preference to any one life over any other? Did not Schweitzer argue that there is no ethically justified distinction between living organisms?

The whole issue is even more complicated when we remember the double aspect of reverence for life: good consists (1) in preserving life and (2) in furthering it. In order to preserve one life, it may be necessary to kill another. But may it not also be necessary to kill another life in order to enhance the life we favor? Or does necessity arise only with respect to the negative aspect of reverence for life? Regardless, when deciding if killing is necessary, must not Schweitzer resort to the same anthropocentric, pragmatic, or instrumentalist criteria he rejected when he defended the universality and absoluteness of his ethics?

Schweitzer did not think so. He first pointed out that no general principle could be given that would resolve all possible cases:

> It is not by receiving instruction about agreement between ethical
> and necessary that a man makes progress in ethics, but only by com-
> ing to hear more and more plainly the voice of the ethical, by becom-
> ing ruled more and more by the longing to preserve and promote
> life, and by becoming more and more obstinate in resistance to the
> necessity for destroying or injuring life.[34]

Like Gandhi, Schweitzer insisted that our decision concerning when it is necessary to kill another life depends not only on the universal sanctity of life, nor only on the context and its pragmatic and utilitarian considerations, but also on the level of our ethical maturity. The more we develop our sense of reverence for life, the more responsive and caring we will be toward other living beings. Schweitzer hoped that, with the cultivation of our moral sensitivity, the line that separates necessary from unnecessary killing will gradually shift, so that what,

33. Schweitzer, *Philosophy of Civilization*, 318 [reprinted in this volume, p. 144].
34. Schweitzer, *Philosophy of Civilization*, 317 [reprinted in this volume, p. 144].

in the past, appeared to be cases of necessary killing do not look so anymore. Yet, when we have to kill, when there is no other acceptable solution to the problem at hand, we need to kill with reverence.

Thus, Schweitzer did not maintain that killing should never be allowed. His position was more balanced. While he was unequivocal about claiming that the expression of the command not to kill is one of the greatest events in the spiritual history of mankind, he did not assume that this absolute prohibition could be carried out fully. Schweitzer ascribed the initial pronouncement of the command not to kill to Jainism, which was later accepted by Hinduism and other religious traditions. Yet he praised Gandhi for his flexible approach and his realization that, despite the absolute nature of this prohibition, the fate of animals was probably sadder in India than in any other country. Gandhi's own principles demanded complete compassion toward animals, rather than blind submission to a commandment against killing them. Gandhi offended many of his Hindu adherents when he ended the suffering of a calf in prolonged agony by giving it poison. Schweitzer sided with Gandhi in this particular case and insisted that Gandhi compelled Hindu ethics to come to grips with reality. Like Gandhi, Schweitzer refused to exclude the demands of reality from his own ethics of reverence for life. The confrontation with reality involves conflicts that require us to make what can only be subjective decisions. Yet we live truthfully only when we experience these conflicts in all their profundity.

The confrontation with reality forced Schweitzer to accept that killing of other lives will always continue. Life is full of conflicts, but the existence of such conflicts is not necessarily a sign that there is something wrong with his ethical theory. Reverence for life "offers itself as the realistic answer to the realistic question of how man and the universe are related to each other."[35] Nevertheless, reverence for life is not a matter of charity, not an attitude that we may or may not take toward other lives. Reverence for life is our moral obligation; it is an absolute moral obligation. This belief led Schweitzer to argue that the ethics of reverence for life implies an unlimited responsibility toward other living beings: "In the matter also of our relation to other men, the ethics of reverence for life throw upon us a responsibility so unlimited as to be terrifying."[36]

It is far from clear that "terrifying responsibility" and "constant guilt" really follow from the core of the ethics of reverence for life, or that Schweitzer himself should defend such a radical stance.[37] "Responsibility" must be proportionate

---

35. Schweitzer, *Out of My Life and Thought*, 233.

36. Schweitzer, *Philosophy of Civilization*, 320 [reprinted in this volume, p. 145]. For further discussion, see Brabazon, *A Biography*, 280–87.

37. For further discussion, see Mike W. Martin, *Albert Schweitzer's Reverence for Life: Ethical Idealism and Self-Realization* (Burlington, VT: Ashgate, 2007), 21–24.

to our deeds. An unlimited responsibility obscures the difference between the meritoriousness of our acts, and perhaps also between the necessary and unnecessary killing of living beings. Furthermore, would not such a constant and unlimited sense of guilt and responsibility be paralyzing, for no matter what we do in the present or the future, the same sense of guilt and responsibility would persist? Schweitzer urged moral agents to act; but for our engagement to make sense, there must be a sense of responsibility proportionate to human activity.

Various commentators explained Schweitzer's excessive preoccupation with guilt as "overly Lutheran." They pointed out that one of the German words that Schweitzer uses, *Schuld,* means both "guilt" and "indebtedness." We should put emphasis more on the latter rather than on the former meaning, and think of regret, responsibility, and healthy realism, rather than constant guilt, as the appropriate response to the never fully satisfactory decisions we must make.[38]

While these suggestions are reasonable, it is important to realize that the reason for Schweitzer's emphasis on guilt was ethical, not theological. The sense of guilt in question has essentially to do with the high standards and ideals that the ethics of reverence for life establishes. This guilt is due not only to the awareness of how far we are from achieving the full development of the ideal of civilization, but even more so to the awareness of how feeble our efforts are to live up to the high standards that the ethics of reverence for life sets for us. The fact that the ideals of this ethics are never fully achievable is no excuse for our lack of enthusiasm, commitment, and effort to make the world better than it is. Every ethics deserving of its name, thought Schweitzer, must contain some absolute elements; it must demand of us what is actually beyond our strength. "Take the question of man's duty to his neighbor. The ethics cannot be fully carried out, without involving the possibility of complete sacrifice of self."[39] When we refrain from such sacrifices, we should feel a sense of guilt and responsibility because there is so much more that we could have done for our neighbors and for living beings in general.

One further objection to Schweitzer's ethics of reverence for life concerns his sometimes confusing differentiation between rationalism and mysticism (together with the related distinctions between knowledge and will, reason and spirit). Although Schweitzer maintained that one virtue of his ethics was that it is based on thought and reflection, he seemed equally eager to limit, and, in some cases, even dismiss, the relevance of knowledge and rationality. He

---

38. See Marvin Meyer, "Introduction," xiii, and Mike W. Martin, "Rethinking Reverence for Life," 181–83, both in *Reverence for Life: The Ethics of Albert Schweitzer for the Twenty-First Century,* ed. Marvin Meyer and Kurt Bergel. For further development of this line of criticism, see Mike W. Martin, *Albert Schweitzer's Reverence for Life,* 55–64.

39. Schweitzer, "Ethics of Reverence for Life," 187 [reprinted in this volume, p. 159].

argued that our knowledge of the world cannot be the foundation of ethics and that, moreover, our knowledge brings into doubt whether the world is created with any purpose and by an intentional agent. All life for him was a mystery, and science would never be able to resolve this riddle. Thus, instead of basing ethics on a rational worldview, Schweitzer maintained that our ethical outlook must be based on our life view, which is the contribution of our emotions and intuitions or, as he also put it, of the experience of our will to live. Ethics thus becomes a self-devotion to all life, a life- and world-affirmation that is independent of our knowledge of the universe.

Schweitzer's line of reasoning invites numerous questions. Did he not too quickly dismiss the contribution of science and rationally oriented philosophy? Did he not resort too easily to mysticism? Did he really give us a clear sense of direction when he claimed that the goal of civilization is the spiritual perfecting of every individual, which he then interpreted in the sense of reverence for and unity with all living beings? Could he not defend the ethics of reverence for life without resorting to sacredness, spirituality, and the mystical unity of all beings?

Schweitzer's reply was that he was not a defender of irrationalism and obscure spirituality. As he poignantly explained in the preface to *Ethics and Civilization,*

> All valuable conviction is non-rational and has an emotional character because it cannot be derived from knowledge of the world but arises out of the thinking experience of our will to live, in which we stride out beyond all knowledge of the world. It is this fact that the rational thought that thinks itself out to a conclusion comprehends as the truth by which we must live. The way to true mysticism leads up through rational thought to deep experience of the world and of our will to live.[40]

Even if Schweitzer was right about this, he could not deny that the attitude of reverence for life is constantly in conflict with itself. In its countless manifestations, life clashes with other life; the creative force is, at the same time, the destructive force. All life, Schweitzer agreed with the pessimist Schopenhauer, involves suffering and death. How, then, can we resolve the issue of optimism and pessimism? Does the ethics of reverence for life lead to optimism, or does it entangle itself in the maze of optimism and pessimism?

---

40. Schweitzer, *Philosophy of Civilization,* 80–81 [reprinted in this volume, p. 111].

Schweitzer did not always help resolve this issue. What he did state clearly was that his position is a mixture of pessimism and optimism: he was an agnostic and theoretical pessimist, but he nonetheless considered his brand of ethical mysticism to be of an optimistic kind. As he phrased it, "My knowledge is pessimistic, but my willing and hoping are optimistic."[41] Pessimism signifies world- and life-denial, the logical outcome of which is the extinction of the will to live, and Schweitzer admitted that he was pessimistic about the current situation in the world: "I see before me, in all its dimensions, the spiritual and material misery to which mankind has surrendered because it has renounced thinking and the ideals that thought engenders."[42] But this pessimism was not his last word: "Because I have confidence in the power of truth and of the spirit, I believe in the future of mankind. Ethical acceptance of the world contains within itself an optimistic willing and hoping that can never be lost. It is, therefore, never afraid to face the somber reality as it really is."[43]

Schweitzer's optimism, the "optimism notwithstanding," as his critic Oskar Krauss called it, is "groundless" and "unfounded."[44] No rational thought can ground and found it, and Schweitzer was the first to admit that. Yet did his confidence "in the power of truth and of the spirit" entitle Schweitzer to assert that truth and spirit will triumph in the world?

Our optimism may be rationally "groundless" and "unfounded," but it is not irrational and illusory if we think that the ethics of reverence for life, when taken seriously and applied widely, may help our civilization recuperate. Yet, whether the truth and the spirit will triumph, whether our planet will ever turn into the Kingdom of God, no ethical view that aspires toward any respectability can assert.

V. Relevance of Schweitzer's Ethics

Schweitzer's ethics of reverence for life stands in need of further development. The most urgent area of improvement deals with providing a more detailed handling of what is generally called conflicts of values. We simply do not have enough guidelines with regard to when killing of other lives is necessary.

41. Quoted from Schweitzer's epilogue to *Out of My Life and Thought*, 242 [reprinted in this volume, p. 241]. For further discussion of optimism and pessimism, see *Philosophy of Civilization*, 94–100.

42. Schweitzer, *Out of My Life and Thought*, 243 [reprinted in this volume, p. 241].

43. Schweitzer, *Out of My Life and Thought*, 243 [reprinted in this volume, p. 242].

44. Oskar Krauss, *Albert Schweitzer: His Work and His Philosophy*, trans. E. G. McCalman (London: Adam and Charles Black, 1944); quotes are from pages 37, 40, and 57.

Schweitzer said that he cannot give a general rule and that much of it depends on the context and on how developed our moral sense is. This is all true, but it is not all that can be done. There are further distinctions that need to be taken into account; for instance, the one between intentional and unintentional killing. What should also be provided is a more systematic analysis of various types of conflicting situations and conflicting values. Roughly speaking, some of them deal with the preservation of the entire human species, some with the preservation of smaller groups or individuals. Then there are types of situations in which killing occurs in order to enhance, rather than merely sustain, one's existence. The modes of enhancement (scientific, cultural, educational, technological, etc.) can be compared and ranked. In ranking them, there is no reason to consider the choices between our ethical criteria for such decisions on the one hand, and pragmatic and utilitarian criteria on the other, in terms of an irreconcilable either/or dichotomy. We cannot but use both kinds of standards, and their interdependence should be more carefully examined.

What this consideration suggests is ultimately a need to develop Schweitzer's ethics in the direction of an elaborate theory of value. Reverence for life would certainly be the central value of such a theory, yet it would not be the only one. Like Isaiah Berlin, Schweitzer was a value pluralist, which means that a map of values (including those of justice, love, happiness, compassion, truthfulness, and so on) should be carefully developed. Berlin promoted a stronger version of pluralism (the diverse values cannot be unified), whereas Schweitzer defended its weaker version (despite the existence of diverse and non-reducible values, reverence for life is the most important moral value).[45] The relationship of the value of reverence for life to a whole network of connected values needs to be further elaborated. Such elaborations will not eliminate the burden of making decisions with regard to when it is permissible to kill another life, but they may considerably assist us in making such difficult choices.

Schweitzer's theory should also be developed in the direction of a systematic philosophical anthropology. The coordinate system of such anthropology is already outlined by the ethics of reverence for life. On the one hand, human life is one among many forms of life, all of which deserve our reverence and devotion. On the other hand, we cannot but treat other forms of life from the human point of view; when Schweitzer talks about the situations in which it is inevitable to kill other forms of life, he mostly has a human point of view in mind. In a Schweitzer-inspired anthropology, the task of humanity would be to

---

45. For Isaiah Berlin's view, see his two classical essays: "The Pursuit of the Ideal," and "Two Concepts of Liberty," both reprinted in Berlin, *The Proper Study of Mankind* (New York: Farrar, Straus and Giroux, 1998), 1–16, 191–242. I make the distinction between the stronger and weaker versions of pluralism following Robert Nozick, *Philosophical Explanations* (Cambridge, MA: Harvard University Press, 1981), 447.

harmonize with nature and other living creatures, rather than to exploit them for the short-term gains. Unlike most thinkers, Schweitzer would put will and spirit, rather than reason and consciousness, in the center of his anthropological conception. This bare outline of an anthropological theory may sound promising, but how fruitful such an approach would be cannot be said without further development.

Schweitzer's ethics of reverence for life also contains within itself the seeds of a promising political philosophy. In this philosophy, moral values would have the principal role. In "Toward Perpetual Peace," the essay to which Schweitzer alluded in several of his writings, Kant insisted that politics must bend its knee in front of morality. Schweitzer would expand Kant's principle and say that economy must also bend its knee in front of morality. When this is not the case, humanity is pushed from one war to another, from one form of colonization to another. In the triangle of economy, politics, and ethics, that dominates our lives, the only hierarchy that can create a foundation for perpetual peace and cooperation among nations is the one in which ethics dominates from the top of the triangle.

Schweitzer considered our civilization, the civilization in which economy and politics take precedence over morality, as analogous to a sick patient. He diagnosed this patient as very ill because it lives an unbalanced life whose habits, if unchanged, might easily lead to the patient's self-destruction. He prescribed what he believed to be a fairly simple cure for its regeneration: (1) cooperation between the material and the spiritual aspects of civilization; (2) faith in humanity, idealism, and thoughtfulness; and (3) a focus on the individual, for only the spiritual transformation of individuals can lead to a desired regeneration. All three points are implicit in his ethics of reverence for life.

Schweitzer diagnosed the malaise of our civilization accurately. His prescription also pointed in the right direction. His main mistake consisted in underestimating how vastly more complicated civilization is than an individual patient, and, consequently, how vastly more complex it is to cure an entire civilization. Schweitzer's prescription appears good for the initial stages of the treatment, but it unquestionably demands supplementation.

Despite his plans and efforts, Schweitzer did not succeed in completing his ethics of reverence for life. Thus, we must appraise this ethical outlook as Schweitzer left it. We could approach this task in various ways, but I suggest that we here follow Iris Murdoch's view that the essential questions of every ethical theory are: (1) What is a good man like? (2) How can we make ourselves morally better? and (3) Can we make ourselves morally better?[46]

46. Iris Murdoch, *The Sovereignty of Good* (London: Routledge, 2001), 51.

Most ethical theories, especially those dealing with the ethics of conduct, address the first and the third questions in passing, and discuss the second question in detail. Schweitzer's answer to the second question was his theory of reverence for life, but he also paid considerable attention to the third question, which Murdoch declared to be "a central problem in moral philosophy." In her formulation, the problem amounts to the following: "How is one to connect the realism which must involve a clear-eyed contemplation of the misery and evil of the world with a sense of uncorrupted good without the latter idea becoming the merest consolatory dream?"[47] Schweitzer treated this problem very seriously, and his struggle to find a viable path between pessimism and optimism was his response to this problem.

Despite the uncontested significance of the second and third questions, it may nonetheless be the case that the most important question is the first one: What is a good man like? This question deserves full attention, and Schweitzer clearly understood its relevance: "If any age lacks the minds that force it to reflect about the ethical, the level of its morality sinks, and with it its capacity for answering the questions that present themselves."[48] To answer the first question, Schweitzer used the examples of Socrates and Jesus, Goethe and Gandhi; but his own life and work also provide more than an adequate illustration of what a good man is like. For Schweitzer, it was more important to set an example than to provide a strict ethical code. Let us then clarify exactly what kind of example he provided.

Schweitzer's friend and admirer Albert Einstein once remarked: "There must be, after all, an indestructible good core in many people. Or else they would never have recognized [Schweitzer's] simple greatness."[49] Schweitzer also believed in that "indestructible good core in many people." There is, however, a significant gap between that good core in most of us and what his personal example and his ethics of reverence for life demand of us. Schweitzer's example opened many eyes to the misfortune and suffering of human beings not only in Africa but all over the world. In every unspoiled soul this awareness creates a desire to render active assistance to those in need. Yet, in most of us, this desire results in a passing concern and a quickly forgotten impulse. Life brings new stories and creates new heroes, while the old ones fade away.

Schweitzer himself was different than most of us because in him that good core and that desire to help others led to a changed lifestyle and a lifelong commitment. He knew well what was at stake: "I have given up the ambition

47. Murdoch, *Sovereignty of Good*, 59.
48. Schweitzer, *Philosophy of Civilization*, 103.
49. Albert Einstein, "Out of Inner Necessity," in *To Dr. Albert Schweitzer: A Festschrift Commemorating His 80th Birthday*, 38.

to become a great scholar, I want to be more—*simply a human.*"[50] This imperative—to be human, to become more human than he already is—was the central
motivation of Schweitzer's thought and his life and his personal answer to the
question: What is a good man like? It is also the foundation of the lasting legacy
of Albert Schweitzer: no matter what objections we may have to his philosophy
of reverence for life, Schweitzer's example should always serve as a reminder
that our ultimate goal is to be more than we already are: human, in the full
sense of this word.

50. Schweitzer's letter to Hélène Bresslau, February 25, 1905; quoted from *The Albert Schweitzer—Hélène
Bresslau Letters 1902–1912*, ed. Rhena Schweitzer Miller and Gustav Woytt, trans. Antje Butman Lemke (Syracuse,
NY: Syracuse University Press, 2003), 65. According to Lewis Mumford, "Albert Schweitzer's life, therefore, is
a sign and a pledge. His life says, better than any book he has written, that however deeply our own lives suffer
from the passive breakdown or the active destruction of our civilization, it is still possible to create a plan of
life based on more solid foundations and directed toward higher ends: a life more organic in structure, more
personal in expression, no longer the victim of specialism, nihilism, and automatism"; *The Conduct of Life* (New
York: Harcourt Brace Jovanovich, 1970), 214–15.

PART I

A Foundation of the Ethics of Reverence for Life: Philosophy of Religion and Philosophy of Civilization

1

Western and Indian Thought

In the Preface of his book Indian Thought and Its Development, *Schweitzer admits that as a young man he became interested in Indian thought while reading Schopenhauer. His interest proved to be lifelong because Indian ethics stresses our relations not only with other human beings but with all living creatures. Schweitzer outlines two major differences between the two schools of thought, which help us understand some of the categories that underlie his entire philosophical outlook. While the Western view is, in principle, life- and world-affirming, Indian thought is almost exclusively life- and world-negating. Life- and world-affirmation consists in human beings' regarding their existence as something of value in itself; accordingly, they strive to perfect as much of their existence as possible. Life- and world-negation consists in regarding our existence as meaningless and sorrowful, which leads to a mortification of the self or to a renunciation of all activity that aims at the improvement of life conditions in this world. The second major difference between the two traditions is that Western thought is mostly dualistic and rationally oriented, whereas Indian thought is almost exclusively monistic and mystical. Although Schweitzer favors the life- and world-affirmation of Western thought, he gives preference to the mystical monism of Indian philosophy. He believes that, even though our natural impulses lead us toward life- and world-affirmation, the dualistic worldview does not square with facts. It is the monistic–mystical*

Selection from *Indian Thought and Its Development*, trans. Mrs. Charles E. B. Russell (Boston: Beacon, 1936), Ch. 1: "Western and Indian Thought," 1–18.

view of the spiritual union of man with an infinite Being that is "the only method (of thought) in harmony with reality."

We know very little about any thought except our own, especially about Indian thought. The reason that it is so difficult to become familiar with it is that Indian thought in its very nature is so entirely different from our own because of the great part that the idea of what is called world- and life-negation plays in it. Whereas our modern European worldview, like that of Zarathustra and the Chinese thinkers, is, on principle, world- and life-affirming.

World- and life-affirmation consists in this: that man regards existence as he experiences it in himself and as it has developed in the world as something of value, per se, and accordingly strives to let it reach perfection in himself, while within his own sphere of influence he endeavors to preserve and to further it.

World- and life-negation, on the other hand, consists in his regarding existence as he experiences it in himself and as it is developed in the world as something meaningless and sorrowful, and he resolves accordingly (a) to bring life to a standstill in himself by mortifying his will to live, and (b) to renounce all activity that aims to improve the conditions of life in this world.

World- and life-affirmation unceasingly urges human beings to serve their fellows, society, the nation, mankind, and, indeed, all that lives, with their utmost will and in lively hope of realizable progress. World- and life-negation takes no interest in the world, but regards man's life on earth as either merely a stage-play in which it is his duty to participate, or as only a puzzling pilgrimage through the land of Time to his home in Eternity.

People commonly speak of an optimistic and a pessimistic worldview. But these expressions do not define the distinction in its essential nature. What determines a man's worldview is not whether, according to his disposition, he takes things more or less lightly or whether he has been gifted with or denied the capacity to have confidence; what is decisive is his inner attitude toward Being, his affirmation or negation of life. Worldview consists in a determination of the will. The question is not so much what man expects or does not expect from existence, but what use he aims at making of it. Naturally, the attitude toward existence determined by the will can be influenced by a more optimistic or more pessimistic disposition, just as it may be by favorable or unfavorable events. But it is not simply the result of that. The most profound world- and life-affirmation is that which has been hard won from an estimate of things unbiased by illusion and even wrested from misfortune, while the most profound world- and life-negation is that which is developed in theory, in spite of a naturally serene disposition and happy outward circumstances.

The battle for world- and life-affirmation and world- and life-negation must be constantly fought and won afresh.

World- and life-affirmation is natural because it corresponds with the instinctive will to live that is in us. World- and life-negation seems to us Europeans an unnatural and incomprehensible thing because it contradicts this instinctive and intuitive force within us.

The fundamental difference in worldviews has nothing to do with difference of race. The Indian Aryans show an inclination to world- and life-negation; the Iranian-Persian and the European Aryans lean toward world- and life-affirmation. This difference in attitude had its origin in events, and these were reflected in thought.

This does not mean that Indian thought is completely governed by world- and life-negation and ours by world- and life-affirmation. In the *Upanishads* there is also a certain element of world- and life-affirmation, and in many writings in Indian literature it even finds quite strong expression. The problem is just this: the relationship between world- and life-affirmation and world- and life-negation as they are found side by side in Indian thought, where world- and life-negation occupies a predominant position.

In European thought, too, there have been periods when world- and life-negation was found alongside world- and life-affirmation. Hellenic thought, in later periods, began to have misgivings about the world- and life-affirmation from which it started. Neo-Platonism and Greco-oriental Gnosticism abandoned it in the first centuries of our era. They were no longer concerned with the activity to which man has to devote himself in the world but with his redemption from the world.

This attitude of despair as it confronts life and the universe becomes apparent in the Greco-Roman thought of the late-classical period because it was obliged to admit that it could not succeed in bringing world- and life-affirmation and its knowledge of the universe into harmony with what happens in the universe. The men of that time were oppressed by the experience of historical events of calamitous import to themselves. Bere of hope in both philosophy and actual world events, they turned in despair to world- and life-negation.

Christianity also brought European thought into relationship with world- and life-negation. World- and life-negation is found in the thought of Jesus insofar as he did not assume that the Kingdom of God would be realized in this natural world. He expected that this natural world would very speedily come to an end and be superseded by a supernatural world in which all that is imperfect and evil would be overcome by the power of God.

But this form of world- and life-negation found in Jesus is different from that of India. Instead of denying the material world because its gaze is directed to pure Being, it only denies the evil, imperfect world in expectation of a good and perfect world that is to come.

It is characteristic of the unique type of the world- and life-negation of Jesus that his ethics is not confined within the bounds of that conception. He does not preach the inactive ethics of perfecting the self alone, but instead preaches active, enthusiastic love of one's neighbor. It is because his ethics contains the principle of activity that it has affinity with world- and life-affirmation.

In the late-classical period, the Greco-oriental and Christian forms of life-negation came together, so that European thought, up to the end of the Middle Ages, was under the influence of world- and life-negation. This is clear from the fact that, in these centuries, the European was so much concerned with the winning of redemption that he took no trouble to move energetically for the improvement of social conditions and the bringing about of a better future for humanity.

But during the period of the Renaissance, and in the centuries that followed, world- and life-affirmation triumphed. This change was brought about by the influence of the revival of the philosophy of Aristotle and Stoicism, by the faith in progress that owed its rise to the great discoveries of science, and by the effect that the ethics of Jesus, with its challenge to active love, had on the minds of men who had been taught by the Reformation to read the Gospels. This form of world- and life-affirmation was so strong that it no longer took any account of the form of world- and life-negation that was present in the thought of Jesus. It assumed, as a matter of course, that Jesus, by his preaching, had intended to found the Kingdom of God on this earth and that it was man's part to work for its further development. Thus, through the principle of activity in his ethics, Christianity, in spite of its original content of world- and life-negation, was able to join forces with the modern European world- and life-affirmation.

In the seventeenth century, therefore, began the period of the great social reforms on which modern European society is based.

In the latest European thought, world- and life-affirmation has in many respects lost the ethical character that it possessed up to the second half of the nineteenth century. But this form of world- and life-affirmation, which has become independent, curiously enough no longer possesses the same strength as that of the earlier period. In the philosophical works of the last decades, world- and life-affirmation is not infrequently expressed in a way that suggests it is wandering on the wrong track and has lost confidence in itself.

Thus, both in Indian and in European thought, world- and life-affirmation and world- and life-negation are found side by side: but in Indian thought, the latter is the predominant principle, and in European the former.

In the profoundest form of world- and life-affirmation, in which man lives his life on the loftiest spiritual and ethical plane, he attains to inner freedom from the world and becomes capable of sacrificing his life for some end. This profoundest world- and life-affirmation can assume the appearance of world- and life-negation. But that does not make it world- and life-negation: it remains what it is—the loftiest form of world- and life-affirmation. He who sacrifices his life to achieve any purpose for an individual or for humanity is practicing life-affirmation. He is taking an interest in the things of this world and, by offering his own life, wants to bring about in the world something that he regards as necessary. The sacrifice of life for a purpose is not life-negation but the profoundest form of life-affirmation, placing itself at the service of world-affirmation. World- and life-negation is present only when man takes no interest whatever in any realizable purpose or in the improvement of conditions in this world. As soon as he in any way withdraws from this standpoint, whether he admits it to himself or not, he is already under the influence of world- and life-affirmation.

The difficulty of the worldview of world- and life-negation consists in the fact that it is impracticable. It is compelled to make concessions to world- and life-affirmation.

It really ought to demand of man that, as soon as he reaches the conviction that Non-Being is to be regarded as higher than Being, he shall quit existence by a self-chosen death. It gives a reason for not demanding this of him by explaining that it is not so important to make an end of life as soon as possible as it is to mortify as thoroughly as we can the will to live in our hearts. The worldview of world- and life-negation is therefore in contradiction with itself in that it does want to be lived. With this desire it enters on the path of concession to world- and life-affirmation that it must then follow to the end.

To remain alive, even in the most miserable fashion, presupposes some activity conducive to the maintenance of life. Even the hermit, who is most strict of all men in his world- and life-negation, cannot escape from that. He picks berries, goes to the spring, fills his drinking-cup, perhaps even washes himself now and then, and feeds his companions the birds and the deer as a proper hermit should.

Passing from concessions to concessions, which have to be made if men who live the worldview of world- and life-negation are to remain alive, the decision is reached that what really matters is not so much actual abstention from action as that men should act in a spirit of non-activity and in inner freedom from the world so that action may lose all significance. In order not to be obliged to confess to themselves how much of world- and life-negation is abandoned, they have recourse to a method of regarding things that savors of relativity.

But the greatest difficulty for the worldview of world- and life-negation comes from ethics. Ethics demands of man that he should interest himself in the world and in what goes on in it and, what is more, ethics simply compels him to action. So if world- and life-negation really becomes concerned with ethics at all, it is driven to make such great concessions to world- and life-affirmation that it ceases to exist.

To escape this fate it has to try to confine itself to a non-active ethics. This ethics that keeps within the bounds of world- and life-denial can demand only two things of man, namely, that in a spirit of kindliness completely free from hatred he should seek true inner perfection, and that he should show forth this by refraining from destroying or damaging any living thing, and in general by abstaining from all acts not inspired by love and sympathy. Active love it cannot demand of him.

But ethics can be adapted to this renunciation demanded by world- and life-negation only so long as it has not yet reached its full development. When morality really attains to consciousness of itself, to further the work of love becomes a matter of course that cannot be avoided.

In measure as the worldview of world- and life-negation becomes ethical, it necessarily, therefore, renounces itself.

As a fact, the development of Indian thought follows the line of ever-greater concessions until, at last, as ethics gradually expands, it is forced either to unconfessed or to admitted abandonment of world- and life-denial.

But on the circuitous paths that it follows, the thought of India encounters questions and forms of knowledge that we who follow the straight road of our modern world- and life-affirmation either do not meet at all or do not see so plainly.

We modern Europeans are so much occupied with our activity within the world that we give little or no heed to the question of our spiritual future. But the worldview of world- and life-negation sets the question of man becoming spiritually more perfect at the center of all reflection and deliberation. It holds before man as the highest aim that he should endeavor to attain to the right composure, the right inwardness, the right ethical attitude of mind, and to true peace of soul. Although the ideal set up by Indian world- and life-negation of becoming spiritually more and more perfect is of necessity one-sided and inad- equate, it nevertheless has great significance for us in affording an insight into a system of thought that is occupied with a great problem of which we take far too little notice.

Our world- and life-affirmation needs to try conclusions with the world- and life-negation that is striving after ethics in order that it may arrive at greater clarity and depth.

In ethics, too, Indian thought, starting from world- and life-negation, presses forward to a stage of knowledge that is quite outside the purview of European thinking. It reaches the point of taking into account the fact that our ethical behavior must concern not only our human neighbor but all living things. The problem of the boundlessness of the field of ethics and the boundlessness of the claims that ethics makes upon us—a problem from which, even today, European thought is trying to escape—has existed for Indian thought for more than two thousand years, although Indian thought, too, has not yet felt its whole weight or recognized the whole range that it covers.

When distinguishing the Indian worldview from ours, there is yet another difference, which lies just as deep as that between world- and life-affirmation and world- and life-denial. The Indian worldview is monistic and mystical; ours is dualistic and doctrinaire.

Mysticism is the perfected form of worldview. In this worldview man endeavors to arrive at a spiritual relationship to the infinite Being to which he belongs as a part of Nature. He studies the universe to discover whether he can apprehend and become one with the mysterious will that governs it. Only in spiritual unity with infinite Being can he give meaning to his life and find strength to suffer and to act.

And if, in the last resort, the aim of a worldview is our spiritual unity with infinite Being, then the perfect worldview is of necessity mysticism. It is in mysticism that man realizes spiritual union with infinite Being.

Mysticism alone corresponds to the ideal of a worldview. All other worldviews are in their nature incomplete and fail to correspond with the facts. Instead of providing a solution to the fundamental question of how man is to become spiritually one with infinite Being and, from this solution as a beginning, deciding in detail what is to be his attitude to himself and to all things in the universe, these other forms of worldview lay down precepts about the universe to instruct man about what part he ought to play in it.

The theory of the universe that these doctrinaire worldviews represent is dualistic. They assume two principles in the history of events, starting from the very origins of Being. One principle is conceived as an ethical personality who guarantees that what happens in the universe has an ethical goal; the other is represented as the natural force dwelling within the universe and operative in a course of events governed by natural laws. This dualistic worldview exists in very many variations. In the teaching of Zarathustra, in that of the Jewish prophets, and in Christianity, what happens in the universe is interpreted as a battle in which the supernatural ethical power winds its way through in conflict with the natural non-ethical. Where a more critical form of thought engages in the problem, it strives, insofar as it can, to cover up the dualism. But it is there nevertheless. Even the philosophy of Kant is dualistic. It works with the idea, derived from Christianity, of an ethical Creator of the universe, without making clear to itself how it can succeed in identifying him with the Primal Cause of Being.

The dualistic worldview does not correspond with reality, for it comprises doctrines about the universe that cannot be made to square with the facts. It derives from a habit of thought that is under the influence of ethical belief.

So while Indian thought rests in the perfected form of worldview, in mysticism, our own thought strives after a form of worldview that is essentially naïve and not in agreement with facts.

How can this be explained?

It is true that mysticism is, in its nature, the perfected kind of worldview. But if we regard the contents, all mysticism down to the present is unsatisfying because it denies the world and life and has no ethical content. And the reason for this is that, in the history of the universe and, therefore, also in the first origins of Being, no ethical principle can be discovered.

No ethics can be won from knowledge of the universe. Nor can ethics be brought into harmony with what we know of the universe.

For this reason, thought finds it impossible to attain to the conception of a spiritual union with infinite Being from which shall emerge the idea of self-devotion to the world in ethical activity. This explains why, up to now, mysticism really understands that, by man's becoming spiritually one with infinite Being, he is merely passively absorbed into that Being.

So the remarkable paradox emerges that thinking, when it is in agreement with facts, is unable to justify the worldview of ethical world- and life-affirmation. If, nevertheless, it wants to advocate this because natural feeling holds it for true and valuable, it must substitute for real knowledge of the universe a dualistic ethical explanation. It may no longer regard the universe as something that has issued and continues to issue from the mysterious Primal Cause of Being, but must assume a Creator of the universe who has an ethical character and sets an ethical purpose before world events.

According to this ethical explanation of the universe, man, by ethical activity, enters the service of the divine world-aim.

As long as thought is still naïve, the ethical–dualistic explanation of the world causes it no difficulty. But in measure as thought develops, so it comes more or less clearly to take account of the unreliability of such an explanation. That is why the dualistic method of thought in European philosophy is not unopposed. A monistic–mystical tendency repeatedly rises in revolt against it. In the Middle Ages, Scholasticism had to be on the defense against a mysticism that goes back to Neo-Platonism and grows strong in independent thinking. The pantheism of Giordano Bruno is a confession of monistic mysticism. Spinoza, Fichte, Schelling, and Hegel are concerned with the spiritual union of man with infinite Being. Although their philosophy does not pose as mysticism, it is mysticism, nevertheless, in its essentials. It is monistic thought under the influence of modern natural science that undertakes the great forward push against dualism.

In actual fact the monistic method of thought, the only method in harmony with reality, has already gained the victory over the dualistic. But it is not able to make full use of what it has won. For it is not in a position to replace the world-affirming ethical worldview of dualism by another worldview of anything like the same value. What monism makes known as its own worldview is altogether beggarly. And what little worldview it has is for the most part borrowed from the worldview of dualism. European monism is not clear as to the necessity of creating a worldview that, in its essence, is mysticism and that has, for its object, the question of the spiritual union of man with infinite Being.

The dualistic method of thinking is maintained in Europe because it belongs to the worldview of ethical world- and life-affirmation, which stands firm because of its inner content of truth and its inner worth. So far as is possible, it fits in with monism. The confusion in modern European thought has its origin in the fact that dualism wears the cloak of monism and monism gets its worldview from dualism.

In India, again, monistic mysticism has to make concessions to dualism in measure as it assumes an ethical and world- and life-affirming character. It does this in such a way that it passes from the Brahmanic mysticism of being merged in the original source of Being into the Hindu mysticism of loving self-surrender to the one and only God. It arrives, therefore, at a position that it originally avoided, a position where it comprehends the primal source of existence as a divine Being. Here, as a matter of fact, it abandons monism. But it cannot do otherwise. In order to absorb into itself thoughts of ethical world- and life-affirmation, and to give correspondingly more satisfaction as a worldview, it is forced to develop into a mysticism of spiritual union with God. Insofar, then, as an ethical nature is attributed to God, ethical world- and life-affirmation does gain a footing in mysticism.

The ethical conception of God in modern Indian thought is no longer essentially different from that in European thought.

But in spite of these concessions to the dualistic mode of thinking, modern Indian thought holds unswervingly fast to the conviction that worldview is mysticism. It holds to the principle that all the ideas contained in a worldview must together result from the nature of the spiritual union of man with infinite Being. That this worldview is a personal experience of the thought of the individual, by which he clarifies his relationship to Being and, along with this, clarifies what he wants to make of his life—to this truth the Indian thinkers remain faithful today, just as they did in the past.

It is true they cannot make a reality of the ideal of which they confess themselves adherents. Their mysticism is inadequate in its nature as in its content. But what a magnificent thing it is that they do not abandon the ideal!

European thought, on the contrary, has difficulty holding fast to the right conception of worldview. Indeed, insofar as it admits dualism, it completely surrenders this. Dualism regards worldview as a doctrine that the individual has to acquire, instead of claiming, as does mysticism, to be a conviction that is born, and is constantly being renewed, within him.

But once the true conception of worldview is abandoned, there arises the danger that tenets that are no longer worldview at all nevertheless make their appearance as such. This is happening in the European thought of our own time. Opinions and convictions that have arisen from no kind of reflection about man and the universe, but that are concerned only with man and human society, are given out as worldview and accepted as such, in the same way as we are content to call the history of the miserable wars waged on our little earth universal history. Nothing is so characteristic of the want of thought of our time as that we have lost the consciousness of what worldview really is.

It is necessary that we come back to the understanding that the only true worldview is that which arises from meditation in which man is alone with the universe and himself.

If such confusion and perplexity reign in European thought, it is not only due to the difficulties that it has to overcome, but also to the fact that it is not sufficiently clear about its real task, namely, the task of creating a worldview. European thought finds its right bearings only when all the single problems that affect human existence converge into the fundamental problem of how man can arrive at the right spiritual relationship to Being. It raises its head only when it again sets the highest goal before it.

There is, then, a twofold interest for European thought in the study of Indian thought, which is so different in its nature, let alone the stimulus of becoming acquainted with a foreign mode of thinking.

In the first place, European thought represents a world- and life-affirmation that is wanting in depth because it has not yet come to a thorough understanding of its position in relation to world- and life-negation and to ethics. In Indian thought, after a long struggle against world- and life-negation, ethical world- and life-affirmation prevails. The problem with which we are concerned is here unfolded like a scroll from the opposite end.

Secondly, European thought allows itself to be guided by the knowledge that the worldview of ethical world- and life-affirmation is, from its content, the most valuable, while Indian thought is determined by the other fact, that mysticism is the perfect kind of worldview. European thought, then, has to make an effort to attain to a worldview of ethical world- and life-affirmation that, in its nature, is mysticism, and Indian thought has to strive to give to mysticism ethical world- and life-affirmation as its content. Again, then, the problem with which our thinking is concerned is unrolled in Indian thought from the opposite end.

In Indian thought we learn to understand better what is going on in our own thought.

From a comparison of European and Indian thought, it becomes clear that the great problem of thought in general consists in the attainment of a mysticism of ethical world- and life-affirmation. Thought has not yet succeeded in uniting into a single whole the worldview that, in its method, is perfect and the worldview that, in its content, is most valuable. It cannot master the puzzling difficulties that are in the way of this apparently so simple synthesis. But it must not, on that account, cease to aim at that worldview that alone is really satisfying. Up to now it has directed its efforts far too little toward this end.

2

The Historical Jesus

According to Schweitzer, we can know Jesus not by means of a complete reconstruction of the details of his life, but by understanding his will. In the case of Jesus, the will is centered upon the Kingdom of God and manifested through his hope for ethical perfection of the world and his dedication to this end. In our era, asserts Schweitzer, there could be no vital fellowship with Jesus because our age is utterly devoid of all enthusiasm for the ultimate aims of humanity and human existence; we are drifting in precisely the opposite direction.

The philosophical significance of this piece consists in its arguing for the far greater significance of will over knowledge (and reason), and for the need to rededicate ourselves to morally perfecting the world (which Schweitzer calls life- and world-affirmation). Unlike contemporary moral philosophers, who try to direct us by means of various moral precepts, Schweitzer simply points out the relevance of rediscovering our moral enthusiasm within ourselves: "The ideals lie within us; they are given within the ethical will."

What is the historical Jesus to us when we preserve him from any spurious admixture of the present with the past? We are struck by a direct awareness that his personality, despite all its strange and

Selection; the concluding part of *Geschichte der Leben-Jesu-Forschung* (Tübingen: J. C. B. Mohr, 1913); the enlarged version of *Von Reimarus zu Wrede: Eine Geschichte der Leben-Jesu-Forschung* (1906); translated by Henry Clark and reprinted here from *The Ethical Mysticism of Albert Schweitzer*, by Henry Clark (Boston: Beacon, 1962), Appendix II, 195–205.

enigmatic qualities, has something great to say to all ages so long as the world shall last, no matter how much the knowledge and attitudes of men may change. We know that he can enrich our religion profoundly. We feel ourselves called upon to articulate clearly this elemental feeling, so that it does not soar away in dogmatic formulas or lure historical research into the inevitably hopeless attempt to modernize Jesus by diluting or explaining away whatever is historically conditioned in his preaching—as though he would mean more to us thereby.

In the final analysis, the whole scientific quest for the historical Jesus has only this single aim: to set forth accurately the natural and unforced interpretation of the oldest accounts. To know Jesus and to understand him requires no preliminary erudition. Nor is it necessary that we know the details of his public ministry or be able to reconstruct a "life of Jesus." His very being, that which he is and wills, manifests itself in a few of his lapidary sayings and thrusts itself upon us. We know him without knowing much about him, and we sense his eschatological significance even without having a scholarly knowledge of this concept. For the characteristic thing about Jesus is the way in which he looks beyond the perfection and blessedness of the individual to the perfection and blessedness of the world and of an elect humanity. His will and his hope are centered upon the Kingdom of God.

In every worldview, historically conditioned elements are intertwined with timeless elements. The crucial factor is the will, which penetrates and molds the conceptual materials out of which the worldview is made. Since these materials are subject to change, there is no worldview, regardless of how great and profound it may be, that does not contain some historically conditioned elements. But the will itself is timeless: it reveals the unfathomable and irreducible essence of a person and it also exercises a decisive influence on the ultimate development of the worldview held by that person. However great a change may occur in conceptual materials or in the worldviews to which they belong, that makes no difference: the distance separating any two worldviews will be only so great as the distance separating the direction of the wills that determine these worldviews. Although the variations that result from differing conceptual materials may seem to be decisive, they are ultimately of secondary importance only. For the same will, regardless of the conceptual materials through which it manifests itself, always creates a worldview in which it can express itself.

Since the presuppositions of perception and cognition, which in our sense can be defined as a worldview, became set—that is, since the individual began to take into account the totality of being, the world as a whole, and to reflect on the changing relationships (both passive and active) between the All and himself as a knowing, willing subject—no further developments of far-reaching significance have occurred in the spiritual life of mankind. The problems that occupied the Greeks still concern the most modern philosophy, and contemporary skepticism is essentially the same as that which found a hearing in classical thought.

Because of the fact that Jesus expressed his worldview in the primitive metaphysics of late-Jewish apocalypticism, it is exceedingly difficult to translate his ideas into our modes of expression. The task is simply impossible so long as one tries to go about it by separating the permanent from the transitory in detail. This approach is so lacking in force and decisiveness that its apparent contributions to our religion are bound to be illusory.

Actually, there is no point in seeking to separate the permanent from the transitory. What is needed is a translation of the fundamental thought of that worldview into concepts that are familiar to us. What we need to know is this: How would the will of Jesus—grasped in all its directness and concreteness and comprehensiveness—how would it invigorate our conceptual material and create from it a worldview of sufficient ethical vitality and power to be counted the modern equivalent of the worldview that he created in terms of late Jewish metaphysics and eschatology?

Up to now, those who have tried to reconcile Jesus' worldview with ours have weakened the distinctiveness of his thought. In so doing, they have also weakened the will, which is expressed in this thought. It [the thought] loses its originality and ceases to exert an elemental influence upon us. That is why the Jesus of modern theology is so remarkably lifeless. Jesus is greater, despite his strangeness, when allowed to remain in the eschatological world. And he affects us more deeply than the modern Jesus.

The work of Jesus was to fill the late-Jewish eschatology with his natural and profound morality, and thereby to express, in the conceptual materials of that age, a hope for ethical perfection of the world and a will dedicated to that end. All attempts to ignore his worldview as a totality, and to reduce his significance for us to nothing more than his revelation of the "fatherhood of God," "the brotherhood of man," and so forth, will inevitably lead to a narrow and peculiarly insipid interpretation of his religion. In reality he is an authority for us, not in the sphere of knowledge, but only in the realm of the will. It is his destiny to clarify and heighten the driving forces of hope and will that we and our fellow men bear within us, until they reach an intensity that would have been impossible without the impact of his personality. Thus it is that, in spite of all differences in conceptual materials, he forms our worldview according to the essence of his and arouses in ours the energies that surge in his.

The last and deepest knowledge of things comes from the will. Hence, thought that strives to frame a final synthesis of observation and knowledge in order to construct a worldview is directed by the will. For the primary and ultimate essence of the persons and ages in question is the will.

If our age and our religion have failed to apprehend the greatness of Jesus, if they have shied away from the eschatological coloring of his thought, the fault is not merely their inability to accommodate themselves to the strangeness of it. The crucial reason is to be found elsewhere. Their willing and hoping had not been stamped with the indelible mark of an intense yearning for the moral perfection of the world—and this is what was decisive for Jesus and his worldview. Eschatology, in the broadest and most general sense of the term, was missing. They found in themselves no equivalents for the thoughts of Jesus; consequently, they were in no position to transpose his worldview from the key in which late-Jewish apocalypticism was played into one that would be familiar to their ear.

There was no answering chord of sympathy between their worldview and that of Jesus. As a result, the historical Jesus remained a stranger to them, not only in his thought material but also in his very essence. His ethical enthusiasm and the directness and power of his thought remained inaccessible to them because they knew nothing similar to this in their own thought and experience. So they continually endeavored to make of this "fanatic" a contemporary man and theologian, one who would be duly observant of the accepted rules of moderation and propriety in all that he did. Conservative theology, like the older orthodoxy to which it is akin, could not appropriate the historical Jesus, for it also neglected the great ethical ideals that were struggling for vital expression in his eschatology.

Our civilization and our religion have found it impossible to attain a real knowledge of the historical Jesus and a religious relationship with him because their willing and hoping and longing have not been tuned to the same pitch as his. There could be no vital fellowship between him and a generation utterly devoid of all directness and all enthusiasm for the ultimate aims of humanity and existence. In spite of all its progress in historical perception, it really remained more foreign to him than was the rationalism of the eighteenth or early nineteenth century, which was drawn close to him by virtue of its enthusiastic faith in the advancing moral progress of mankind.

If we read through the expositions of Christian faith and Christian ethical theories that have appeared in recent decades, we are amazed to discover how feebly most of them set forth the elemental moral thought of the yet-to-be-achieved general perfection of mankind. These studies seem to have produced only a quavering tone that echoes as it fades away, whereas they ought to have resounded with the stirring basic theme of every true ethical worldview.

Thus, the real essence of Jesus remains inoperative. He has been changed from a living man into an "Agent of Revelation" and a "Symbol." In [Arthur] Drews's interpretation of religion (an interpretation influenced by the period of Greek–Oriental decadence), the ethical and eschatological currents are so weak that there is no longer any place at all for the historical Jesus.

Only insofar as the conceptual materials of an age are charged with ethical–eschatological vitalities does that age have a real and living relationship to Jesus. This means that its worldview must exhibit the equivalent of the will and hope that were central for him; that is, it must be dominated by the thoughts that are found in Jesus' concept of the Kingdom of God.

If the signs of the time do not mislead us, we are entering into an age that is drifting in precisely the opposite direction. All progress in knowledge notwithstanding, we have experienced in the past few decades a stagnation of our civilization, which manifests itself in every area of life. There are even numerous signs of a genuine retrogression. The sickness displays manifold symptoms, but the root cause is to be found in this condition: nothing in our civilization, including religion, is providing enough ethical ideals and energies. It has lost the great aim of the moral perfection of all mankind, and it is hemmed in by the walls of national and sectarian ideals instead of encompassing the whole world in its vision. Its greatness and its goodness pretend to be self-sufficient, whereas they ought to put themselves at the service of that general ethical perfection that, in accordance with the preaching of Jesus, one may call the Kingdom of God. These values of civilization possess genuine ethical worth only to the extent that they do serve this end.

But the abandonment of the mighty striving for perfection of the world, a striving that was so very passionately intent upon achieving its goal, has brought about a weakening of our religion and our ethics. As a result, our worldview is deficient in judgment concerning events and relationships and in devotion to its task it has of providing a great compass that could point out to people the road ahead and show them their highest duties at all times.

This abandonment of ethical eschatology is avenged. Instead of fighting for the triumph of the ethical spirit of God, through which individuals, sectarian groups, and people at large might be filled with sustaining inspiration, mankind today is on the verge of delivering itself into the hands of the spirits of thoughtlessness and resigning itself to the stagnation and decline of civilization. And this means the repudiation of all that lifts mankind to the heights of true humanity. Those who see where we are headed and do not allow themselves to become insensitive to the tragedy of our situation, but rather experience again and again the woe that hangs over the future of the world, are ready to encounter the historical Jesus and to understand what he has to say to us despite the strangeness of his language. With him (who also experienced a similar despair in the terms of thought current in his day) they perceive that we shall be saved from present conditions through a mighty hope for the Kingdom of God and a will dedicated to it. With him they know that such a hoping and willing can afford to be scornful of the circumstances as they appear. With him they perceive that we must find support, freedom, and peace in our faith in the invincible power of the moral spirit; that we must spread this faith and the convictions that it involves concerning daily life; that we must find the highest good in the Kingdom of God and live for it.

Of greatest importance in this worldview are its qualities of enthusiasm and heroism, which spring from the will and faith that are centered in the Kingdom of God and which are augmented rather than diminished by unfavorable conditions. A religion possesses just so much of an understanding of the historical Jesus as it possesses of a strong, passionate faith in the Kingdom of God. The other claims that religion might make concerning its bond with him are unreal; they exist only in words and formulas. We possess only so much of him as we permit him to preach to us of the Kingdom of God. All lesser disputes over metaphysics and conceptual materials simply fall into the background. The only thing that matters is this: that the significance of the concept of the Kingdom of God for our worldview is the same as it was for him, and that we experience in the same way that he did the urgency and the power of that concept.

The important thing is a *will to will understanding* of Jesus, for in this the essence of the worldview is communicated. An analysis of the details of his activities and his preaching, the intention of which is to distinguish between enduring and obsolete elements, is unnecessary. His words translate themselves, as it were, automatically in the idiom appropriate to our conceptual materials. Many of these words that at first strike us as strange become true in a profound and eternal sense even for us, when we accept with open minds the power of the spirit that speaks in him. When confronted with the difficulties of making his message clear and alive for present-day hearers, one could almost call to mind his saying, "Seek ye first the Kingdom of God and his righteousness, and all these things shall be added unto you."

The change in conceptual material requires, of course, that the ultimate perfection that he expected as a supernatural event be expected by us only as the result of ethical endeavor. One ought not to employ violent exegesis to read into his words our concept of gradual development. What matters, though, is that our allegiance to the ideal of a Kingdom created by ethical endeavor should be pursued with the same ardor that inflamed his devotion to the divine intervention that he awaited, and that we should be prepared to give up everything for it.

Even the part of his preaching that modern man normally regards as a stumbling block can no longer disturb us if he is known will to will. He saw no intrinsic value in work, property, and many other things that we value as ethically good because for him these things were not included in the blueprint of the Kingdom. But for us the plans appear to have been redrawn, so that some things that were formerly excluded are now a prominent part of the building. At any rate, we work in the service of the Kingdom of God and thus maintain fellowship with him because we regard the Kingdom as the measure of all moral worth.

The late-Jewish thought material made it inevitable that he should think in predestinarian terms and accept nationalistic limitations on his ministry. Of this fact there can be no doubt. And there are many other aspects of his thought that must be acknowledged to be strange and offensive. But these are always historically conditioned elements, part of the conceptual material that simply fades from view as soon as the will of Jesus manifests itself to us.

So the eschatological interpretation of Jesus is not, as is so often supposed, something that makes his preaching more difficult for our age to comprehend. If we focus our attention upon all that is self-authenticating in his person and in his Sermon on the Mount, then all that is strange and offensive can be dealt with at our leisure. All that takes care of itself as soon as we recognize that he was conditioned by the conceptual materials with which he had to work. Neither long speeches nor great learning is required. In reality, the true Jesus is easier to proclaim than the modernized Jesus, if only one lets that which is elemental in him speak out, in order that he may really be for us, too, the one who preaches with authority and not as the scribes.

Even the fact that the historical Jesus regarded the Kingdom of God as something transcending morality and thus proclaimed only an "ethics of the interim" does not affect what he has to say to us because this drawback is removed if we translate his preaching into our metaphysics. His mighty personal ethics teaches us that whoever wishes to work for the Kingdom of God can accomplish something only if he continually purifies himself inwardly and makes himself free from the world.

Our relationship to the historical Jesus must be simultaneously truthful and free. We give history its due and then make ourselves free from its conceptual materials. But we bow before the mighty will that stands behind it, and we seek to serve this will in our time, that it may be born in us in new vitality and fruitfulness, and that it may work toward fulfillment in us and in the world.

But it is not true to say that we possess the idea of the moral perfection of the world and the ideas we have of what must be done in our time because we have obtained them through historical revelation. These ideas lie within us; they are given with the ethical will. Because Jesus, as one who stood in the line of succession of the greatest among the prophets, summed up these ideas and taught them with the utmost thoroughness and directness, and because he embodied them in his own great personality, he helps us be similarly dedicated and become ethical forces in our own time.

This interpretation of religion and of the person Jesus is usually dismissed as one-sidedly moralistic and rationalistic. In order to overcome this reaction, we need call to mind only the fact that if this interpretation is really alive and potent, it encompasses religion in its totality. For all that man can really say about salvation boils down to this: it means being set free from the world and from ourselves through a fellowship of the will with Jesus, and being filled with power and peace and courage for life. Let no one forget that Jesus himself was essentially a rationalist and a moralist. That he was conditioned by late-Jewish metaphysics is incidental.

In the final analysis, our relationship to Jesus is of a mystical sort. No personality of the past can be transported to the present by means of historical reflection or affirmations about his authoritative significance. We enter into relationship with him only by being brought together in the recognition of a common will, and by experiencing a clarification, enrichment, and quickening of our will through his. Thus do we find ourselves again in him. In this sense, every deeper relationship between men partakes of a mystical quality. So our religion, insofar as it is to be regarded as specifically Christian, is not so much a "Jesus-cult" as it is a Jesus-mysticism.

Only in this manner does Jesus also create fellowship among us. He does this, not by being a symbol or anything of that sort, but in the following way: to the extent that we, with one another and with him, are of one will—to put the Kingdom of God above everything else, and to serve in behalf of this faith and hope—to this extent is there fellowship between him and us and the men of all generations who have lived and do live in the same thought.

This is the touchstone by which all movements for religious unity must be evaluated. False compromises are of no avail. All concessions by means of which liberal religion seeks a rapprochement with dogmatic religion will result only in ambiguities and inconsistencies which weaken its own position. The differences are rooted in the conceptual materials presupposed by each side, and all efforts for agreement in this area are futile. These differences loom so large because there is a dearth of elemental, living religion. Two thin streams of water run side by side through the boulders and gravel of a great riverbed. It really does not matter that here and there someone tries to clear away the piles of rock that separate them in a vain effort to make them flow together. But when the water rises and overflows the boulders—then the two will become one. Thus, dogmatic and liberal religion shall be united when willing and hoping are once again directed toward the Kingdom of God, when the spirit of Jesus once again becomes something elemental and powerful in them. When this occurs, they shall be drawn together so closely in the essence of their worldview and religion that the differences of conceptual material, though not done away with, will sink beneath the surface, just as boulders are covered by a rising flood and finally cast only a faint glimmer out of the depths.

Jesus was hailed by men who thought of him in terms of the late-Jewish conceptual materials as Messiah, Son of Man, and Son of God—but for us these names have become historical parables. If he applied these titles to himself, that was because they were historically conditioned expressions of his awareness that he was a master and a leader. We have no designation that defines what he is for us.

He comes to us as one unknown, without a name, as of old, by the lakeside, he came to those men who knew him not. He speaks to us the same word: "Follow thou me!" and sets us to the tasks that he has to fulfill for our time. He commands. And to those who obey him, whether they be wise or simple, he will reveal himself in the toils, the conflicts, the sufferings that they shall pass through in his fellowship, and, as an ineffable mystery, they shall learn in their own experience who he is.

3

The Kingdom of God

Schweitzer considers this essay to be the best summary of his philosophy of religion. He starts from the premise that the essential element of Jesus' faith was his belief in the immanent coming of the Kingdom of God. Jesus' denial of this world is quite different from Indian thinkers' life- and world-negation. Jesus preaches not resignation and passivity but a positive love, a love that leads to action. The apostle Paul also accepts the idea of the Kingdom of God, with the provision that its coming is postponed for a short time. With the passing centuries, the idea of the Kingdom of God became a burden and an embarrassment. To avoid this embarrassment, the Orthodox Church turned its attention toward Jesus' resurrection, while the Western Church has focused on the forgiveness of sins and the possibility of redemption. Schweitzer argues that what is needed is a new rendering of the ideal of the Kingdom of God that will be adequate for our time. In his words, "We are no longer content, like the generations before us, to believe in the Kingdom that comes of itself at the end of time. Mankind today must either realize the Kingdom of God or perish. The very tragedy of our present situation compels us to devote ourselves in faith to its realization."

The philosophical significance of this piece consists in its showing how an event, previously understood as cosmological, can be interpreted in ethical and spiritual terms. Schweitzer insists on the faithfulness to the

Complete essay; originally published as "The Conception of the Kingdom of God in the Transformation of Eschatology," in appendix to E. N. Mozley, *The Theology of Albert Schweitzer* (New York: Macmillan, 1951), 79–103.

original message of Jesus and challenges us to find the most appropriate way for its realization in our time. Our ultimate service to Jesus is the service of truth, for faith and truth are impossible without each other: "Devotion to truth . . . is the essence of spiritual life. Faith that refuses to face indisputable facts is but little faith. Truth is always gain, however hard it is to accommodate ourselves to it. To linger in any kind of untruth proves to be a departure from the straight way of faith."

The primitive Christian hope of an immediate coming of the Kingdom of God was based on the teaching of Jesus; yet, the fact that it remained unfulfilled did not shatter Christian faith. How was the catastrophe dealt with? What transformation of the faith enabled it to survive the surrender of the original expectation?

Although the eschatological problem has been under discussion for more than a generation, until quite recently only three factors have usually been taken into consideration as determining the development and reshaping of Christian belief, namely, the struggle for unity, the conflict with second-century Gnosticism, and accommodation to Greek metaphysics. But these do not cover the whole ground. A fourth factor was at work, much more strongly than has been admitted, namely, the inescapable abandonment of the early hope of a speedy coming of the Kingdom of God. The effect of this has been studied in detail for the first time by Martin Werner in *The Origin of the Christian Dogmas.*

The apostle Paul had to wrestle with the problem, but it did not seriously affect him because he took the view that the coming of the Kingdom was postponed only for a short time. He was thus able to hold to his conviction that the Kingdom must come as the immediate consequence of the self-sacrifice of Jesus on the Cross. His theory is that the Kingdom of God has actually come in the death and resurrection of Jesus and is actually present, though not yet revealed. Those events inaugurated the transformation of the world of nature into the supernatural world of the Kingdom of God. Through mystical fellowship with the crucified and risen Jesus Christ, believers already share with him the supernatural quality of life in the Kingdom; they are already risen, though they look like ordinary people.

This view enables Paul to distinguish between the coming of the Kingdom and its manifestation. He regards the earlier view, with its hope fixed simply on the future, as falling short of the truth. His whole theology rests on this antedating, which is bound up with the assurance that Jesus himself expected the Kingdom to arrive with his resurrection as the result of his death.

The greatest thinker in the early Church thus holds both views side by side; the Kingdom is to come, and it is growing—and the latter tends to displace the former. But the new view cannot cover the whole ground because it starts from the theory of a brief postponement, which time will soon disprove. The early Church as a whole rejected this doctrine, holding that the death and resurrection of Jesus simply made it possible for the Kingdom to come some time and that they must be content to wait for it.

From the second generation onward, the arrival of the Kingdom becomes "one far-off divine event," and in later days it is infinitely far away. This change, of necessity, affects the nature of the expectation. Originally, it held a dominant position at the very center of the faith; now it falls into the background. Instead of being the very essence of belief, it is now just one article among others.

When the Kingdom was expected immediately, it had a meaning for the present, which it overshadowed. The believer looked for a redemption that would lift him, with the multitude of his fellow believers, into a world no longer subject to mortality and evil. With such a hope, he felt himself already delivered out of this world. But the Kingdom has no such meaning for the present, when it is imagined as being far away; the believer knows that he is condemned to live out his life in the same old world.

Denial of the world is a different thing when the end is not impending. It presented little difficulty to those for whom the other world was so near; but to those who can cherish no hope of seeing the arrival of the new world, life must mean the denial of this world from first to last. These can have no hope for the world and its inhabitants; hopelessness about the present situation goes along with belief in the coming of the Kingdom of God at the end. Moreover, the fact that the Kingdom is merely something to be awaited has an unfortunate corollary. It made no difference to those who expected it immediately; but it obviously creates an unnatural situation for those whose faith compels them to do nothing but wait for the Kingdom, which comes entirely of itself. Both by their denial of the world and by their belief that the Kingdom comes of itself, they are condemned to refrain from all efforts to improve the present situation.

While Christianity has to tread this path, it cannot be to the surrounding Greco-Roman world what it ought to be. It cannot use its moral energy as power for regenerating the empire and its peoples. It conquers paganism; it becomes the religion of the state. But owing to its peculiar character it must leave the state to its fate. This world is not the dough in which its leaven can work.

The idea of redemption was also affected by the change of outlook. Originally, the dominant thought of the Kingdom of God meant that believers shared with one another the blessings of a new creation. But now the experience of the individual took precedence over that of the community. Each separate believer is now concerned with his own redemption. He cares nothing for the future of mankind and of the world. There is something cold and unnatural about the naïve egoism of such piety.

The abandonment of eager expectation meant that Christianity lost the joy that characterized it in the days of Paul and the early Church. It started in bright sunshine but had to continue its journey in the chilly gloom of a vague and uncertain hope. The idea of the Kingdom of God is no longer at the center of faith, and this has led to a far-reaching impoverishment.

The substitution of the distant view for the near view of the coming of the Kingdom of God necessitates the elaboration and reshaping of the faith. Originally, the believer expected to come into possession of the blessedness of redemption through immediate admission into the Kingdom opened by the death and resurrection of Jesus. But when these blessings are postponed until the end of time, demands are made of faith that cannot be met by the earlier doctrine of redemption. The old assurance of the immediate attainment of the blessedness of redemption has now faded and must be replaced by the assurance of a right, secured by the death and resurrection of Jesus, to the blessedness of the Kingdom of God at the end of time. The early Christians thought of redemption and blessedness as different aspects of the same experience. Later they were separated in time, and each came to have its own meaning. Instead of blessedness as such, the believer had the blessedness of being assured of his right to redemption; and this gave him strength to bear the burden of life in this world.

It became necessary, in the development of the doctrine of redemption, to have a comprehensive interpretation of the death and resurrection of Jesus, showing how these guarantee future blessedness to the believer. Faith feels that it must be clear on this point. Christian theology was entirely occupied, in the first centuries, with meeting the demand of faith for a fuller understanding of the death and resurrection of Jesus.

Assurance of a share in the coming blessedness naturally depends upon the assurance of having received the forgiveness of sins and the power of the resurrection already in this present life. Resurrection and acquittal on the Day of Judgment on the grounds that sins have already been forgiven: these are the conditions of entrance into the Kingdom of God and its blessedness. Christianity had been the religion of faith in the Kingdom of God; now it became the religion of faith in the resurrection and the forgiveness of sins.

Greek theology is chiefly interested in the problem of reaching certainty with regard to the possession of power to rise again from the dead; in the West it is the forgiveness of sins of which theology wants to make sure. The task was made easier in both cases by the work that Paul had done. He was the first to tackle the question of being actually redeemed before the full revelation of the Kingdom of God; and he solved it in his own way. Later generations, however, could not simply adopt his solution, since they lacked the glowing eschatological expectation that lay behind his doctrine of the possession of eternal life and the forgiveness of sins through mystical union with Christ. But Paul's theology is a magnificent structure, and it provided material that could be used for buildings of another style.

The creators of Greek theology are known to us through their writings: Ignatius, bishop of Antioch, who suffered martyrdom in Rome in the second decade of the second century; Justin Martyr, born in Palestine, who shared the same fate in Rome in 165; and Irenaeus, from Asia Minor, who was made bishop of Lyons in 178.

Their teaching starts from Paul's view of the power of resurrection, which the Spirit imparts to the physical nature of Jesus and of believers. Appropriating this, they develop and reshape it. Their reshaping consists in placing the work of the Spirit, which follows upon the death and resurrection of Jesus, in the long-continuing course of the natural order, whereas Paul assigned it to the era during which the natural world was being transformed into the supernatural world of the Kingdom of God.

Greek theology found it possible to assert, as if it were quite obvious, only that the Spirit prepares the body for the coming resurrection because this was stated in Paul's epistles. There was nothing in the primitive Christian doctrine of the Spirit to justify the idea, but Paul's teaching gave it apostolic authority. His sovereign treatment of the Jewish eschatological doctrine of the work of the Spirit gave to the Christian faith something that Greek religious thought could appropriate. Ignatius, Justin, and Irenaeus turned the eschatological mysticism of being "in Christ" into Greek mysticism.

The fundamental idea in Greek theology is that the Spirit first entered into union with human flesh in the person of Jesus and thus gained the power to work upon man's physical nature. This power was further exercised among men after Jesus was separated from the world by his death and resurrection. As a new principle of life, it regenerates men spiritually and physically, so that they are fitted for eventual entrance into the Kingdom of God. The new life, which is for Paul the effect of being already risen with Christ, is regarded by Greek theology as being born again through the Spirit; the theory of dying and rising again with Christ is gone. The effect is the same as it was for Paul, but the sole cause is now said to be the working of the Spirit.

The Greek Fathers agree with Paul that the transformation of believers is due to the death and resurrection of Jesus, but for them it takes place with the Kingdom of God in view, and not, as for him, in the Kingdom already present. According to their teaching, believers live no longer in the world but in the intermediate realm of the Spirit, until the Kingdom comes. Ignatius and Justin set the seal of martyrdom on this doctrine—noblest of its kind—of world-renunciation through the Spirit.

Western theology is concerned mainly with the doctrine of the forgiveness of sins, and its task is to interpret the death of Jesus in such a way that men may find in it forgiveness ever available, ever renewed, for all the lapses of which they become guilty. Only thus can believers have the assurance that their redemption has already been achieved; for them the Kingdom is not at hand, but far away, and the whole of their life in this world has to be lived in the midst of temptation.

Neither Jesus himself nor Paul offers this view of the efficacy of the atoning death on the Cross.

Jesus takes it for granted, in his preaching, that God in his tender mercy guarantees forgiveness to those who truly repent. The Lord's Prayer attaches the condition that the petitioner must have forgiven all his debtors.

Two sayings of Jesus, from the later period of his activity, give an atoning significance to his death:

> The Son of man came not to be ministered unto, but to minister, and to give his life a ransom for many (Mark 10:45).
> This is my blood of the covenant, which is shed for many (Mark 14:24).
> (. . . unto remission of sins; Matt. 26:28).

The atoning value of his death, according to Jesus, does not interfere with the direct flowing of forgiveness from the tender mercy of God but adds something to it. Its object, as he sees it, is not to enable God to forgive but to save the faithful from having to pay the penalty of their sins in the tribulation preceding the advent of the Messiah, to put an end to the power of the evil one without exposing them to his final onslaught, and to bring in the Kingdom of God without this ghastly prelude.

Jesus undertakes his Passion in order that the last petition of the Lord's Prayer may be fulfilled: "Lead us not into temptation, but deliver us from evil." "Temptation" means "trial," and refers to the pre-Messianic tribulation that was to take place before the coming of the Kingdom, according to late-Jewish eschatology. The words and deeds of Jesus can be understood only when due attention is paid to his preoccupation with this dreadful anticipation.

No teaching about the atonement is given by Jesus to his disciples; he demands of them no theory about it, no faith in it. It remains his secret. He neither poses as the coming Messiah nor seeks faith in himself as such. It is enough that his followers believe in the coming of the Kingdom of God and prepare for entrance into it by repentance and fulfillment of his higher moral law. Who he is and what he has done for them will come home to them when the Kingdom is there and they have entered into it without passing through the great tribulation.

The meaning of the Passion for Jesus himself is rooted in eschatology, its object being to destroy the force of a certain prediction. The many, who are to be ransomed, are believers who await with him the coming of the Kingdom, not mankind as a whole. His own generation is the last. The end of this world is close at hand.

We cannot tell how far the disciples and the first Christians were concerned with the problem of the pre-Messianic tribulation or how far they were persuaded that, for them, atonement, having been wrought by the death of Jesus, would not involve this tribulation. After the crucifixion they found themselves in a situation that left no room for that way of thinking. They knew, from the hints that he had given them, that he was the Messiah and the Son of Man, about to be revealed in his glory, and that his death effected an atonement, involving their own forgiveness, and the coming of the Kingdom.

Having no precise doctrine of the atonement, the apostles and first believers took the simple view that through his death Jesus had gained the forgiveness of sins for them, and so they would escape condemnation in the judgment that would take place upon the coming of the Kingdom of God. Thus, the atoning death of Jesus was given a new meaning at the very beginning; the original idea of Jesus himself was displaced by the view that it was actually the necessary condition of the divine forgiveness of sins. This created an insoluble problem. How is it conceivable that God forgives sins only on the grounds that Jesus has died? How is such a view to be reconciled with the fact that, in the Lord's Prayer, Jesus teaches us to ask for forgiveness as if it could be granted only through the mercy of God to those who forgive their debtors?

It was centuries before anybody had the courage to face this problem. The first really to do so was the Schoolman Anselm of Canterbury (1033–1109), in his famous writing *Cur Deus homo* (Why must God become man?). He argues that God's honor has been damaged by man's sin and that there can be no forgiveness without satisfaction. This cannot be provided by sinful man. But, in his love, God means to forgive. Only a human being who is at the same time God, and, therefore, perfect and sinless, can give adequate satisfaction. Therefore, Jesus came into the world and achieved this through his voluntary death, thus enabling God to act both with justice and with love. All subsequent efforts to solve the problem follow in the track of this completely unsatisfactory explanation.

Those who cannot reconcile their conception of God with a belief that he needs a sacrifice before he can forgive sins are at liberty to look simply to his mercy for forgiveness and to find redemption in the gift of the Spirit of God through Jesus, whereby we are taken out of this world and brought to God.

The fundamental meaning of the death of Jesus for Paul is that he has thereby brought to an end the dominion of the powers of evil in the world and set in motion the process, shown in his resurrection, of transforming the natural world into the supernatural. This is in full harmony with the view held by Jesus himself of the effect of his self-sacrifice in death.

Paul is giving expression to the simple early Christian belief in the forgiveness of sins, when he says that God overlooks the sins committed formerly on the grounds of the atonement wrought by Jesus (Rom. 3:25), not reckoning them (2 Cor. 5:19), and that Jesus delivers believers from the wrath to come (1 Thess. 1:10; Rom. 5:9).

But Paul does not hold to the early view that the death of Jesus makes it possible for the Kingdom to come and, by its atoning efficacy, procures forgiveness for believers on the Day of Judgment. His position is that believers are already free from all sins, basing this on his theory that the transformation of the natural world into the supernatural has already begun and is going on in those who die and rise again with Christ. "We are dead to sin." "He that hath died is justified from sin." "Ye are not in the flesh, but in the spirit." (Rom. 6:2, 7; 8:9). Sin no longer comes into consideration for believers who have, with Paul, the assurance that they are sharers in a real and complete forgiveness of sins.

His polemic against those Christians who are still under the sway of the Jewish view that righteousness is earned by practicing circumcision and observing the Law leads Paul to fashion the doctrine of justification by faith in Jesus Christ alone. "But now apart from the Law a righteousness of God hath been manifested, . . . even the righteousness of God through faith in Jesus Christ; . . . justified freely by his grace through the redemption that is in Christ Jesus" (Rom. 3:21–24).

This assurance of already possessing the full reality of redemption, which goes so far beyond the experience of the first Christians, rested for Paul on his conviction that believers are already risen again, since union with Jesus, through faith and the power of his death, involves dying and rising again with him; they are already in the Kingdom of God. The righteousness that is the qualification for entrance into the Kingdom is no longer something to be striven after. Believers must have it already through their faith in Jesus; otherwise, they could not find themselves sharing in the resurrection, which proves that they are already partakers in the Kingdom of God.

Paul's doctrine is not one of continuous forgiveness but of full forgiveness. He does not take into consideration the possibility of going on sinning after becoming a believer. But his view of justification by faith alone is of fundamental importance for the later rise and development of the doctrine of continuous forgiveness. This made its appearance when Paul's doctrine was separated from eschatology and from the eschatological mysticism of union with Christ in his death and resurrection.

Early Christianity did not contemplate the possibility that further generations of men would make their appearance upon the earth after the death of Jesus. But that is what happened. So it became necessary to widen the scope of the doctrine of the atonement, in order to make it possible for men, yet to be born, to obtain the forgiveness of sins on becoming believers.

If forgiveness becomes available for men of all ages, it must be thought of as being continuous. That was not necessary at the beginning, when the Kingdom was expected immediately. What men needed then was the forgiveness of sins committed before their conversion. The early Christians' view was that this was procured by the death of Jesus and became theirs in baptism. The presumption was that they would continue sinless during the short period of waiting for the Kingdom. Forgiveness takes place, for them as for Paul, only once (cf. Rom. 3:25). But those who have to live the whole of their life in the natural, sinful world need to be assured that believers go on being forgiven again and again for the lapses of which they are guilty in the course of time.

There was, however, a great difficulty in the development of the new doctrine. Baptism could mean only what it had meant from the beginning, namely, the bestowal of forgiveness for past sins. Its character could not be altered, and it remained unaffected by the abandonment of an immediate expectation of the coming of the Kingdom. The problem thus arose as to whether post-baptismal sins can be forgiven at all, and if they can, by what means this is to be accomplished.

At first the possibility was strongly denied. The author of the epistle to the Hebrews, writing between the years 70 and 80, says that "as touching those who were once enlightened . . . and were made partakers of the Holy Spirit, and tasted the good word of God, and the powers of the age to come, and then fell away, it is impossible to renew them again unto repentance, seeing they crucify to themselves the Son of God afresh, and put him to an open shame" (Heb. 6:4–6).

Hermas, a Roman layman, at the beginning of the second century, asserts the possibility of obtaining forgiveness for later sins by means of a second repentance, in addition to that which led to baptism. He does this on the strength of a revelation brought to him by an "Angel of repentance" who appeared to him in the form of a shepherd. In his book, *The Shepherd of Hermas*, which appeared about AD 130, he announces that God in his mercy is willing to give believers the possibility of regaining their standing in grace by means of a repeated repentance. The Church could do no other than accept this view, which allowed her to take back sinners whom she had been compelled to excommunicate, after they had renewed their repentance.

But the atoning death of Jesus happened only once; and the same is true of the forgiveness that he procured. The recognition of a forgiveness for sins committed after baptism places the Church in the peculiar position of having to admit that besides the forgiveness made possible by the death of Jesus, there is another, not resting on that foundation but granted directly through God's mercy to those who, by repentance and other good works, are found worthy of this grace. Among good works recognized, in addition to public repentance, as having satisfaction-value are: suffering, which has atoning virtue, faithfulness under persecution, deeds of love, and the conversion of heretics.

The Church is the stewardess of this supplementary forgiveness. She prescribes what the sinner must do in the way of repentance and satisfaction, exercises oversight, and assesses to what degree he has done his duty. When she judges that he can have found forgiveness with God, she takes him back into the congregation. She makes no claim to forgive but feels herself to be the announcer of the forgiveness that God has granted.

But the matter cannot rest there, with the permission of only one supplementary forgiveness; it gradually comes to repentance procuring forgiveness again and again. And then there is the problem of differentiating between venial sins and those that are too serious to be forgiven. Thus, in the course of time, the idea of continuous forgiveness was reached.

Augustine (354–430) lays it down as a principle that forgiveness is available within the Church for all sins committed after baptism, provided appropriate satisfaction is made. Outside the Church there is no pardon. Not to believe in the continuous forgiveness of sins within the Church is to commit the sin against the Holy Spirit.

Contemporary new ideas mentioned by Augustine in connection with continuous forgiveness are that of purgatory and that of the offering of prayer, alms and the sacrifice of the Mass by the living on behalf of the dead, that they may find forgiveness.

Purgatory is not punishment in hell, but only a possibility, held out to the sinner after death, of completing, by the endurance of torment, the repentance of which he fell short in his earthly life.

The idea that in the Mass the body and blood of Jesus are offered up afresh as an atoning sacrifice to God appears first in Cyprian, bishop of Carthage, who died as a martyr in 258. Augustine understands this in a purely spiritual sense. The realistic view established itself under Pope Gregory I (590–604), namely, that in the Mass Jesus is offered as a sacrifice sacramentally again and again, to bring the benefit of the atonement to the living and the dead. This sacramental repetition implies that the forgiveness brought about by Jesus on Golgotha avails, not only for sins committed before baptism, but also—as it were, by a side-channel—for those committed after. By letting its priests carry out this repetition of the atoning sacrifice of Jesus, the Church helps establish the view that it brings about and bestows the forgiveness of sins, instead of merely announcing it as something that God does when adequate satisfaction is offered.

Subsequently it became customary for more and more Masses to be celebrated. These were no longer congregational acts of worship but were intended only to convey the atoning power of the sacramental repetition of the death of Jesus to those, living or dead, on whose behalf they were held. Toward the end of the Middle Ages, all Churches had, in addition to the high altar, side altars at which these special Masses were said.

Continuous forgiveness became generally easier and easier to obtain during the Middle Ages—and more and more dependent upon outward performances. It gradually became the custom to secure exemption from the penance ordered by the priests on the grounds of merits or of payments to the Church. Those who took part in the Crusades obtained full exemption. From the twelfth century, those who did not go to war against the infidel could get their indulgence by the payment of money. The Schoolmen justified the dispensation of indulgences by the popes on the grounds that they were the custodians of the accumulated merits of the saints. In the year 1477 Pope Sixtus IV (1471–1484) announced that indulgences were also valid for souls in purgatory and would shorten the time of their purification.

It was widely felt at the end of the Middle Ages that this state of affairs was unsatisfactory. But simply to reform the doctrine of continuous forgiveness and return to the purity of its original formulation would not meet the case.

Then there appeared on the scene Martin Luther (1483–1546), a man of outstanding religious personality, who first objected to the unspiritual practices that had come to be associated with the Church's doctrine of continuous forgiveness, and then proceeded to question its underlying principle.

As a monk, Luther tried to reach the assurance of forgiveness along the orthodox lines. He did not succeed. In his agony, he asked himself whether he was not one of those predestined to damnation, since all his penance, and the absolution that he received, failed to bring him the deliverance for which he looked.

Through Augustine he was led to Paul, whose doctrine of justification by faith alone, without works, was the light that penetrated his darkness. His final spiritual deliverance took place in 1512, and he owed it to Paul. We have, in his lectures at the University of Wittenberg on the Psalms (1513–1515), Romans (1515–1516), Galatians (1516), and Hebrews (1517), the working out of his new conception of continuous forgiveness on the grounds of faith in the operation of the atoning death of Jesus.

Luther inevitably discovered that the Catholic view of baptism was the basis of the doctrine of continuous forgiveness as dependent on justification by works and not by faith. It was this that ruled out the attribution of continuous forgiveness to the atoning death of Jesus. It was responsible for the view that post-baptismal sins required justification by works to obtain forgiveness.

But the effect of baptism should not be confined to the forgiveness of past sins through Jesus' death; it ought to secure for the believer the possibility of finding continuous forgiveness at the Cross. So Luther propounded the doctrine that baptism "is the beginning and gateway of all grace and forgiveness." The pardon that men need every day is just the renewal of baptismal grace, freely given by God on the grounds of faith in the atoning work of Christ.

The conflict between Luther and the Catholic Church turned finally upon the doctrine of baptism. Historically, Luther was in the wrong. He intended to restore the simple original doctrine, from which he thought the Church had departed. But it was the Church, and not Luther, that held the old idea of baptism. Religiously, however, his view was right, for it made it possible to believe in the continuous forgiveness of sins as coming directly from God through Christ.

The Catholic doctrine of baptism is the only thing that has been preserved unaltered throughout the centuries from the first age of eschatological faith. It was a big step in the movement away from eschatology when Luther formulated his doctrine of baptism without any reference to the last things.

Luther's doctrine of forgiveness is not identical with Paul's; it is a restatement of it without the primitive eschatology. It was because Paul was the only great thinker in the early Church who saw clearly that redemption, like the Kingdom, was not something in the future, but a present reality, that Luther found in him the substance and the spirit of his own doctrine of salvation now through the continuous forgiveness of sins. The latter meant for him what the nearness of the Kingdom meant for Paul.

So Luther sounds the same note of victory as Paul, a note that had not been heard in Christian preaching since Paul's day. His sense of triumph leads him away from that denial of the world to which the Church was still committed in spite of its weakened eschatology. He does not ask for renunciation of the world as the expression of true Christianity; what he enjoins is faithful performance of daily duties in the way of our earthly calling and the practice of love to our neighbor. He erects an ideal of Christian perfection that attaches real value to the state, to marriage, and to lawful occupations, and views daily labor, however humble, as service required by God. He feels himself moved to agree with the affirmation of life and the world, although he does not break away from that pessimistic judgment of the world that is involved in the later form of eschatology. In this he was prophetic of what was to happen later in the history of Protestantism.

Luther also combines the conservative with the progressive in that he attaches great importance to the acknowledgment that his doctrine agrees with that of the Church of the first centuries and yet does not make this agreement a rallying point for Protestants but summons them to study the Gospel in the New Testament, recognizing it as their supreme and sole authority.

This principle is the inspiration for the free and dauntless search for religious truth. Luther could not measure the scope of this study of the original Gospel and the recognition of its supreme authority; the road, which he opened up, led further afield than he could ever have imagined. And yet, by following this road, Protestantism completed what Luther had begun. His rejection of the Catholic doctrine of continuous forgiveness as based on primitive Christian baptism, in favor of a new doctrine, constitutes the penultimate stage in the movement of Christianity away from eschatology. The last stage is the surrender of the eschatological idea of the Kingdom of God, with the acceptance of a view that is not determined by its relation to the last things. This is the experience for which Protestantism was destined in its effort to get back to the true Gospel.

What then, is being done to effect this surrender and eliminate eschatology from the conception of the Kingdom? How are matters going?

The fundamental presupposition necessary for this change is provided by the existence of a new attitude toward the world. The affirmation and acceptance of the world begin to take their place beside the traditional Christian denial and rejection of it, which resulted from eschatology.

When it first makes its appearance in the fourteenth century, the positive attitude can hardly be described as a philosophy; it consists, rather, in the rejection of the spirit of the Middle Ages and all that it comprises.

With the contemporary rise and growth of natural science, a more profound level is reached. The order and harmony of the universe come into view as the result of the astronomy of a Copernicus (1473–1543), a Kepler (1571–1630), and a Galileo (1564–1642). Advances in knowledge and skill encourage a belief in progress, and this adds to the strength and vitality of the acceptance of life and the world. The spirit of man acquires an unprecedented confidence in human capacity and creative power in every field. Thus, by the time of a Giordano Bruno (1548–1600), the new attitude has attained the stature of a philosophy.

Clarified and deepened under the influence of the achievements of natural science, the movement then gains strength by appropriating the ethics of later Stoicism, as found in the writings of Cicero (106–43 BC) and developed by Seneca (4 BC–AD 65), Epictetus (50–138), and Marcus Aurelius (120–180). Hugo Grotius (1583–1645) shows how completely the modern acceptance of life and the world is under the influence of the Stoic ideal of humanity. Here is something absolutely new in the intellectual history of Europe: a philosophical acceptance of the world with a moral outlook. Herein lies the differentia of modern European man, as compared with man in earlier times. He has a new intellectual attitude, believing in progress, determined to do all he can to help the world onward and upward, and disposed to universal charity.

The ethical quality of the new outlook makes it acceptable to Christians, who are prepared for it by the ethical teaching of Jesus. For although the latter adopted a negative attitude to life and the world, it did not lose itself in absolute pessimism. That would have involved accepting the ideal of inactivity, whereas Christianity means active love.

The reason that the ethics of Jesus is practical is to be found in the fact that the eschatological denial of the world does not go as far as the Indian. It does not reject existence as such in favor of nonexistence, like the Indian, but only the natural, imperfect, painful world in prospect of the world of the Kingdom of God. Its view is that man must prove and demonstrate his calling to take part in the perfecting of existence by living an active moral life in the natural world. The ethics of Jesus has an affinity with the ethical philosophy of world-acceptance in so far as its ideal is one of activity.

Modern Protestant Christianity takes a long time to break away from world-denial. The hymns of the Church remain under its influence until late in the eighteenth century. Escape from the world provides the leading motif in the cantatas of Johann Sebastian Bach (1685–1750); yet, the Protestantism of that time is moving irresistibly in the direction of a philosophy of world-acceptance. It is not conscious of the step that it is taking; the passage from the old to the new is concealed by the fact that there is so much in common between Christianity and ethical world-acceptance. The point of contact is in the ethics: the Stoic ideal of humanity comes very close to Jesus' ideal of love. So the passage of Christianity in the new age from the ethical negative to the ethical positive view takes place without observation and without conflict.

Belief in the Kingdom of God now takes a new lease of life. It no longer looks for its coming, self-determined, as an eschatological cosmic event, but regards it as something ethical and spiritual, not bound up with the last things, but to be realized with the cooperation of men.

In ancient and medieval times, Christians had no faith in progress, no urge to go forward, no idea that things could be moving onward and upward; yet, it never occurred to them that they were in an unnatural situation so long as their religious life was based on the idea that the Kingdom of God lay far away in the future. It seemed obvious to them that passivity concerning the Kingdom was the only possible attitude.

It is otherwise with those of the new age who are under the influence of the ethical affirmation of the world. What they think is that the Kingdom is something ethical and religious, to be conceived as developing in this world, and requiring ethical effort on the part of believers. This is so obvious to them that they can conceive of no other way of looking at the subject; they understand the Gospels to say that Jesus came into this world to found the Kingdom and to call men into it as fellow workers. Just as Luther substituted his non-eschatological view of baptism for that of the early Church, convinced that it was the authentic teaching of the Gospels, so modern Protestantism substitutes its view of the Kingdom of God and its coming for the eschatological view that Jesus presented, as if it really represented the original. Historically, both are wrong; but, religiously, both are right.

Only as it comes to be understood as something ethical and spiritual, rather than supernatural, as something to be realized rather than expected, can the Kingdom of God regain, in our faith, the force that it had for Jesus and the early Church. Christianity must have a firm hold of this, if it is to remain true to itself, as it was at the beginning—religion dominated by the idea of the Kingdom of God. What the Kingdom of God is, in reality, is shown by the part that it plays in the life of faith. The precise conception that is held of its coming is a matter of secondary consideration. In spite of many fundamental differences from the past, modern Protestant Christianity remains true to the Gospel since it is still the religion of a living faith in the Kingdom of God.

About the end of the eighteenth and the beginning of the nineteenth century, "Lives of Jesus" began to appear, these being the first efforts to reach a historical understanding of his earthly life and teaching. Mention may be made of the works of Johann Jakob Hess (1768–1772)—in three volumes—Franz Volkmar Reinhard (1781), Johann Gottfried Herder (1796), Heinrich Eberhard Gottlob Paulus (1828), and Karl August Hase (1829).

According to these, Jesus appeared before the Jews, whose hopes of the Kingdom of God and the Messiah were materialistic and mundane, as the true Messiah, quite different in character, who made the beginning of a Kingdom of God, which meant the control of human life by the Spirit of God. The idea that Jesus spiritualized the Jewish hope of the Kingdom continued to dominate historical and critical theology during the second half of the nineteenth century. It was set forth by Adolf Harnack in his famous lectures at Berlin University in the winter of 1899–1900 under the title, "What Is Christianity?"

Even at that time, there were grounds for questioning this idea. More careful study of the documents of later Jewish eschatology revealed the fact that their fundamental conceptions were shared by sayings of Jesus concerning the Kingdom of God and the Messiah. This is especially clear in the records of Matthew and Mark, which, in this respect, are shown to be the oldest. But it seemed impossible to believe that Jesus should not have held views about the Kingdom of God and his own Messianic calling that were in harmony with the inwardness and depth of his ideal of love.

At the beginning of this century, therefore, the difficulty was overcome by putting forward the theory that the sayings in question were not actually uttered by Jesus. They had been introduced into the tradition by the early Church, which was still under the influence of the later Jewish eschatology. Harnack and others even suggested that Jesus was able to combine elements of that eschatology with his own spiritual view of the Kingdom in some way that is beyond our comprehension.

But already in 1892 Johannes Weiss, of Heidelberg, had shown that it is impossible to differentiate the eschatological view of the Kingdom and the Messiah, held by Jesus, from that of later Judaism—in his study, *The Preaching of Jesus Concerning the Kingdom of God,* based on Matthew and Mark. I carried Johannes Weiss's argument to its conclusion in my sketch of the life of Jesus, *The Mystery of the Kingdom of God* (1901) and my *Quest of the Historical Jesus* (1906), showing that eschatology not only colored the thoughts of Jesus but also determined his actions.

Those who have the courage to let Matthew and Luke mean what they say must agree that Jesus shared the later Jewish view of the advent of the Kingdom of God, not spiritualizing it but using it as a vehicle for his profound and powerful ideal of love.

It is hard for us to bring ourselves to the point of admitting that Jesus, who is uniquely endowed with the Spirit of God, and is for us the supreme revealer of religious and spiritual truth, does not stand above his age in the way that might seem to be demanded by the significance that he has for all ages.

What we should prefer is that we, and men of every age, might find in Jesus the final truth of religion available in a form that need never be changed. And now we are confronted by the fact that he shared the outlook of an age long past, which is to us mistaken and unacceptable. Why should Christianity have to endure this? Is it not a wound for which there is no balm? Ought we not to maintain the absolute inerrancy of Jesus in matters of religion? Are we not rejecting his authority?

Both Johannes Weiss and I have suffered severely through the compulsion that truth laid upon us to put forward something that was bound to offend Christian faith.

To me, however, Jesus remains what he was. Not for a single moment have I had to struggle for my conviction that in him is the supreme spiritual and religious authority, though his expectation of the speedy advent of a supernatural Kingdom of God was not fulfilled, and we cannot make it our own.

The difficulty can be overcome only by a right apprehension of what is meant by the inerrancy of Jesus.

Our assumption of the limitation of his knowledge does not mean that he had an understanding of nature equal to that attained, or ever attainable, by modern science, but refrained from using it. The historical Jesus stands before us as one who, naturally, shared the outlook of his time. This is not a pose but an actual reality. Anything else would involve a dissimulation, which we can never associate with him.

If Jesus thinks like his contemporaries about the world and what happens in it, then his view of the coming of the Kingdom of God must resemble that of later Judaism.

It is perfectly clear to anyone who studies deeply the way in which progress is achieved in history that what is absolutely new does not easily establish itself, and if, for any reason, it does succeed, it is apt to appear unnatural and questionable. So we must believe that, if Jesus had appeared with a fully spiritualized view of the Kingdom and its coming, his proclamation of it would never have been believed. The ancient world, Jewish, Greek, and Roman, would have had no point of contact with such an announcement. To enable it to do its work naturally, every new idea must be in some way embedded in what is old, and thus be linked with that which preceded it. Jesus ends a series of parables of the Kingdom of God with the remarkable saying, "Therefore every scribe who hath been made a disciple to the Kingdom of heaven is like unto a man that is a householder, which bringeth forth out of his treasure things new and old" (Matt. 13:52).

Truth cannot dissociate itself from the time process; it must work within it. Jesus spiritualizes the conception of the Kingdom of God, in that he brings it into subjection to his ideal and ethics of love. In due time this transforms the conception of the Kingdom.

Spiritual truth is concerned with the knowledge of what we must become spiritually in order to be in a right relationship to God. It is complete in itself. It is intuitive knowledge of what ought to be in the realm of the spirit. All other knowledge is of a different kind, having to do not with what happens in us but with what goes on in the world—a field in which understanding can only be limited and liable to change.

The conception of the realization of a spiritual idea on a universal scale is conditioned by the conception of the world and its events that prevails at a particular time. The fact that Jesus thinks of the realization of the Kingdom of God in a way that is not justified by events does not call into question his authority as a unique revealer of spiritual truth; it challenges only the traditional view of his personality and authority. Christian faith, under the influence of Greek metaphysics, was pleased to confer upon him a divinity and a divine inerrancy to which he made no claim. We shall deal successfully with the problem of his unfulfilled promise only when we turn back to see exactly how he confronts us in the two oldest Gospels. He is so great that the discovery that he belongs to his age can do him no harm. He remains our spiritual Lord.

All attempts to avoid the admission that Jesus held a view of the Kingdom of God and its coming that was not fulfilled and cannot be adopted by us involve the shirking of the truth. Devotion to truth in this matter is of the essence of spiritual life. Faith that refuses to face indisputable facts is but little faith. Truth is always gain, however hard it is to accommodate ourselves to it. To linger in any kind of untruth proves to be a departure from the straight way of faith.

The modern view of the Kingdom of God and its coming creates a spiritual situation comparable to that of Jesus and his little flock and of the early Church. Again, after many centuries, the Kingdom of God has become a live question. Again, mankind as a whole is changing its mind as to what it really means.

Modern faith finds the beginning of the Kingdom of God in Jesus and in the Spirit, which came into the world with him. We no longer leave the fate of mankind to be decided at the end of the world. The time in which we live summons us to new faith in the Kingdom of God.

We are no longer content, as were the generations before us, to believe in the Kingdom that comes of itself at the end of time. Mankind today must either realize the Kingdom of God or perish. The very tragedy of our present situation compels us to devote ourselves in faith to its realization.

We are at the beginning of the end of the human race. The question before it is whether it will use for beneficial purposes or for purposes of destruction the power that modern science has placed in its hands. So long as its capacity for destruction was limited, it was possible to hope that reason would set a limit to disaster. Such an illusion is impossible today, when its power is illimitable. Our only hope is that the Spirit of God will strive with the spirit of the world and will prevail.

The last petition of the Lord's Prayer has again its original meaning for us as a prayer for deliverance from the dominion of the evil powers of the world. These powers are no less real to us as working in men's minds, instead of being embodied in angelic beings opposed to God. The first believers set their hope solely upon the Kingdom of God in expectation of the end of the world; we do it in expectation of the end of the human race.

The Spirit shows us the signs of the time and their meaning.

Belief in the Kingdom of God makes the biggest demands of all the articles of the Christian faith. It means believing the seemingly impossible—the conquest of the spirit of the world by the Spirit of God. We look with confidence for the miracle to be wrought through the Spirit.

The miracle must happen in us before it can happen in the world. We dare not set our hope on our own efforts to create the conditions of God's Kingdom in the world. We must indeed labor for its realization. But there can be no Kingdom of God in the world without the Kingdom of God in our hearts. The starting point is our determined effort to bring every thought and action under the sway of the Kingdom of God. Nothing can be achieved without inwardness. The Spirit of God will strive against the spirit of the world only when it has won its victory over that spirit in our hearts.

4

Religion in Modern Civilization

In this essay Schweitzer emphasizes the problematic role of religion in our time and criticizes several philosophical views for undermining the status of religion in contemporary civilization. He first points out that religion is not a force in our time, and as proof he draws on World War I: during this war religion put itself in the service of politics. Religion is not a force because it has become dogmatic and has lost the vital connection with ethics and critical thinking. Religion's preoccupation is with personal redemption, rather than with the pursuit of moral perfection for all of humanity. Schweitzer criticizes four philosophical orientations that lead to the dogmatization of religion: (1) materialism, which he calls "the religion of natural science" and which he criticizes for focusing primarily on the material good of the community, (2) Kantianism, which unlike material- ism, accepts the existence of God but reduces the role of God to something of secondary importance, (3) the philosophy of values and pragmatism, which Schweitzer traces back to Hume, and which advocates an irrevoca- ble dualism of spiritual and theoretical truths, and (4) "obscurism," which denies the role of reason and thought for our ethical orientation and relies solely on mystical intuition.

I am going to discuss religion in the spiritual life and civilization of our time. The first question to be faced, therefore, is: "Is religion a force in the spiritual life of our age?" I answer, in your name and

Complete essay; originally published in *The Christian Century*, November 21 and 28, 1934, 1483–1484, 1519–1521.

mine, "No!" There is still religion in the world; there is much religion in the Church; there are many pious people among us. Christianity can still point to works of love and to social works of which it can be proud. There is a longing for religion among many who no longer belong to the churches. I rejoice to concede this. And yet we must hold fast to the fact that religion is not a force. The proof? The war!

Religion was powerless to resist the spirit through which we entered the war. It was overcome by this spirit. It could bring no force against the ideals of inhumanity and unreasonableness that gave birth to the war, and when war had broken out, religion capitulated. It became mobilized. It had to join in helping keep up the courage of the peoples. To give each people courage to go on fighting, one had to explain that they were fighting for their existence and for the spiritual treasures of humanity. Religion helped give this conviction. It is easy to understand why it did this. It seemed a necessity. It remains true, however, that in the war religion lost its purity, and lost its authority. It joined forces with the spirit of the world. The one victim of defeat was religion. And that religion was defeated is apparent in our time. For it lifts up its voice but only to protest. It cannot command. The spirit of the age does not listen. It goes its own way.

How did it come about that ethical ideals could not oppose the inhuman ideals of the war? It was due to the spirit of practical realism. I place at opposite extremes the spirit of idealism and the spirit of realism. The spirit of idealism means that men and women of the period arrive at ethical ideals through thinking and that these ideals are so powerful that they say: We will use them to control reality. We will transform reality in accordance with these ideals. The spirit of idealism desires to have power over the spirit of realism. The spirit of practical realism, however, holds it false to apply ideals to what is happening. The spirit of realism has no power over reality. If a generation lives with these ideas, it is subject to reality. This is the tragedy that is being enacted in our age. For what is characteristic of our age is that we no longer really believe in social or spiritual progress but face reality powerless.

The religion of our age gives the same impression as an African river in the dry season—a great riverbed, sandbanks, and between, a small stream that seeks its way. One tries to imagine that a river once filled that bed, that there were no sandbanks but that the river flowed majestically on its way, and that it will someday be like that again. Is it possible, you say, that once a river filled this bed? Was there a time when ethical religion was a force in the spiritual life of the time? Yes, in the eighteenth century. Then, ethical religion and thinking formed one unity. Thinking was religious, and religion was a thinking religion. Because it was conditioned by ethical religious ideas, the thinking of that period undertook to represent reality to itself as it should be. It possessed ethical ideals in accordance with which it transformed reality.

And, as a matter of fact, because it was filled with ideals of this kind, it had power over reality. It undertook a great work of reform. It waged war against superstition and ignorance. It obtained recognition for humanity in the eyes of the law. Torture was abolished, first in Prussia in the year 1740 through a cabinet order of Frederick the Great. It was demanded of the individual that he should place himself at the service of the community. English emigrants formulated in America for the first time the rights of man. The idea of humanity began to gain in significance. People dared to grasp the thought that lasting peace must reign on earth. Kant wrote an essay, "Toward Perpetual Peace" (1795), and in it represented the thought that even politics must submit to the principles of ethics. Finally came the abolition of slavery, as an achievement that the spirit of the eighteenth century brought about in the nineteenth century.

The religious–ethical spirit of the eighteenth century desired then to make the Kingdom of God a reality on earth.

Then, in the nineteenth century the spirit of realism rose against this spirit of idealism. The first personality in which it was realized was Napoleon I. The first thinker in whom it announced itself was the German philosopher Hegel. Men, Hegel maintained, do not have to transform reality in order to bring it into accord with ideals devised by thinking. Progress takes place automatically in the natural course of events. The passions of ruling personalities and of peoples in some way or other are in the service of progress—even war is. The view that ethical idealism is a form of sentimentality of which no use can be made in the world of reality began with Hegel. He was the first to formulate the theory of rationalism. He wrote: "What is reasonable is real, and what is real is reasonable." On the night of June 25, 1820, when that sentence was written, our age began, the age that moved on to the world war—and which perhaps some day will end civilization!

Hegel dares to say that everything serves progress. The passions of rulers and of peoples—all are the servants of progress. One can say only that Hegel did not know the passions of people as we know them, or he would not have dared to write that!

One truth stands firm. All that happens in world history rests on something spiritual. If the spiritual is strong, it creates world history. If it is weak, it suffers world history. The question is, shall we make world history or only suffer it, passively? Will our thinking again become ethical–religious? Shall we again win ideals that will have power over reality? This is the question before us today.

In religion there are two different currents: one free from dogma, and one that is dogmatic. That which is free from dogma bases itself on the preaching of Jesus; the dogmatic bases itself on the creeds of the early Church and the Reformation. The religion free from dogma is to some extent the heir of rationalistic religion. It is ethical, limits itself to the fundamental ethical verities, and endeavors, so far as is in its power, to remain on good terms with thinking. It wants to realize something of the Kingdom of God in the world. It believes itself identical with the religion of Jesus. All the efforts of historical–theological science in the nineteenth century are aimed at proving that Christian dogma began with Paul and that the religion of Jesus is non-dogmatic, so that it can be adopted in any age.

But it constituted a great difficulty for the non-dogmatic religion when theological science, at the end of the nineteenth century, was forced to admit that the ethical religion of Jesus shared the supernatural ideas of late-Jewish belief in the Messianic Kingdom and indeed that it also shared with it its expectation of the approaching end of the world. Here it becomes clear that there is no purely historical foundation for religion. We must take the ethical religion of Jesus out of the setting of his worldview and put it in our own. Whereas he expected the Kingdom of God to come at the end of the world, we must endeavor, under the influence of the spirit of his ethical religion, to make the Kingdom of God a reality in this world by works of love.

Dogmatic religion is based on the creeds, the early Church, and the Reformation. It has no relations with thinking but emphasizes the difference between thinking and believing. This religion, further, is more dominated by the thought of redemption than by that of the Kingdom of God. It has no wish to influence the world. That is the characteristic of all the ancient creeds—that the idea of the Kingdom of God finds no expression in them.

Why did the idea of the Kingdom of God have no significance in the early Church? It was closely connected with the expectation of the end of the world. And when hope of the coming of the end of the world had faded, the idea of the Kingdom of God lost its force as well. So it came about that the creeds were not at the same time preoccupied with the idea of redemption. Only after the Reformation did the idea gradually arise that we men and women in our own age must so understand the religion of Jesus that we endeavor to make the Kingdom of God a reality in this world. It is only through the idea of the Kingdom of God that religion enters into relationship with civilization.

In recent times a tendency has appeared in dogmatic religion that completely turns its back on thinking and at the same time declares that religion has nothing to do with the world and civilization. It is not its business to realize the Kingdom of God on earth. This extreme tendency is mainly represented by Karl Barth.

Karl Barth, who is the most modern theologian, because he lives most in the spirit of our age, more than any other has that contempt for thinking that is characteristic of our age. He dares to say that religion has nothing to do with thinking. He wants to give religion nothing to do with anything but God and man, the great antithesis. He says a religious person does not concern himself with what happens to the world. The idea of the Kingdom of God plays no part with him. He mocks what he calls "civilized Protestantism." The Church must leave the world to itself. All that concerns the Church is the preaching of revealed truth. Religion is turned aside from the world.

Yet Karl Barth—whom I, personally, value greatly—came to the point when he had to concern himself with the world, which, in theory, he did not want to do. He had to defend the freedom of religion against the state. And he did it with courage. But it shows that his theory is false! It is something terrible to say that religion is not ethical. Karl Barth is a truly religious personality, and in his sermons there is much profound religion. But the terrible thing is that he dares to preach that religion is turned aside from the world and, in so doing, expresses what the spirit of the age is feeling.

The spirit of the age dislikes what is simple. It no longer believes the simple can be profound. It loves the complicated and regards it as profound. It loves the violent. That is why the spirit of the age can love Karl Barth and Nietzsche at the same time. The spirit of the age loves dissonance, in tones, in words, and in thought. That shows how far from right thinking it is, for right thinking is a harmony within us.

If one reviews the development of religion since the middle of the nineteenth century, one understands the tragic fact that, although really living religion is to be found among us, it is not the leaven that leavens the thinking of our age.

Let us examine four "paths" along which thinking seeks to arrive at a religion. The first is the path of materialism—the religion of natural science. Materialism proclaims war against metaphysics. It wants only the positive—what one can really know—and by that it declares its intention of living. The ethics of materialism consists in saying: You must live for the good of the community. Has this form of ethics really the significance of a religion? Can a man understand the purpose of his life when he says: I live for the good of the community? No! The ethics of materialism is incomplete. It hangs in the air.

Further, the ethics of materialism is unnecessary. Society has no need that the individual should serve it. Society does not need his morality; it can force upon him the sociology that it holds to be best. Herbert Spencer was not only a great thinker but a great prophet. He expressed anxiety lest the state should by violence force the individual to submit to it. He was right. The ethics of materialism has not triumphed, for in our days we have experienced the state destroying the individual in order to make the individual its servant. Therefore, the ethics of materialism is no religion.

The second path is that followed by Kant and by nearly all the major philosophers of the latter half of the nineteenth century. What do they seek in order to arrive at religion? They no longer venture to say that from ethics we derive the idea of the existence of God and the immortality of the soul. They are more cautious. They ask: Does thinking arrive at anything we can call God? They seek to show that the existence of an ethical God is necessary in some way and try to prove to the materialist that without this idea he cannot rightly live.

But this ethical religion of the philosophers of the second half of the nineteenth century is not firmly grounded. Its idea of God is quite incomplete. What is ethical in such teaching has no force. It lacks compulsive power and enthusiasm, and so this fine philosophical religion has had no significance for the thinking of the world in general. It is something that cannot be placed in the center of things: it is too delicate, too cautious; it utters no commands.

The third path is that of the philosophy of values and pragmatism. The philosophy of values resorts to a type of thinking that becomes dualistic. It asserts that there are spiritual truths alongside theoretical truths and that all valuable conviction has truth in itself—a dangerous assertion. The real father of this doctrine of double truth is Hume. To escape skepticism, Hume says, we need convictions, which will help us live, and in regard to which we ask not, Are they true? but, Are they necessary for our life?

What is pragmatism compared with this philosophy of values? It is a philosophy of values that has given up the criterion of ethics. Pragmatism says: Every idea that helps me live is truth. Europeans got this pragmatism sent, all ready for use, from America, in William James. So, modern thinking arrives at the doctrine of double truth. The theory of double truth is a spiritual danger. If there is a double truth, there is no truth. The sense of sincerity is blunted, and the last thing that thinking can give humanity is a feeling for truth—for sincerity is fundamental in all spiritual life, and when this fundamental is shaken, there is no spiritual life remaining. In pragmatism, not only sincerity and truth but also ethics is in danger. For ethics is no longer the criterion of what is valuable. Pragmatism is filled with the spirit of realism. It permits men to take their ideals from reality.

The fourth path is that trod by modern thinkers emancipated from Kant. They are obscure thinkers—their thinking is obscure and, moreover, they have a talent of writing obscurely! They want to get at religion by saying: All this knowledge of the world through science is only a description of the world, from which man derives nothing. What we must know is not the essential nature of the universe. The thing we must be preoccupied with is the mystery of our life. How we understand the mystery of our life is the mystery of the universe. They say: We know the universe by intuition, not by reason. Our life knows the life in the world, and through our life we become one with the life of the universe. This thinking, therefore, is mysticism.

But ethics plays no part in this form of thought. The great problem of what man is aiming at plays no part in it.

In modern thinking the same thing happens as in religion. Thinking drops the tiller from its hand in the middle of the storm. It renounces the idea of giving to human beings ideals by the help of which they can get on with reality. It leaves them to themselves, and that in a most terrible moment. For the present moment is terrible. Man has won power over the forces of nature and by that has become superman—and, at the same time, most miserable man! For this power over the forces of nature is not being used beneficially but destructively.

Because he has power over the forces of nature, man built machines, which took work away from man, and this makes social problems of such magnitude that no one would have dreamed of them forty years ago. In some cities now air-raid practices are held, with sirens shrieking and all lights out. People shove something over their heads that makes them look like beasts and rush into cellars, while flying through the air appears the superman, possessing endless power for destruction.

Humanity has always needed ethical ideals to enable it to find the right path that man may make the right use of the power he possesses. Today his power is increased a thousand-fold. A thousand-fold greater is now the need for man to possess ethical ideals to point the way. Yet at the very moment that this happens, thinking fails. In this period of deepest need, thinking is not giving to humanity the ideals it needs so that it may not be overwhelmed. Is that our destiny? I hope not. I believe not. I think that in our age we are all carrying within us a new form of thought that will give us ethical ideals.

All thinking must renounce the attempt to explain the universe. We cannot understand what happens in the universe. What is glorious in it is united with what is full of horror. What is full of meaning is united to what is senseless. The spirit of the universe is at once creative and destructive—it creates while it destroys and destroys while it creates, and therefore it remains to us a riddle. And we must inevitably resign ourselves to this.

Thinking that keeps contact with reality must look up to the heavens; it must look over the earth and dare to direct its gaze to the barred windows of a lunatic asylum. Look to the stars and understand how small our earth is in the universe. Look upon earth and know how minute man is upon it. The earth existed long before man came upon it. In the history of the universe, man is on the earth for but a second. Who knows but that the earth will circle round the sun once more without man upon it? Therefore, we must not place man in the center of the universe. And our gaze must be fixed on the barred windows of a lunatic asylum, in order that we may remember the terrible fact that the mental and spiritual are also liable to destruction.

Only when thinking thus becomes quite humble can it set its feet upon the way that leads to knowledge. The more profound a religion is, the more it realizes this fact—that what it knows through belief is little compared with what it does not know. The first active deed of thinking is resignation—acquiescence in what happens. Becoming free, inwardly, from what happens, we pass through the gate of recognition on the way to ethics.

The deeper we look into nature, the more we recognize that it is full of life and the more profoundly we know that all life is a secret and that we are united with all life that is in nature. Man can no longer live his life for himself alone. We realize that all life is valuable and that we are united to all this life. From this knowledge comes our spiritual relationship to the universe.

In the mysticism of the Middle Ages there was this wonderful phrase, *docta ignorantia*—"knowing ignorance." That is our condition. This *docta ignorantia* has been brought to us by natural science. Have no fear of natural science—it brings us nearer to God.

There is a development under way by which the circle of ethics always grows wider, and ethics becomes more profound. This development has been in progress from primitive times to the present. It is often halted, hindered by the absence of thought among men—I dare to say, through that absence of thought that characterizes thought! But yet the development goes on to its end. The circle described by ethics is always widening. Primitive man has duties only toward his nearest relations. All other living beings are to him only things; he mistreats them and kills them, without compunction. Then the circle widens to the tribe, to the people, and grows ever wider until, at last, man realizes his ethical association with the whole of humanity. This represents an enormous act of thinking.

Consider Plato and Aristotle. Their ethics is narrow-hearted. They were occupied only with their fellow citizens. Slaves and foreigners did not concern them. Then, with Stoicism the circle begins to widen. That was the greatest manifestation of Greek thought. (Forgive me this heresy!) Then, in Seneca, Epictetus, Marcus Aurelius, the idea suddenly crops up that ethics is concerned with all humanity. Thought arrives at that intuitive knowledge that you find already in the prophets of Israel and that is explained by Jesus.

Surely, ethics thinks, the circle is wide enough. But no! The force that causes the circle to enlarge enlarges it further. Slowly in our European thought comes the notion that ethics has not only to do with mankind but with the animal creation as well. This begins with St. Francis of Assisi. The explanation that applies only to man must be given up. Thus, we shall arrive at saying that ethics is reverence for all life.

Let me give you a definition of ethics: It is good to maintain life and further life; it is bad to damage and destroy life. However much it struggles against it, ethics arrives at the religion of Jesus. It must recognize that it can discover no other relationship to other beings as full of sense as the relationship of love. Ethics is the maintaining of life at the highest point of development—my own life and other life—by devoting myself to it in help and love, and both these things are connected.

And this ethics, profound, universal, has the significance of a religion. It is religion.

In our age there is an absence of thinking that is characterized by contempt for life. We waged war for questions that, through reason, might have been solved. No one won. The war killed millions of men, brought suffering to millions of men, and brought suffering and death to millions of innocent animals. Why? Because we did not possess the highest rationality of reverence for life. And because we do not yet possess this, every people is afraid of every other, and each causes fear to the others. We are mentally afflicted one for another because we are lacking in rationality. There is no other remedy than reverence for life, and at that we must arrive.

Thinking has not given us that, but thinking is preparing it—in natural science, which allows us to know the inner nature of being, and in ethics, which is developing in a direction by which it reaches its conclusion in reverence for life. Reverence for life dwells within our thought. We have only to go deep enough through absence of thought until we come to this profound ethics, which is already a religion.

We wander in darkness now, but one with another we all have the conviction that we are advancing to the light, that again a time will come when religion and ethical thinking will unite. This we believe, and hope and work for, maintaining the belief that if we make ethical ideals active in our lives, then the time will come when peoples will do the same. Let us look out toward the light and comfort ourselves in reflecting on what thinking is preparing for us.

5

The Decay of Civilization

*This selection contains two opening chapters from Schweitzer's most
important philosophical work,* The Philosophy of Civilization, *first
published in 1923. Every civilization consists of the interaction between its
material and spiritual aspects. Starting with the middle of the nineteenth
century, the development of Western civilization has tipped heavily in
favor of the material element. According to Schweitzer, this development is
the result of philosophy betraying its fundamental role and doing violence
to reality. Although the ultimate vocation of philosophy is to be the guide
and the guardian of general reason, philosophy has abandoned this role
and become engrossed in abstractions detached from life. Schweitzer then
explains in more detail his thesis of the decay of civilization. He emphasizes the dependent economic position of modern man, whose work consists
more and more of being the helper of a machine, rather than the other
way around. The growing economic dependence of man also means the
increase of superficiality and indifference with regard to the spread of violence and destruction, both in peaceful times and in times of war. According to Schweitzer, modern man is in danger of losing his humanity.*

We are living today under the sign of the collapse of civilization. The
situation has not been produced by the war; the latter is only a

Selection from *The Decay and the Restoration of Civilization*, Part I of *The Philosophy of Civiliza-
tion*, Part I; first translated by C. T. Campion as *The Decay and the Restoration of Civilization* (New
York: Macmillan, 1932); reprinted here from *The Philosophy of Civilization* (Amherst, NY: Prometheus
Books, 1987), 1–20.

manifestation of it. The spiritual atmosphere has solidified into actual facts, which again react on it with disastrous results in every respect. This interaction of material and spiritual has assumed a most unhealthy character. Just below a mighty cataract we are driving along in a current full of formidable eddies, and it will need the most gigantic efforts to rescue the vessel of our fate from the dangerous side channel into which we have allowed it to drift, and bring it back into the main stream, if, indeed, we can hope to do so at all.

We have drifted out of the stream of civilization because there was among us no real reflection upon what civilization is. It is true that at the end of the last century and the beginning of this there appeared a number of works on civilization with the most varied titles; but, as though in obedience to some secret order, they made no attempt to settle and make clear the conditions of our intellectual life, and instead devoted themselves exclusively to its origin and history. They gave us a relief map of civilization marked with roads that men had observed or invented, and that led us over hill and dale through the fields of history from the Renaissance to the twentieth century. It was a triumph for the historical sense of the authors. The crowds whom these works instructed were filled with satisfied contentment when they understood that their civilization was the organic product of so many centuries of the working of spiritual and social forces, but no one worked out and described the content of our spiritual life. No one tested its value from the point of view of the nobility of its ideas and its ability to produce real progress.

Thus, we crossed the threshold of the twentieth century with an unshakable conceit of ourselves, and whatever was written at that time about our civilization only confirmed us in our ingenuous belief in its high value. Anyone who expressed doubt was regarded with astonishment. Many, indeed, who were on the road to error, stopped and returned to the main road again because they were afraid of the path that led off to the side. Others continued along the main road but in silence; the understanding and insight that were at work in them only condemned them to isolation.

It is clear now to everyone that the suicide of civilization is in progress. What yet remains of it is no longer safe. It is still standing, indeed, because it was not exposed to the destructive pressure that overwhelmed the rest, but, like the rest, it is built upon rubble, and the next landslide will very likely carry it away.

But what was it that preceded and led up to this loss of power in the innate forces of civilization?

The age of the Enlightenment and of rationalism had put forward ethical ideals, based on reason, concerning the development of the individual to true manhood, his position in society, the material and spiritual problems that arose out of society, the relations of the different nations to each other, and their issue in a humanity that should be united in the pursuit of the highest moral and spiritual objects. These ideals had begun, both in philosophy and in general thought, to get into contact with reality and to alter the general environment. In the course of three or four generations, there had been such progress made, both in the ideas underlying civilization and in their material embodiment, that the age of true civilization seemed to have dawned upon the world and to be assured of an uninterrupted development.

But, in about the middle of the nineteenth century, this mutual understanding and cooperation between ethical ideals and reality began to break down, and in the course of the next few decades it disappeared more and more completely. Without resistance, without complaint, civilization abdicated. Its ideas lagged behind, as though they were too exhausted to keep pace with it. How did this come about?

The decisive element in the production of this result was philosophy's renunciation of her duty.

In the eighteenth century and the early part of the nineteenth, it was philosophy that led and guided thought in general. She had busied herself with the questions that presented themselves to mankind at each successive period, and had kept the thought of civilized man actively reflecting upon them. Philosophy at that time included within herself an elementary philosophizing about man, society, race, humanity, and civilization, which produced in a perfectly natural way a living popular philosophy that controlled the general thought and maintained the enthusiasm for civilization.

But that ethical, and at the same time optimistic, view of things in which the Enlightenment and rationalism had laid the foundations of this healthy popular philosophy was unable in the long run to meet the criticism leveled at it by pure thought. Its naïve dogmatism raised more and more prejudice against it. Kant tried to provide the tottering building with new foundations, undertaking to alter the rationalistic view of things in accordance with the demands of a deeper theory of knowledge, without, however, making any change in its essential spiritual elements. Goethe, Schiller, and other intellectual heroes of the age showed, by means of criticism both kindly and malicious, that rationalism was popular philosophy rather than real philosophy, but they were not in a position to put into the place of what they destroyed anything new that could give the same effective support to the ideas about civilization that were current in the general thought of the time.

Fichte, Hegel, and other philosophers, who, for all their criticism of rationalism, paid homage to its ethical ideals, attempted to establish a similar ethical and optimistic view of things by speculative methods; that is, by logical and meta-physical discussion of pure being and its development into a universe. For three or four decades, they succeeded in deceiving themselves and others with this supposedly creative and inspiring illusion and in doing violence to reality in the interests of their theory of the universe. But, at last, the natural sciences, which all this time had been growing stronger and stronger, rose up against them and, with a plebeian enthusiasm for the truth of reality, reduced to ruins the magnifi-cent creations of their imagination.

Since that time the ethical ideas on which civilization rests have been wan-dering about the world, poverty-stricken and homeless. No theory of the uni-verse has been advanced that can give them a solid foundation; in fact, not one has made its appearance that can claim for itself solidity and inner consistency. The age of philosophic dogmatism had come definitely to an end, and after that nothing was recognized as truth except the science that described reality. Complete theories of the universe no longer appeared as fixed stars; they were regarded as resting on hypothesis and ranked no higher than comets.

The same weapon that struck down the dogmatism of knowledge about the universe struck down also the dogmatic enunciation of spiritual ideas. The early simple rationalism, the critical rationalism of Kant, and the speculative rationalism of the great philosophers of the nineteenth century had all alike done violence to reality in two ways. They had given a position above that of the facts of science to the views that they had arrived at by pure thought, and they had also preached a series of ethical ideals that were meant to replace by new ones the various existing relations in the ideas and the material environ-ment of mankind. When the first of these two forms of violence was proved to be a mistaken one, it became questionable whether the second could still be allowed the justification that it had hitherto enjoyed. The doctrinaire methods of thought that made the existing world nothing but material for the produc-tion of a purely theoretical sketch of a better future were replaced by sympa-thetic attempts to understand the historical origin of existing things for which Hegel's philosophy had prepared the way.

With a general mentality of this description, a real combination of ethi-cal ideals with reality was no longer possible; there was not the freedom from prejudice that that required, and so there came a weakening of the convictions that were the driving power of civilization. So, too, an end was put to that jus-tifiable violence to human convictions and circumstances without which the reforming work of civilization can make no advance because it was bound up with that other unjustifiable violence to reality. That is the tragic element in the psychological development of our spiritual life during the latter half of the nineteenth century.

Rationalism, then, had been dismissed; but with it went also the optimistic convictions as to the moral meaning of the universe and of humanity, of society and of man, to which it had given birth, though the conviction still exerted so much influence that no attention was paid to the catastrophe that had really begun.

Philosophy did not realize that the power of the ideas about civilization that had been entrusted to it was becoming a doubtful quantity. At the end of one of the most brilliant works on the history of philosophy, which appeared at the close of the nineteenth century, philosophy is defined as the process "by which there comes to completion, step by step, and with ever clearer and surer consciousness, that conviction about the value of civilization the universal validity of which it is the object of philosophy itself to affirm." But the author has forgotten the essential point, namely, that there was a time when philosophy did not merely convince itself of the value of civilization but also let its convictions go forth as fruitful ideas destined to influence the general thought; while from the middle of the nineteenth century onward, these convictions had become more and more of the nature of hoarded and unproductive capital.

Once, philosophy had been an active worker producing universal convictions about civilization. Now, after the collapse in the middle of the nineteenth century, this same philosophy had become a mere drawer of dividends, concentrating her activities far from the world on what she had managed to save. She had become a mere science, which sifted the results of the historical and natural sciences and collected from them material for a future theory of the universe, carrying on, with this objective in view, a learned activity in all branches of knowledge. At the same time she became more and more absorbed in the study of her own past. Philosophy came to mean practically the history of philosophy. The creative spirit had left her. She became more and more a philosophy that contained no real thought. She reflected, indeed, on the results achieved by the individual sciences, but she lost the power of elemental thought.

Philosophy looked back with condescending pity on the rationalism that she had outstripped. She prided herself on having got beyond the ideas of Kant, on having been shown by Hegel the inner meaning of history, and on being at work today in close sympathy with the natural sciences. But, for all that, she was poorer than the poorest rationalism because she now carried on in imagination only, and not in reality, the recognized work of philosophy, which rationalism had practiced so zealously. Rationalism, for all its simplicity, had been a working philosophy, but philosophy herself had now become, for all her insight, merely a pedantic philosophy of degenerates. She still played, indeed, some sort of role in schools and universities, but she had no longer any message for the great world.

In spite of all her learning, philosophy had become a stranger to the world, and the problems of life that occupied men and the whole thought of the age had no part in her activities. Her way lay apart from the general spiritual life, and just as she derived no stimulus from the latter, so she gave none back. Refusing to concern herself with elemental problems, she contained no elemental philosophy that could become a philosophy of the people.

From this impotence came the aversion to all generally intelligible philosophizing that is so characteristic of her. Popular philosophy was for her merely a review—prepared for the use of the crowd, simplified, and therefore rendered inferior—of the results given by the individual sciences that she had herself sifted and put together in view of a future theory of the universe. She was wholly unconscious of several things, namely, that there is a popular philosophy that arises out of such a review; that it is just the province of philosophy to deal with the elemental, inward questions about which individuals and the crowd are thinking, or ought to be thinking, to apply to them more comprehensive and more thorough methods of thought, and then restore them to general currency; and, finally, that the value of any philosophy is, in the last resort, to be measured by its capacity, or incapacity, to transform itself into a living philosophy of the people.

Whatever is deep is also simple and can be reproduced as such, if only its relation to the whole of reality is preserved. It is then something abstract, which secures for itself a many-sided life as soon as it comes into contact with facts.

Whatever of inquiring thought there was among the general public was therefore compelled to languish because our philosophy refused either to acknowledge or to help it. It found in front of it a deep chasm that it could not cross.

Of gold coinage, minted in the past, philosophy had abundance; hypotheses about a soon-to-be-developed theoretical theory of the universe filled her vaults like unminted bullion; but food with which to appease the spiritual hunger of the present she did not possess. Deceived by her own riches, she had neglected to plant any ground with nourishing crops, and, therefore, ignoring the hunger of the age, she left the latter to its fate.

That pure thought never managed to construct a theory of the universe of an optimistic, ethical character, and to build up on that for a foundation the ideals that go to produce civilization, was not the fault of philosophy; it was a fact that became evident as thought developed. But philosophy was guilty of a wrong to our age in that it did not admit the fact but remained wrapped up in its illusion, as though this were really a help to the progress of civilization.

The ultimate vocation of philosophy is to be the guide and guardian of the general reason, and it was her duty, in the circumstances of the time, to confess to our world that ethical ideals were no longer supported by any general theory of the universe but were, until further notice, left to themselves, and must make their way in the world by their own innate power. Philosophy ought to have shown us that we have to fight on behalf of the ideals on which our civilization rests. She ought to have tried to give these ideals an independent existence by virtue of their own inner value and inner truth, and so to keep them alive and active without any extraneous help from a corresponding theory of the universe. No effort should have been spared to direct the attention of the cultured and the uncultured alike to the problem of the ideals of civilization.

But philosophy philosophized about everything except civilization. She went on working undeviatingly at the establishment of a theoretical view of the universe, as though by means of it everything could be restored, and did not reflect that this theory, even if it were completed, would be constructed out of history and science only, and would accordingly be unoptimistic and unethical, and would remain forever an "impotent theory of the universe," which could never call forth the energies needed for the establishment and maintenance of the ideals of civilization.

So little did philosophy philosophize about civilization that she did not even notice that she herself and the age along with her were losing more and more of it. In the hour of peril, the watchman who ought to have kept us awake was himself asleep, and the result was that we put up no fight at all on behalf of our civilization.

Even if the abdication of thought has been, as we have seen, the decisive factor in the collapse of our civilization, there are yet a number of other causes that combine with it to hinder our progress in this regard. They are to be found in the field of spiritual in addition to that of economic activity and depend, above all, on the interaction between the two, an interaction that is unsatisfactory and continually becoming more so.

The capacity of the modern man for progress in civilization is diminished because the circumstances in which he finds himself placed injure him psychically and stunt his personality.

The development of civilization comes about—to put it quite generally—by individual men thinking out ideals that aim at the progress of the whole, and then so fitting them to the realities of life that they assume the shape in which they can influence most effectively the circumstances of the time. A man's ability to be a pioneer of progress, that is, to understand what civilization is and to work for it, depends, therefore, on his being a thinker and on his being free. He must be the former if he is to be capable of comprehending his ideals and putting them into shape. He must be free in order to be in a position to launch his ideals out into the general life. The more completely his activities are taken up in any way by the struggle for existence, the more strongly will the impulse to improve his own condition find expression in the ideals of his thought. Ideals of self-interest then get mixed up with and spoil his ideals of civilization.

Material and spiritual freedom are closely bound up with one another. Civilization presupposes free men, for only by free men can it be thought out and brought to realization.

But among mankind today both freedom and the capacity for thought have been sadly diminished.

If society had so developed that a continually widening circle of the population could enjoy a modest, but well-assured, condition of comfort, civilization would have been much more helped than it has been by all the material conquests that are lauded in its name. These do, indeed, make mankind as a whole less dependent upon nature, but at the same time they diminish the number of free and independent lives. The artisan who was his own master becomes the factory hand through the compulsion of machinery. Because in the complicated business world of today only undertakings with abundant capital behind them can maintain their existence, the place of the small, independent dealer is being taken more and more completely by the employee. Even the classes that still possess a larger or smaller amount of property or maintain a more or less independent activity get drawn more and more completely into the struggle for existence because of the insecurity of present conditions under the economic system of today.

The lack of freedom that results is made worse still because the factory system creates continually growing agglomerations of people who are thereby compulsorily separated from the soil that feeds them, from their own homes, and from nature. Hence comes serious psychical injury. There is only too much truth in the paradoxical saying that abnormal life begins with the loss of one's own field and dwelling place.

Civilization is, it is true, furthered to a certain extent by the self-regarding ideals produced by the groups of people who unite and cooperate in defense of their similarly threatened interests insofar as they seek to obtain an improvement in their material, and thereby also in their spiritual, environment. But these ideals are a danger to the idea of civilization as such because the form that they assume is either not at all, or very imperfectly, determined by the really universal interests of the community. The consideration of civilization as such is held back by the competition between the various self-regarding ideals that go under its name.

To the want of freedom we have to add the evil of overstrain. For two or three generations, numbers of individuals have been living merely as workers, not as human beings. Whatever can be said in a general way about the moral and spiritual significance of labor has no bearing on what they have to do. An excessive amount of labor is the rule today in every circle of society, with the result that the laborer's spiritual element cannot possibly thrive. This overwork hits him indirectly even in his childhood, for his parents, caught in the inexorable toils of work, cannot devote themselves to his upbringing as they should. Thus, his development is robbed of something that can never be made good, and later in life, when he himself is the slave of overlong hours, he feels more and more the need of external distractions. To spend the time left to him for leisure in self-cultivation, or in serious intercourse with his fellows or with books, requires a mental collectedness and a self-control that he finds very difficult. Complete idleness, forgetfulness, and diversion from his usual activities are a physical necessity. He does not want to think and seeks not self-improvement but entertainment, that kind of entertainment, moreover, that makes least demand upon his spiritual faculties.

The mentality of this mass of individuals, spiritually relaxed and incapable of self-collectedness, reacts upon all those institutions that ought to serve the cause of culture, and therewith of civilization. The theater takes a second place behind the pleasure resort or the picture show, and the instructive book behind the diverting one. An ever-increasing proportion of periodicals and newspapers have to accommodate themselves to the necessity of putting their matter before their readers in the shape that lets it be assimilated most easily. A comparison of the average newspapers of today with those of fifty or sixty years ago shows how thoroughly such publications have had to change their methods in this respect.

When once the spirit of superficiality has penetrated into the institutions that ought to sustain the spiritual life, these exercise, on their part, a reflex influence on the society that they have brought to this condition, and force on all alike this state of mental vacuity.

How completely this want of thinking power has become a second nature in men today is shown by the kind of sociability that it produces. When two of them meet for a conversation, each is careful to see that their talk does not go beyond generalities or develop into a real exchange of ideas. No one has anything of his own to give out, and everyone is haunted by a sort of terror, lest anything original should be demanded from him.

The spirit produced in such a society of never-concentrated minds is rising among us as an ever-growing force, and it results in a lowered conception of what man should be. In ourselves, as in others, we look for nothing but vigor in productive work and resign ourselves to the abandonment of any higher ideal.

When we consider this want of freedom and of mental concentration, we see that the conditions of life for the inhabitants of our big cities are as unfavorable as they could be. Naturally, then, those inhabitants are in most danger on their spiritual side. It is doubtful whether big cities have ever been foci of civilization in the sense that in them there has arisen the ideal of a man well and truly developed as a spiritual personality; today, at any rate, the condition of things is such that true civilization needs to be rescued from the spirit that issues from them and their inhabitants.

But, besides the hindrance caused to civilization by the modern man's lack of freedom and of the power of mental concentration, there is a further hindrance caused by his imperfect development. The enormous increase of human knowledge and power, in specialized thoroughness as well as in extent, necessarily leads to individual activities being limited more and more to well-defined departments. Human labor is organized and coordinated so that specialization may enable individuals to make the highest and most effective possible contribution. The results obtained are amazing, but the spiritual significance of the work for the worker suffers. There is no call upon the whole man, only upon some of his faculties, and this has a reflex effect upon his nature as a whole. The faculties that build up personality and are called out by comprehensive and varied tasks are ousted by the less comprehensive ones, which from this point of view are, in the general sense of the word, less spiritual. The artisan of today does not understand his trade as a whole in the way in which his predecessor did. He no longer learns, like the latter, to work the wood or the metal through all the stages of manufacture; many of these stages have already been carried out by men and machines before the material comes into his hands. Consequently, his reflectiveness, his imagination, and his skill are no longer called out by ever varying difficulties in the work, and his creative and artistic powers are atrophied. In place of the normal self-consciousness that is promoted by work into the doing of which he must put his whole power of thought and his whole personality, there comes a self-satisfaction that is content with a fragmentary ability that, it may be admitted, is perfect, and this self-satisfaction is persuaded by its perfection in mastering details to overlook its imperfection in dealing with the whole.

In all professions, most clearly perhaps in the pursuit of science, we can recognize the spiritual danger with which specialization threatens not only individuals but the spiritual life of the community. It is already noticeable, too, that education is carried on now by teachers who have not a wide enough outlook to make their students understand the interconnection of the individual sciences and to be able to give them a mental horizon as wide as it should be.

Then, as if specialization and the organization of work, where it is unavoidable, were not already injurious enough to the soul of the modern man, it is pursued and built up where it could be dispensed with. In administration, in education, and in every kind of calling, the natural sphere of activity is narrowed as far as possible by rules and superintendence. How much less free in many countries is the elementary school teacher of today compared with what he was once! How lifeless and impersonal has his teaching become as a result of all these limitations!

Thus, through our methods of work we have suffered loss spiritually and as individuals just in proportion as the material output of our collective activity has increased. Here, too, is an illustration of that tragic law that says that every gain brings with it, somehow or other, a corresponding loss.

But man today is in danger not only through his lack of freedom, of the power of mental concentration, and of the opportunity for all-round development: he is in danger of losing his humanity.

The normal attitude of man to man is made very difficult for us. Owing to the hurry in which we live, to the increased facilities for intercourse, and to the necessity for living and working with many others in an overcrowded locality, we meet each other continually, and in the most varied relations, as strangers. Our circumstances do not allow us to deal with each other as man to man, for the limitations placed upon the activities of the natural man are so general and so unbroken that we get accustomed to them and no longer feel our mechanical, impersonal intercourse to be something that is unnatural. We no longer feel uncomfortable that in such a number of situations we can no longer be men among men, and at last we give up trying to be so, even when it would be possible and proper.

In this respect, too, the soul of the townsman is influenced most unfavorably by his circumstances, and that influence, in its turn, works most unfavorably on the mentality of society.

Thus, we tend to forget our relationship with our fellows and are on the path toward inhumanity. Wherever there is lost the consciousness that every man is an object of concern for us just because he is man, civilization and morals are shaken and the advance to fully developed inhumanity is only a question of time.

As a matter of fact, the most utterly inhuman thoughts have been current among us for two generations past in all the ugly clearness of language and with the authority of logical principles. There has been created a social mentality that discourages humanity in individuals. The courtesy produced by natural feeling disappears, and in its place comes a behavior that shows entire indifference, even though it is decked out more or less thoroughly in a code of manners. The standoffishness and want of sympathy that are shown so clearly in every way to strangers are no longer felt as being really rudeness but pass for the behavior of the man of the world. Our society has also ceased to allow to all men, as such, a human value and a human dignity; many sections of the human race have become merely raw material and property in human form. We have talked for decades with ever-increasing light-mindedness about war and conquest, as if these were merely operations on a chessboard; how was this possible, save as the result of a tone of mind that no longer pictured to itself the fate of individuals but thought of them only as figures or objects belonging to the material world? When the war broke out, the inhumanity within us had a free course. And what an amount of insulting stuff, some decently veiled, some openly coarse, about the colored races, has made its appearance during the last decades, and passed for truth and reason, in our colonial literature and our parliaments, and so become an element in general public opinion! Twenty years ago there was a discussion in one of our continental parliaments about some deported Negroes who had been allowed to die of hunger and disease; and there was no protest or comment when, in a statement from the tribune, it was said that they "had been lost," as though it were a question of cattle!

In the education and the schoolbooks of today, the duty of humanity is relegated to an obscure corner, as though it were no longer true that it is the first thing necessary in the training of personality, and as if it were not a matter of great importance to maintain it as a strong influence in our human race against the influence of outer circumstances. It has not been so always. There was a time when it was a ruling influence not only in schools but in literature, even down to the book of adventures. Defoe's hero, Robinson Crusoe, is continually reflecting on the subject of humane conduct, and he feels himself so responsible for loyalty to this duty that when defending himself he is continually thinking how he can sacrifice the smallest number of human lives; he is so faithful, indeed, to this duty of humanity, that the story of his adventures acquires thereby quite a peculiar character. Is there among works of this kind today a single one in which we shall find anything like it?

Another hindrance to civilization today is the over-organization of our public life.

While it is certain that a properly ordered environment is the condition and, at the same time, the result, of civilization, it is also undeniable that, after a certain point has been reached, external organization is developed at the expense of spiritual life. Personality and ideas are then subordinated to institutions, when it is really these that ought to influence the latter and keep them inwardly alive.

If a comprehensive organization is established in any department of social life, the results are at first magnificent, but after a time they fall off. It is the already existing resources that are realized at the start, but later on the destructive influence of such organization on what is living and original is clearly seen in its natural results, and the more consistently the organization is enlarged, the more strongly its effect is felt in the repression of creative and spiritual activity. There are modern states that cannot recover either economically or spiritually from the effects of over-centralization of government dating from a very early period of their history.

The conversion of a wood into a park and its maintenance as such may be a step toward carrying out several different objects, but it is all over then with the rich vegetation that would assure its future condition in nature's own way.

Political, religious, and economic associations aim today at forming themselves in such a way as will combine the greatest possible inner cohesion with the highest possible degree of external activity. Constitution, discipline, and everything that belongs to administration are brought to perfection hitherto unknown. They attain their objectives, but, just in proportion as they do so, these centers of activity cease to work as living organizations and come more and more to resemble perfected machines. Their inner life loses in richness and variety because the personalities of which they are composed become impoverished.

Our whole spiritual life nowadays has its course within organizations. From childhood up, the man of today has his mind so full of the thought of discipline that he loses the sense of his own individuality and can see himself as thinking only in the spirit of some group or other of his fellows. A thorough discussion between one idea and another or between one man and another, such as constituted the greatness of the eighteenth century, is never met with now. But at that time fear of public opinion was a thing unknown. All ideas had then to justify themselves to the individual reason. Today it is the rule—and no one questions it—always to take into account the views that prevail in organized society. The individual starts by taking it for granted that both for himself and his neighbors there are certain views already established that they cannot hope to alter, views that are determined by nationality, creed, political party, social position, and other elements in one's surroundings. These views are protected by a kind of taboo and are not only kept sacred from criticism, but are not considered a legitimate subject of conversation. This kind of intercourse, in which we mutually abjure our natural quality as thinking beings, is euphemistically described as respect for other people's convictions, as if there could be any convictions at all where there is no thought.

The modern man is lost in the mass in a way that is without precedent in history, and this is perhaps the most characteristic trait in him. His diminished concern about his own nature makes him susceptible, to an extent that is almost pathological, to the views that society and its organs of expression have put, ready made, into circulation. Since, over and above this, society, with its well-constructed organization, has become a power of as yet unknown strength in the spiritual life, man's want of independence in the face of it has become so serious that he is almost ceasing to claim a spiritual existence of his own. He is like a rubber ball that has lost its elasticity and preserves indefinitely every impression that is made upon it. He is under the thumb of the mass, and he draws from it the opinions on which he lives, whether the question at issue is national or political or one of his own belief or unbelief.

Yet this abnormal subjection to external influences does not strike him as being a weakness. He looks upon it as an achievement, and in his unlimited spiritual devotion to the interests of the community he thinks he is preserving the greatness of the modern man. He intentionally exaggerates our natural social instincts into something fantastically great.

It is just because we thus renounce the indefeasible rights of the individual that our race can neither produce new ideas nor make current ones serviceable for new objectives; its only experience is that prevailing ideas obtain more and more authority, take on a more and more one-sided development, and live on till they have produced their last and most dangerous consequences.

Thus, we have entered on a new medieval period. The general determination of society has put freedom of thought out of fashion because the majority renounces the privilege of thinking as free personalities and let themselves be guided in everything by those who belong to the various groups and cliques.

Spiritual freedom, then, we shall recover only when the majority of individuals become, once more, spiritually independent and self-reliant and discover their natural and proper relation to those organizations in which their souls have been entangled. But liberation from the Middle Ages of today will be a much more difficult process than that which freed the peoples of Europe from the first Middle Ages. The struggle then was against external authority established in the course of history. Today the task is to get the mass of individuals to work themselves out of the condition of spiritual weakness and dependence to which they have brought themselves. Could there be a harder task?

Moreover, no one as yet clearly perceives what a condition of spiritual poverty is ours today. Every year the spread of opinions that have no thought behind them is carried further by the masses, and the methods of this process have been so perfected, and have met with such a ready welcome, that our confidence in being able to raise to the dignity of public opinion the silliest of statements, wherever it seems expedient to get them currently accepted, has no need to justify itself before acting.

During the war the control of thought was made complete. Propaganda definitely took the place of truth.

With independence of thought thrown overboard, we have, as was inevitable, lost our faith in truth. Our spiritual life is disorganized, for the over-organization of our external environment leads to the organization of our absence of thought.

Not only in the intellectual sphere, but in the moral also, the relation between the individual and the community has been upset. With the surrender of his own personal opinion, the modern man surrenders also his personal moral judgment. In order that he may find good what the mass declares to be such, whether in word or deed, and may condemn what it declares to be bad, he suppresses the scruples that stir in him. He does not allow them to find utterance either with others or with himself. There are no stumbling blocks that his feeling of unity with the herd does not enable him to surmount, and thus he loses his judgment in that of the mass, and his own morality in theirs.

Above all, he is thus made capable of excusing everything that is meaningless, cruel, unjust, or bad in the behavior of his nation. Unconsciously to themselves, the majority of the members of our barbarian civilized states give less and less time to reflection as moral personalities, so that they may not be continually coming into inner conflict with their fellows as a body and continually having to get over things that they feel to be wrong.

Public opinion helps them by popularizing the idea that the actions of the community are not to be judged so much by the standards of morality as by those of expediency. But they suffer injury to their souls. If we find among men of today only too few whose human and moral sensibility is still undamaged, the chief reason is that the majority have offered up their personal morality on the altar of their country, instead of remaining at variance with the mass and acting as a force that impels the latter along the road to perfection.

Not only between the economic and the spiritual, then, but also between the mass of men and individuals, there has developed a condition of unfavorable action and reaction. In the days of rationalism and serious philosophy, the individual got help and support from society through the general confidence in the victory of the rational and moral, which society never failed to acknowledge as something that explained and justified itself. Individuals were then carried along by the mass; we are stifled by it. The bankruptcy of the civilized state, which becomes more manifest every decade, is ruining the man of today. The demoralization of the individual by the mass is in full swing.

The man of today pursues his dark journey in a time of darkness, as one who has no freedom, no mental collectedness, no all-round development, as one who loses himself in an atmosphere of inhumanity, who surrenders his spiritual independence and his moral judgment to the organized society in which he lives, and who finds himself in every direction up against hindrances to the temper of true civilization. Of the dangerous position in which he is placed, philosophy has no understanding and therefore makes no attempt to help him. She does not even urge him to reflect on what is happening to himself.

The terrible truth that with the progress of history and the economic development of the world it is becoming not easier, but harder, to develop true civilization has never found utterance.

PART II

The Ethics of Reverence for Life

6

Civilization and Ethics

Against the philosophical tradition that goes all the way back to the pre-Socratics, Schweitzer argues that our view of life and the meaning of life is not dependent on our knowledge of the world. It is instead rooted in a more primordial phenomenon, which he calls the will to live. When we try to build our life view on knowledge of the world, we inevitably end with a dualism that cannot be reconciled, the dualism of knowing and willing. Once we realize that the worldview is the product of the life view and the will to live, this dualism does not present a problem anymore. The most direct and the most profound manifestation of the will to live is reverence for life: "From an inner necessity I exert myself in producing values and practicing ethics in the world even though I do not understand the meaning of the world. Reverence for life is not justified by any corresponding knowledge of the world but is the disposition that determines our relation to the world." Such reverence for life is, according to Schweitzer, both "the highest truth and the highest practicality."

My subject is the tragedy of the Western worldview.

While still a student I was surprised to find the history of thought always written merely as a history of philosophical systems, never as the history of man's effort to arrive at a conception of the universe. Later, when reflecting on the current of civilization in which I found

Selection; Preface to *Civilization and Ethics*, Part II of *The Philosophy of Civilization*; first translated by C. T. Campion and published as *Civilization and Ethics* (New York: Macmillan, 1929); reprinted here from *The Philosophy of Civilization* (Amherst, NY: Prometheus Books, 1987), 71–84.

myself living, I was struck by the strange and inexorable connections that exist between civilization and our view of the world as a whole. Next I felt a still stronger compulsion to put to Western thought the question of what it has been aiming at, and what result it has reached in the matter of a philosophy of life. What is there left of the achievements of our philosophy when it is stripped of its tinsel of learning? What has it to offer when we demand from it those elemental ideas that we need, if we are to take our position in life as men who are growing in character through the experience given by work?

So I came to an unsparing effort to come to an understanding with Western thought. I recognized and admitted that it has sought for that outlook on life from which alone a deep and comprehensive civilization can come. It has wanted to reach a position of world- and life-affirmation and with that as a foundation decree that it is our duty to be active, to strive for progress of all kinds, and to create values. It has wanted to reach an ethical system and, on that foundation, establish that for the sake of serviceable activity we have to place our life at the service of ideas and of the other life around us.

But it did not succeed in grounding its world- and life-affirming ethical worldview convincingly and permanently in thought. Our philosophy did nothing more than produce again and again unstable fragments of the serviceable outlook on life that hovered before its mind's eye. Consequently, our civilization has also remained fragmentary and insecure.

It was a fatal mistake that Western thought never admitted to itself the unsatisfying result of its search for a stable and serviceable outlook on the universe. Our philosophizing became less and less elemental, losing all connection with the elementary questions that man must ask of life and of the world. More and more it found satisfaction in the handling of philosophic questions that were merely academic, and in expert mastery of philosophical technique. It became more and more the captive of secondary things. Instead of real music, it produced again and again mere bandmaster's music, often magnificent for its kind but still only bandmaster's music.

Through this philosophy that did nothing but philosophize instead of struggling for a worldview founded on thought and serviceable for life, we came to be without any worldview at all and therefore lacking in civilization.

Signs of an awakening of thought on this point are beginning to be visible. It is admitted here and there that philosophy must again try to offer a conception of the universe. This is generally expressed by saying that people are encouraging it to venture once more on "metaphysics," that is to say, to put forward definitive views about the spiritual nature of the world, whereas hitherto it has been occupied with the classification of scientific facts and the emission of cautious hypotheses.

Not only in philosophy but in thought generally, this awakening of the need for a worldview expresses itself as a need for "metaphysics." Fantastic systems of "metaphysics" are sought and offered. Individuals who believe that they have at their disposal peculiar psychic experiences, and assert that with their aid they can look behind the actual nature of phenomena, come forward as producers of a worldview.

But neither the cautious academic, nor the much-claiming fantastic "metaphysics," can really give us a worldview. That the road to this leads through "metaphysics" is a fatal error that has already enjoyed too long a span of life in our Western thought. It would be tragedy if we renewed its vigor just now, when we are faced by the necessity of working our way out of that shortage of a philosophy of life in which our misery, both spiritual and material, is grounded. No further wandering along the traditional roads that lead nowhere can save us, whether we advance as the successors of our fathers or on adventurous lines of our own. Only in a deep conception of, and experience in, the problems of worldview lies for us any possibility of advance.

That is why I am undertaking what has never been attempted in this way before, namely, so to pose the problem of Western philosophy as to make the Western search for a worldview come to a halt and take account of itself. There are two points on which it must be clear before it proceeds to further exertion. The first is the overwhelming importance in the search for a worldview of the quality of that which is sought. What is it we want? We want to find the world- and life-affirmation, and the ethical system that we need for that serviceable activity that gives our life a meaning, based on such thought about the world and life as finds a meaning in them also. If our search for a worldview is once thoroughly permeated by the recognition that everything turns upon these two fundamental questions, it is thereby saved from betaking itself to by-paths, thinking that by some happy disposition of fortune it can reach its goal along them. It will then not search for a "metaphysic," thinking to reach a worldview by means of it, but it will search for a worldview and accept with it anything "metaphysical" that may turn up. From every point of view, it will remain elemental.

The second task that the conscious search for a conception of the universe must not shirk is the consideration of what is the real and ultimate nature of the process by which it has hitherto attempted to secure that serviceable worldview that hovered before it. Reflection on this is necessary that it may make up its mind whether further advance along the road it has hitherto followed gives any prospect of success. Our philosophy ought to have been philosophizing long ago about the road along which it was going in search of a worldview. It never did so, and therefore was always running uselessly round and round in a circle.

The process by which Western thought has hitherto sought for a worldview is doomed to be fruitless. It has consisted simply in interpreting the world in the sense of world- and life-affirmation, that is to say, in attributing to the world a meaning that allowed it to conceive the aims of mankind and of individual men as having a meaning within that world. This interpretation is acted upon by all Western philosophy. A few thinkers who venture to be un-Western, and resolutely allow world- and life-negation and ethics to be made subjects of discussion, are side currents that do not affect the main course of the river.

That this process followed by Western thought consists in adopting an optimistic-ethical interpretation of the world will not be clear without further explanation, for it is, indeed, not always openly followed. The optimistic-ethical interpretation is often found imbedded in the results of investigations into the nature of knowledge; it often appears beneath a veil of "metaphysics"; it is often so delicately shaded that it produces none of its usual effects. It is only when one has clearly grasped the fact that Western thought has nothing else in mind than to establish for itself a worldview based on world- and life-affirmation and ethical in character, that one can realize how in its theory of knowledge, in its metaphysics, and in all its movements generally in the game of life, it is guided, consciously or unconsciously, by the effort to interpret the world in some way or other, and in some measure, in the sense of world- and life-affirmation and ethics. Whether in this attempt it goes to work openly or secretly, skillfully or unskillfully, honorably or craftily, does not matter. Western thought needs this interpretation in order that it may be able to give a meaning to human life. Its view of life is to be a result of its view of the world. It has never considered any other course.

But this awakening of Western thought will not be complete until that thought steps outside itself and comes to an understanding with the search for a worldview as this manifests itself in the thought of mankind as a whole. We have too long been occupied with the developing series of our own philosophical systems and have taken no notice of the fact that there is a world philosophy of which our Western philosophy is only a part. If, however, one conceives philosophy as being a struggle to reach a view of the world as a whole, and seeks out the elementary convictions that are to deepen it and give it a sure foundation, one cannot avoid setting our own thought face to face with that of the Hindus, and of the Chinese in the Far East. The latter looks strange to us because in much it has remained till now naïve and embodied in myth, whereas, on the other hand, it has spontaneously advanced to refinements of criticism and to artificialities. But this does not matter. The essential thing is that it is a struggle for a philosophy of life: the form it takes is a secondary matter. Our Western philosophy, if judged by its own latest pronouncements, is much more naïve than we admit to ourselves, and we fail to perceive this only because we have acquired the art of expressing what is simple in a pedantic way.

Among the Hindus we encounter the worldview that is based on world- and life-negation, and the way in which it has laid its foundations in thought is calculated to leave us not knowing what to make of our prejudice in favor of world- and life-affirmation, which, as Westerners, we are inclined to assume to be more or less self-evident.

The attraction and tension that, in Hindu thought, govern the relations between world- and life-negation and ethics afford us glimpses into the problem of ethics for which Western thought offers us no comparable opportunities.

Nowhere, again, has the problem of world- and life-affirmation, both in itself and in its relation to ethics, been felt in so elemental and comprehensive a fashion as in Chinese thought. Lao-tse, Chwang-tse, Kung-tse (Confucius), Meng-tse, Lie-tse, and the rest are thinkers in whom the problems of worldview with which our Western thought is wrestling encounter us in a form, strange indeed, but compelling our attention. Discussing these problems with them means that we ourselves are wrestling with them as well.

That is why I bade our search for a worldview seek to reach clear ideas about itself and come to a halt in order to fix its attention on the thought of mankind as a whole.

My solution to the problem is that we must make up our minds to renounce completely the optimistic–ethical interpretation of the world. If we take the world as it is, it is impossible to attribute to it a meaning in which the aims and objects of mankind and of individual men have a meaning also. Neither world- and life-affirmation nor ethics can be founded on what our knowledge of the world can tell us about the world. In the world we can discover nothing of any purposive evolution in which our activities can acquire a meaning. Nor is the ethical to be discovered in any form in the world-process. The only advance in knowledge that we can make is to describe more and more minutely the phenomena that make up the world and their implications. To understand the meaning of the whole—and that is what a worldview demands—is for us an impossibility. The last fact that knowledge can discover is that the world is a manifestation, and in every way a puzzling manifestation, of the universal will to live.

I believe I am the first among Western thinkers who has ventured to recognize this crushing result of knowledge, and the first to be absolutely skeptical about our knowledge of the world without at the same time renouncing belief in world- and life-affirmation and ethics. Resignation as to knowledge of the world is for me not an irretrievable plunge into a skepticism that leaves us to drift about in life like a derelict vessel. I see in it that effort of honesty that we must venture to make in order to arrive at the serviceable worldview that hovers within sight. Every worldview that fails to start from resignation in regard to knowledge is artificial and a mere fabrication, for it rests upon an inadmissible interpretation of the universe.

Once thought has become clear about the relation in which worldview and life view stand to each other, it is in a position to reconcile resignation as to knowledge with adherence to world- and life-affirmation and ethics. Our view of life is not dependent on our view of the world in the way that uncritical thought imagines. It does not wither away if it cannot send its roots down into a corresponding worldview, for it does not originate in knowledge, although it would like to base itself thereon. It can safely depend upon itself alone, for it is rooted in our will to live.

World- and life-affirmation and ethics are given in our will to live, and they come to be clearly discerned in it in proportion as it learns to think about itself and its relation to the world. The rational thought of other times aimed at getting to know the world and at being able, in that knowledge, to conceive of the highest impulses of our will to live as purposive in view of the universe and its evolution. But that aim was unattainable. We are not meant to unite the world and ourselves in such harmony with one another. We were naïve enough to assume that our view of life must be contained in our view of the world, but the facts do not justify this assumption. The result is that our thought finds itself involved in a dualism with which it can never be reconciled. It is the dualism of worldview and life view, of knowing and willing.

To this dualism, all the problems with which human thought has busied itself ultimately return. Every fragment of the thought of mankind that has any bearing on man's conception of the universe—whether in world religions or in philosophy—is an attempt to resolve this dualism. It is sometimes softened down, but only to let a unitary, monistic worldview be adopted in its place; at other times it is left standing but is transformed into a drama with a monistic issue.

Innumerable are the expedients that thought has used in trying to get rid of dualism. Everything it has undertaken commands respect, even the staggering naïvetés and the meaningless acts of violence to which it committed itself, for it has always been acting under the compulsion of inner necessity: it wanted to rescue a serviceable worldview from the abyss of dualism.

But from this continuous mishandling of the problem, there could issue no solution capable of satisfying thought. We were to be taken over the abyss on tottering bridges of snow.

Instead of going on bridging this abyss with forced logic and imaginative ideas, we must make up our minds to get to the root of the problem and let it bring its influence to bear as it directly encounters us in the facts. The solution is not to try to get rid of dualism from the world but to realize that it can no longer do us any harm. This is possible, if we leave behind us all the artifices and inveracities of thought and bow to the fact that, as we cannot harmonize our life view and our worldview, we must make up our minds to put the former above the latter. The volition that is given in our will to live reaches beyond our knowledge of the world. What is decisive for our life view is not our knowledge of the world but the certainty of the volition that is given in our will to live. The eternal spirit meets us in nature as mysterious creative power. In our will to live, we experience it within us as volition that is both world- and life-affirming and ethical.

Our relation to the world as it is given in the positive certainty of our will to live, when this seeks to comprehend itself in thought: that is our worldview. Worldview is a product of life view, not vice versa.

The rational thought of today, therefore, does not pursue the phantom of getting to know the world. It leaves knowledge of the world on one side as something for us unattainable and tries to arrive at clear ideas about the will to live that is within us.

The problem of worldview, then, brought back to facts and tackled by rational thought without formulating any hypothesis, may be put thus: "What is the relation of my will to live, when it begins to think, to itself and to the world?" And the answer is: "From an inner compulsion to be true to itself and to remain consistent with itself, our will to live enters into relations with our own individual being and with all manifestations of the will to live that surround it, that are determined by the sentiment of reverence for life."

Reverence for life, *veneratio vitae*, is the most direct and, at the same time, the profoundest achievement of my will to live.

In reverence for life my knowledge passes into experience. The simple world- and life-affirmation that is within me just because I am will to live has, therefore, no need to enter into controversy with itself, if my will to live learns to think and yet does not understand the meaning of the world. In spite of the negative results of knowledge, I have to hold fast to world- and life-affirmation and deepen it. My life carries its own meaning in itself. This meaning lies in my living out the highest idea that shows itself in my will to live, the idea of reverence for life. With that for a starting point, I give value to my own life and to all the will to live that surrounds me, I persevere in activity, and I produce values.

Ethics grows out of the same root as world- and life-affirmation, for ethics, too, is nothing but reverence for life. That is what gives me the fundamental principle of morality, namely, that good consists in maintaining, promoting, and enhancing life, and that destroying, injuring, and limiting life are evil. Affirmation of the world, which means affirmation of the will to live that manifests itself around me, is possible only if I devote myself to other life. From an inner necessity, I exert myself in producing values and practicing ethics in the world and on the world even though I do not understand the meaning of the world. For in world- and life-affirmation and in ethics I carry out the will of the universal will to live that reveals itself in me. I live my life in God, in the mysterious divine personality that I do not know as such in the world but only experience as mysterious Will within myself.

Rational thinking which is free from assumptions ends therefore in mysticism. To relate oneself in the spirit of reverence for life to the multiform manifestations of the will to live that together constitute the world is ethical mysticism. All profound worldview is mysticism, the essence of which is just this: that out of my unsophisticated and naïve existence in the world there comes, as a result of thought about self and the world, spiritual self-devotion to the mysterious infinite Will that is continuously manifested in the universe.

This world-affirming, ethical, active mysticism has always been hovering as a vision before Western thought, but the latter could never adopt it because in its search for a worldview it always turned into the wrong road of optimistic–ethical interpretation of the world instead of reflecting directly on the relation that man assumes to the world under the inner compulsion of the profoundest certainty of his will to live.

From my youth onward, I have felt sure that all thought that thinks itself out to an issue ends in mysticism. In the stillness of the African jungle, I have been able to work out this thought and give it expression.

I come forward, therefore, with confidence as a restorer of that rational thought that refuses to make assumptions. I know indeed that our time will have absolutely no connection with anything that is in any way rationalistic and would like to know it renounced as an aberration of the eighteenth century. But the time will come when it will be seen that we must start again where that century came to a stop. What lies between that time and today is an intermezzo of thought, an intermezzo with extraordinarily interesting and valuable moments, but nevertheless unhappy and fatal. Its inevitable end was our sinking into a condition in which we had neither a philosophy of life nor civilization, a condition that contains in itself all that spiritual and material misery in which we languish.

The restoration of our worldview can come only as a result of inexorably truth-loving and recklessly courageous thought. Such thinking alone is mature enough to learn by experience how the rational, when it thinks itself out to a conclusion, passes necessarily over into the non-rational. World- and life-affirmation and ethics are non-rational. They are not justified by any corresponding knowledge of the nature of the world but are the disposition in which, through the inner compulsion of our will to live, we determine our relation to the world.

What the activity of this disposition of ours means in the evolution of the world, we do not know. Nor can we regulate this activity from outside; we must leave entirely to each individual its shaping and its extension. From every point of view, then, world- and life-affirmation and ethics are non-rational, and we must have the courage to admit it.

If rational thought thinks itself out to a conclusion, it arrives at something non-rational that, nevertheless, is a necessity of thought. This is the paradox that dominates our spiritual life. If we try to get on without this non-rational element, there result views of the world and of life that have neither vitality nor value.

All valuable conviction is non-rational and has an emotional character because it cannot be derived from knowledge of the world but arises out of the thinking experience of our will to live, in which we stride out beyond all knowledge of the world. It is this fact that the rational thought that thinks itself out to a conclusion comprehends as the truth by which we must live. The way to true mysticism leads up through rational thought to deep experience of the world and of our will to live. We must all venture once more to be "thinkers," so as to reach mysticism, which is the only direct and the only profound world-view. We must all wander in the field of knowledge to the point where knowledge passes over into experience of the world. We must all, through thought, become religious.

This rational thought must become the prevailing force among us, for all the valuable ideas that we need develop out of it. In no other fire than that of the mysticism of reverence for life can the broken sword of idealism be forged anew.

In the disposition to reverence for life lies enclosed an elementary conception of responsibility to which we must surrender ourselves; in it there are forces at work that drive us to revision and ennoblement of our individual social and political disposition.

It is the disposition to reverence for life, too, that alone is capable of creating a new consciousness of law. The misery prevailing under our political and social condition is due to a great extent to the fact that neither jurists nor laity have in their minds a living and direct conception of law. During the age of rational thought, there was a search made for such a conception, and effort was made to establish fundamental laws that were held to be given in the nature of man and to get them generally recognized. Later on, however, this endeavor was given up, and laws passed at definite dates displaced natural law. Finally, we got to the stage of being satisfied with purely technical law. This was the intermezzo that followed the period of rational thought in the sphere of law.

We have entered into a period in which the feeling for law is hopelessly bereft of force, of soul, and of sense of moral obligation. It is a period of lawlessness. Parliaments produce with easy readiness statutes that contradict the idea of law. States deal arbitrarily with their subjects without regard to the maintenance of any feeling for law. Those, indeed, who fall into the power of a foreign nation are outlaws. No respect is shown for their natural right to a fatherland, or freedom, or dwelling place, or property, or industry, or food, or anything else. Belief in law is today an utter ruin.

This state of things was in preparation from the moment when the search for the natural conception of law, grounded on rational thought, was given up.

The only thing to be done, then, is to make a new connection in the sphere of law also, at the point where the thread of the rational thought of the eighteenth century got broken. We must search for a conception of law that is founded on an idea that grows directly and independently out of a worldview. We have to reestablish human rights that cannot be infringed, human rights that guarantee to each person the greatest possible freedom for his personality within the entity of his own nation, human rights that protect his existence and his human dignity against any foreign violence to which he may be subjected.

Jurists have allowed law and the feeling for law to be ruined. They could not help it, however, for there was no idea provided by the thought of the time to which a living conception of law could have anchored itself. In the complete absence of any worldview, law collapsed entirely, and it is only out of a new worldview that it can be built up again. It is from a fundamental idea about our relation to all that lives, as such, that it must flow in future, as from a spring that can never dry up and never become a swamp. That spring is reverence for life.

Law and ethics spring up together from the same idea. Law is so much of the principle of respect for life as can be embodied in an external code; ethics is what cannot be so embodied. The foundation of law is humanity. It is folly to wish to put out of action the links between law and worldview.

In this way a worldview is the germ of all ideas and dispositions that are determinative for the conduct of individuals and of society.

Airplanes carry men today through the air over a world in which hunger and organized robbery take place. It is not in China only that one recognizes the grotesque character of such progress: it is almost typical for mankind generally, and such grotesque progress cannot be changed to the normal until there prevails a general disposition capable of bringing order again into the chaos of human life through ethics. In the last resort, the practical can be realized only through the ethical.

What a remarkable circle! Rational thought that thinks itself out arrives at something non-rational and subjective which is a necessity of thought, namely, the ethical affirmation of world and life. On the other hand, what, for the purpose of molding the conditions of existence for individual men and mankind as a whole, is rational, that is to say, what is objectively practical in this regard, can be brought about only by individuals perseveringly putting into action the above-mentioned non-rational and subjective. The non-rational principle underlying our activity, a principle that is provided for us by rational thought, is the sole rational and practical principle underlying all the happenings that are to be produced through human action. Thus, the rational and the non-rational, the objective and the subjective, proceed each from the other and return each into the other again. Only when the play of this mutual interchange is in full activity do normal conditions of existence arise for men and mankind. Let it be disturbed, and the abnormal develops.

So, in this book I have written the tragedy of the search for a worldview and have myself trod a new path to the same goal. Whereas Western thought has not arrived at any goal because it would not venture resolutely into the desert of skepticism about knowledge of the world, I make my way through this desert with calm confidence. It is, after all, only a narrow strip, and it lies in front of the ever-green oasis of an elemental philosophy of life that grows out of thought about the will to live. In my attempt, however, to reach a philosophy of life by this new method, I am conscious of having done no more than put together and think out to conclusions many gropings after this new method that were made by other seekers during the period covered.

But I also put into this book my conviction that mankind must renew itself in a new temper of mind, if it is not to be ruined. I entrust to it, further, my belief that this revolution will come about, if only we can make up our minds to become thinking men.

A new Renaissance must come, and a much greater one than that in which we stepped out of the Middle Ages; a great Renaissance in which mankind discovers that the ethical is the highest truth and the highest practicality, and experiences at the same time its liberation from that miserable obsession by what it calls reality, in which it has hitherto dragged itself along.

I would be a humble pioneer of this Renaissance, and throw the belief in a new humanity, like a torch, into our dark age. I make bold to do this because I believe I have given to the disposition to humanity, which hitherto has ranked only as a noble feeling, a firm foundation in a philosophy of life that is a product of elementary thinking and can be made intelligible to everyone. Moreover, it has gained thereby a power of attracting and convincing, which it has not had hitherto, and is capable now of trying conclusions in energetic and consistent fashion with reality, and of proving its full value within it.

7

The Optimistic Worldview in Kant

*Schweitzer's first philosophical work was on Kant's philosophy of religion.
Throughout his entire life, he was a great admirer of Kant but also a sharp
critic. In this selection, Schweitzer emphasizes that Kant properly focuses
ethics on volition ("good will") and directs it toward a higher world order.
Kant's categorical imperative is superior to any utilitarian calculus, yet,
for the exalted character of the moral law, Kant pays the price of having it
devoid of all content; he gains profundity at the cost of vitality. The reasons
for these shortcomings are (1) Kant's ethics is too narrow, limited only to
the duties that human beings have toward each other; (2) Kant blocks
the natural sources of morality and does not allow direct sympathy to be
regarded as ethical; and (3) Kant's ethics is based on a confusion of the
ethical with the intellectual, insofar as the ethical activity is represented as
dependent on the results of his epistemological ("transcendental") idealism.
This idealism cannot result in an ethical, but always in a supra-ethical
worldview: "By its depreciation of the reality of the empirical world, ethical
philosophy is not helped but injured."*

So far as concerns the general tendency of his thought, Immanuel
Kant lives entirely in the optimistic–ethical worldview of rationalism.
He has, however, a feeling that its foundations are not sufficiently

Selection; "The Optimistic–Ethical Worldview in Kant," Ch. 14 of *Civilization and Ethics*, Part II
of *The Philosophy of Civilization*; first translated by C. T. Campion and published as *Civilization and
Ethics* (New York: Macmillan, 1929); reprinted here from *The Philosophy of Civilization* (Amherst, NY:
Prometheus Books, 1987), 181–189.

deep and firm, and he regards it as his task to give them an altogether securer basis. For this purpose, profounder ethics and a less naïve positiveness in assertions about philosophy that touch upon the supra-sensible seem to him desirable.

Like the English intellectualists and intuitionists, Kant is offended by the idea that the ethics in which the modern age finds satisfaction and its impulse to activity is rooted merely in considerations of the universal advantage of morally good actions. Like them, he feels that ethics is something more than this and that, in the ultimate analysis, it has its origin in the compulsion that men experience to strive for self-perfection. But while his predecessors stick fast in the matter provided by semi-scholastic philosophy and theology, he attacks the problem along the lines of pure ethical thought. It follows for him that the fundamental origin and the exalted character of the moral can be preserved only if we always consciously make it an end in itself and never merely a means to an end. Even if moral conduct proves itself to be always advantageous and practical, our motive to it must nevertheless always be a purely inward compulsion. Utilitarian ethics must abdicate before the ethics of immediate and sovereign duty. That is the meaning of the doctrine of the categorical imperative.

The English anti-utilitarians had in common with the utilitarians the thought that moral law was related in essence to empirical natural law. Kant, however, asserts that it has nothing to do with the order of nature but has its origin in supra-natural impulses. He is the first since Plato to feel, like him, that the ethical is the mysterious fact within us. In powerful language he proves in the *Critique of Practical Reason* that ethics is a volition that raises us above ourselves, frees us from the natural order of the world of the senses, and attaches us to a higher world order. That is his great discovery.

In the development of it, however, he falls short of success. Whoever asserts the absoluteness of moral duty must also give the moral an absolute and completely universal content. He must specify a principle of conduct that shows itself as absolutely binding and as lying at the foundations of the most varied ethical duties. If he does not succeed in doing this, his work is only a fragment.

When Plato announces that ethics is supra-natural and mysterious, his worldview provides him with a basic principle of the ethical that corresponds to these qualities and also has a definite content. He is in a position to define ethics as a process of becoming pure and free from the world of sense. This, his own special form of ethics, he develops in the passages where he is consistent with himself. Then, when he cannot complete his argument without active ethics, he has recourse to the popular theory of virtue.

Kant, however, as a child of the modern spirit, cannot let world- and life-negation rank as ethics. Since he can go only a part of the way with Plato, he sees himself faced with the confusing task of letting purposive, activist ethics directed on the empirical world originate in impulses that are not determined by any adaptation to the empirical.

Kant can find no solution of the problem thus set. In the form that he gives it, it is, in fact, insoluble. But he never even realizes that he has arrived at the problem of finding a basic principle of the moral, which is a necessity of thought. He is content with formally characterizing ethical duty as absolutely binding. That duty, unless its content is at once given to it, remains an empty concept, he is unwilling to admit. For the exalted character of his basic principle of the moral, he pays the price of having it devoid of all content.

Beginnings of an attempt to establish a basic moral principle with a content are to be found in his treatise *Foundations of the Metaphysics of Morals* (1785) and again, later, in *The Metaphysics of Morals* (1797). In the 1785 volume he arrives at the dictum: "Act in such a way that you use human nature both in your own person and in everyone else's always as an end, never merely as a means." But instead of seeing how far the totality of ethical duties can be developed out of this principle, in the 1797 treatise he prefers to set before ethics two ends to be aimed at, the perfecting of oneself and the happiness of others, and to enlarge upon the virtues that promote them.

In his investigation of the ethics that aims at personal perfection, he drives his gallery with sure instinct toward the recognition that all virtues that contribute thereto must be conceived as manifestations of sincerity and of reverence for one's own spiritual being. He does not, however, go the length of comprehending these two as a unity. Just as little does he concern himself to make clear the inner connection between effort directed to self-perfecting and effort directed to the common good, and in that way to dig down to the roots of the ethical as such.

How far Kant is from understanding the problem of finding a basic moral principle that has a definite content can be seen from the fact that he never gets beyond an utterly limited conception of the ethical. He obstinately persists in drawing the boundary of his ethics as narrowly as possible, making it concerned with no duties beyond those of man to man. He does not include the relations of man to nonhuman existence. It is only indirectly that he finds room for the prohibition of cruelty to animals, putting this among the duties of man to himself. By inhuman treatment of animals, he says, sympathy with their sufferings is blunted in us and thereby "comes a weakening of a natural disposition that is very helpful to our morality in relation to other men, and it gradually dies out."

Again, the vandalism of the destruction of beautiful, natural objects, which are viewed as entirely without feeling, is said to be unethical only because it violates the duty of man to himself by undermining the desire—itself a support to morality—of having something to love without regard to utility.

If the sphere of the ethical is limited to the relations of man to man, then all attempts to reach a basic principle of the moral with an absolutely binding content are rendered hopeless in advance. The absolute demands the universal. If there really is a basic principle for the moral, it must be concerned in some way or other with the relations between man and life as such in all its manifestations.

Kant, then, does not essay the task of developing a system of ethics that corresponds to his deepened conception of the ethical. On the whole he does nothing more than put the current utilitarian ethics under the protectorate of the Categorical Imperative. Behind a magnificent façade he constructs a block of tenements.

His influence on the ethics of his time is twofold. He furthers it by his challenge to profounder reflection on the nature of the ethical and the ethical destiny of man. At the same time he is a danger in that he robs ethics of its simplicity. The strength of the ethics of the age of reason lies in its naïve utilitarian enthusiasm. It directly enlists men in its service by offering them good aims and objects. Kant makes ethics insecure by bringing this directness in question and calling for ethics derived from much less elementary considerations. Profundity is gained at the cost of vitality because he fails to establish at the same time a basic moral principle with a content, a principle that shall compel acceptance from deep and yet elementary considerations.

Often Kant actually makes it his object to block the natural sources of morality. He will not, for example, allow direct sympathy to be regarded as ethical. The inner feeling for the suffering of another as if it were one's own is not to count as duty in the real sense of the word but only as a weakness by which the evil in the world is doubled. All help to others must have its source in a reasoned consideration of the duty of contributing to the happiness of mankind.

By taking from ethics its simplicity and directness, Kant also loosens the connection that ethics and the belief in progress had formed with one another, with the result that the two together had proved so productive of good. The disastrous separation between them that, later on, in the course of the nineteenth century, became complete, was partly due to him.

He endangers the ethics of his time by wishing to drive out the naïve rationalistic conception of the ethical in favor of a deepened interpretation, without at the same time being in a position to establish for it a basic principle that has been correspondingly deepened, has a definite content of its own, and is directly convincing. He labors at the provision of new foundations without remembering that a house that is not adequately shored up will develop cracks.

Kant passes by the problem of finding a basic principle of the moral with a definite content, because, while attempting to deepen the concept of the ethical, he pursues an object that lies outside ethics. He wishes to bring ethical idealism into connection with an idealistic representation of the world, which has its source in a theory of knowledge. From that source, he hopes there will come an ethical philosophy capable of satisfying critical thought.

Why has Kant, with a rigorism that intentionally depreciates ordinary moral experience, ventured forward to the discovery that the moral law has nothing to do with the natural world order, but is super-sensible? Because he refuses, similarly, to let the world of the senses that is experienced by us in space and time be accepted as anything more than a manifestation of the non-sensible that makes up true reality. The concept of the moral that contains none but inward and spiritual duties is for him the extending ladder that he draws out so as to mount by it to the region of pure Being. He has no feeling of dizziness when, in company with ethics, he climbs above all empirical experience and all empirical aims. He is determined to go right up with ethics, which can never be sufficiently a priori for him, because he sets up another ladder of the same length, that of epistemological idealism, and tries to lean one against the other so that they may give mutual support.

How does it come about that the theoretical assumption that the world of sensible phenomena has a non-sensible world of Being lying behind it has any importance for philosophy? Because within the notion of absolute duty, which man experiences at work within himself, there lies a fact of the world order of that same immaterial world. Hence arises the possibility, thinks Kant, of raising to certainty by means of ethics those great elements in the non-sensible world that are of value for the optimistic–ethical worldview: the ideas of God, of the ethical freedom of the will, and of immortality, which otherwise would always remain merely problematical.

So far as rationalism affirms unhesitatingly, from the standpoint of theoretical knowledge, the ideas of God, of the ethical freedom of the will (virtue), and of immortality, which make up its optimistic–ethical worldview, it builds upon a foundation that cannot bear the weight of critical thought. Kant wishes, therefore, to erect the optimistic–ethical conception of the universe as a lake dwelling built upon piles rammed into place by ethics. These three ideas are to be able to claim real existence as necessary postulates of the ethical consciousness.

This plan, however, of thus securing the position of the optimistic–ethical worldview cannot be carried out. It is only the idea of the ethical freedom of the will that can be made a logical demand of the moral consciousness. To establish the ideas of God and immortality as equally "postulates," Kant has to abandon all respectable logic and argue with bold and ever-bolder sophisms.

There is no way of uniting epistemological and ethical idealism, however enticing the undertaking looks at first sight. When they are set side by side, the happenings that take place according to a law of causation originating in free-dom, and that become conscious in man through the moral law, are seen to be identical with the happenings that are universal in the world of things in them-selves. There ensues a disastrous confusion of the ethical with the intellectual. If the world of the senses is only a manifestation of an immaterial world, then all the happenings that come about in the space and time sphere of causa-tion produced by necessity are only parallel appearances of the events that are brought about in the intellectual sphere of causation produced by freedom. All happenings—human activity just as much as natural happenings—therefore are, according to the point of view, at once immaterial and free, and also natural and necessary. If ethical activity produced by freedom is represented as analo-gous with the results of epistemological idealism, then either everything that happens in the world, conceived as intellectual happening, is ethical, or there is no such thing as an ethical event. Because he has chosen to put side by side these two things, human activity and natural happening, Kant has to renounce all ability to maintain the difference between them. But the very life of ethics depends on this difference being there and effective.

Epistemological idealism is a dangerous ally for ethical idealism. The world order of immaterial happening has a supra-ethical character. From the setting side by side of ethical and epistemological idealism there can never result an ethical, but always only a supra-ethical, worldview.

From epistemological idealism, therefore, ethics has nothing to expect, but everything to fear. By its depreciation of the reality of the empirical world, ethi-cal philosophy is not helped but injured.

Ethics has materialist instincts. It wants to be concerned with empirical happenings and to transform the circumstances of the empirical world. But if that world is only "appearance," derived from an intellectual world that func-tions within it or behind it, ethics has nothing on which to act. To wish to influence a self-determined play of appearances makes no sense. Ethics can, therefore, allow validity to the view that the empirical world is mere appear-ance only with the limitation that activity exerted upon the appearance does at the same time influence the reality lying behind it. But, thereby, it comes into conflict with all epistemological idealism.

Kant is defeated by the same fate that rules in Stoic, Indian, and Chinese monism alike. As soon as thought tries in any way to comprehend ethics in con-nection with the world-process, it falls at once, consciously or unconsciously, into the supra-ethical manner of regarding it. Fully to shape ethics to an ethical worldview means making it come to terms with nature-philosophy. Ethics is thereupon, as a matter of fact, devoured in one way or another by that philoso-phy, even if it is verbally saved from such a fate. The coupling of ethical with epistemological idealism is only bringing ethics and nature-philosophy into relation with one another in a roundabout way by which it is hoped to outwit the logic of facts. But this logic cannot be outwitted. The tragic result lies in the ensuing identification of the ethical with the intellectual.

The ethical is not something irrational that becomes explicable when we betake ourselves from the world of appearance to the region of immaterial Being that lies behind it. Its spiritual character is of a peculiar kind and rests upon the fact that the world-process, as such, comes into contradiction with itself in man. It follows that the ethical will and ethical freedom of the will are not explicable by any theory of knowledge and cannot, moreover, serve as a support to any such theory.

As a result of conceiving the moral law and empirical obedience to natural law as in absolute opposition to each other, Kant finds himself on the road that leads to a dualistic worldview. Afterward, however, in order to satisfy the claims of the unitary and optimistic worldview that the spirit of the age prescribes, he manages, with the stratagems that are provided for him by the combination of ethical and epistemological idealism, to work his way back on to the road that leads to the monistic point of view.

Kant is great as an ethical thinker, great too with his theory of knowledge, but as shaper of a worldview he is not in the first rank. By his deepened conception of the nature of the ethical, a conception that lands him in dualistic thought, the problem of the optimistic–ethical conception of life is unfolded in an entirely new way. Difficulties reveal themselves that till then no one could have imagined. But he does not deal with them. He is blinded by his ambition to be the Copernicus of the optimistic–ethical worldview, believing that he can show the difficulties inherent in that view to be misunderstandings that explain themselves away as soon as, by means of his epistemological idealism, actual relations take the place of these that are apparent but inexplicable. In reality, he does nothing but replace the naïve optimistic–ethical interpretation of the world, which was the basis of action for the rationalists by a fake explanation.

He does not take the trouble to ask himself in what the optimistic ethical worldview really consists, to what final items of knowledge and demands it leads, and how far these are confirmed by experience of the moral law. He takes it over without examination in the formula: "God, Freedom (or Virtue), and Immortality," which was supplied to it by rationalism, and determines to raise it in this naïve form to a certainty!

There is, thus, in Kant's philosophy the most terrible want of thought interwoven with the deepest thinking. Tremendous new truths make their appearance in it. But they get only halfway on their journey. The absoluteness of ethical duty is grasped, but its content is not investigated. Experience of the ethical is recognized as the great secret by means of which we comprehend ourselves as "other than the world"; but the dualistic thinking that goes with it is not worked out any further. That the final perceptions of our worldview are assertions of the ethical will is admitted, but the consequences of this supremacy of the will over knowledge are not thought out to a conclusion.

Kant stimulates powerfully the men of his time but is unable to make secure for them the optimistic–ethical philosophy of life in which they have been living. Although both he and they are content to deceive themselves in the matter, his mission is to deepen it, and . . . to make it become less secure than before.

8

Schopenhauer and Nietzsche's Quest for Elementary Ethics

While Fichte and Hegel interpret Kant's "thing in itself" as "will to action," Schopenhauer understands it as "will to live," and Nietzsche as "will to power." Schweitzer agrees with Schopenhauer and Nietzsche that Fichte and Hegel overvalue the role of state and human organizations, and that morality must be brought back to its most elementary level. Schopenhauer attempts to develop an ethics of universal pity, according to which all life is suffering and we must love even the most insignificant creature of the creation. Yet this pity is for Schopenhauer merely deliberation that does not lead to any action. Schopenhauer's pity is not ethical but theoretical. He feels more contempt than pity for the living beings.

Nietzsche's original goal was to establish a worldview of higher life-affirmation and thereby become anti-Schopenhauerian, anti-Christian, and anti-utilitarian. Schweitzer admires his placing of individual morality before the ethics of society. Nonetheless, Nietzsche's ideal does not lead to a higher spirituality of the will to live but rather to a repression of spiritual impulses. His ideal man becomes a superman who seeks his own ends without any consideration for the rest of mankind. Nietzsche's combination of life-affirmation and world-negation, better known as the will to power, is ethical as much as Schopenhauer's pity for the world.

Selection; "Schopenhauer and Nietzsche," Ch. 20 of *Civilization and Ethics*, Part II of *The Philosophy of Civilization*; first translated by C. T. Campion and published as *Civilization and Ethics* (New York: Macmillan, 1929); reprinted here from *The Philosophy of Civilization* (Amherst, NY: Prometheus Books, 1987), 235–248.

As bad luck will have it, the two most important ethical thinkers of the second half of the nineteenth century, Schopenhauer and Nietzsche, do not help the age in the search for what it needs, namely, a system of social ethics that is also true ethics. Concerned only with individualist ethics from which no social ethics can be developed, they offer incitements that, however valuable in themselves, cannot arrest the demoralization in the general outlook on life that is in progress.

Common to both is the fact that they are elemental moralists. They pursue no abstract cosmic speculations. Ethics is for them an experience of the will to live. They are, therefore, from their very core, cosmic.

In Schopenhauer the will to live tries to become ethical by turning to world- and life-negation; in Nietzsche by devoting itself to a deepened world- and life-affirmation.

From the standpoint of their own elemental ethics, these two thinkers, who stand in such deep contrast to each other, rise as judges of what they find accepted as ethics in their time.

Arthur Schopenhauer (1788–1860) begins to publish at the beginning of the century. His *World as Will and Representation* appears in 1819. But he first obtains a hearing about 1860, when speculative philosophy had definitely gone bankrupt and the unsatisfactory nature of the ethics of popular utilitarianism, and also that of Kant's successors, was generally acknowledged.

The most important among the earlier of these is Johann Friedrich Herbart (1776–1841). His importance lies in the department of psychological investigation. It is on a psychological foundation that he tries to establish ethics in his *General Practical Philosophy* (1808). He traces morality back to five direct and ultimate judgments, which cannot be derived from anything beyond themselves and may be compared with aesthetic judgments. They are: the ideas of inward freedom, of perfection, of benevolence, of right, and of equity. By submitting itself to this mode of outlook, which starts from pure intuition and is confirmed as correct for human beings by the course of their experience, the will becomes ethical.

Instead, therefore, of seeking one basic principle for morality, Herbart accepts several ethical ideas that appear side by side. This anemic ethical theory possesses no convincing power. But in his teaching about society and the state, Herbart does produce something of solid value.

Among the earlier successors of Kant there belongs also Immanuel Hermann Fichte (1797–1879), a son of Johann Gottlieb Fichte, the so-called Younger Fichte, with his *System of Ethics* (2 vols., 1850–1853), which in its time enjoyed considerable repute.

Schopenhauer is the first representative in Western thought of a consistent world- and life-denying system of ethics. The incentive came to him from the philosophy of India, which early in the nineteenth century began to be known in Europe. For the exposition of his worldview he starts, like J. G. Fichte, from Kant's epistemological idealism. Like Fichte he defines the essence of things in themselves, which is to be accepted as underlying all phenomena, to be will— not, however, like Fichte, as will to action, but more directly and more correctly as will to live. The world, he says, I can understand only by analogy with myself. Myself, looked at from outside, I conceive as a physical phenomenon in space and time, but looked at from within, as will to live. Everything, accordingly, that meets me in the world of phenomena is a manifestation of the will to live.

What is the meaning, then, of the world-process? Simply that countless individualities that are rooted in the universal will to live are continually seeking satisfaction, which is never gratified, in aims that they set before themselves in obedience to an inward impulse. Again and again they experience the disappointment that pleasure longed for, not pleasure attained, is real pleasure; they have continually to struggle against hindrances; their own will to live continually comes into conflict with other wills to live. The world is meaningless and all existence is suffering. The knowledge of this is attained by the will to live in the highest living creatures, which are gifted with the power of remaining always conscious that the totality of what is around them, outside themselves, is merely a world of appearances. Surveying in this way the totality of existence, the will is in a position to reach clarity of thought about itself and about existence.

That it must effect something worthwhile in the world is the obsession with which the will to live has befooled itself in European philosophy. When it has attained to knowledge of itself, it realizes that optimistic world-affirmation is of no benefit to it. It can only hurry it on from unrest to unrest, from disappointment to disappointment. What it must try to do is to step out from the terrible game in which, bedazzled, it is taking part, and settle itself to rest in world- and life-negation.

For Spinoza, the meaning of the world-process is that supreme individualities arise, who find their experience within the Absolute; for Fichte, that the urge to activity of the Absolute comprehends itself in supreme individualities as ethical; for Hegel, that the Absolute in supreme individualities arrives at adequate consciousness of itself; for Schopenhauer, that in supreme individualities the Absolute attains to knowledge of itself and finds deliverance from the blind urge to life-affirmation that is within it. The meaning of the world-process, therefore, is always found in this: that the Finite and the Infinite blend their experiences in one another. Spinoza, Fichte, and Hegel—and this is the weakness of their worldview—cannot make it properly intelligible how far this experience in the Finite really has a meaning for the Absolute. In Schopenhauer, however, it has such a meaning. In man the universal will to live begins to turn from the path of unrest and suffering into the path of peace.

The transition from Being to nothingness is introduced. This nothingness is nothingness, it is true, only for the will to live, which is still filled with an urge to life-affirmation and with its conception of the world. What it is in itself, this nirvana of the Buddhists, cannot be defined by our conceptions, which come to us through our senses.

That Schopenhauer develops his pessimistic–ethical, as Fichte his optimistic–ethical, worldview, with the material provided by epistemological idealism has not the importance that he himself attributes to this fact. Indian predecessors have made this connection easier for him. In itself, pessimism can be developed just as well without epistemological idealism. The drama of the tragic experience of the will to live remains the same whatever the scenery and costumes with which it is played.

Although, therefore, it makes its appearance in the dress of Kant's theory of knowledge, Schopenhauer's philosophy is elemental nature–philosophy.

What then is the ethical content of his system?

Like the philosophy of the Indians, it appears in a threefold shape: as ethics of resignation, as ethics of universal pity, and as ethics of world-renunciation.

About resignation, Schopenhauer speaks in forcible words. In language that rises to the level of poetry, he describes how the man who is intent on his own self-perfecting does not meet the destinies of his existence in childish resistance to what is hard, but feels them as incitements to become free from the world. In the disagreeable circumstances that poison his existence, and in the misfortune that threatens to crush him, he suddenly feels himself lifted out of everything on which he sets value and brought to the triumphant feeling that nothing can any longer do him harm. The field of resignation, which the philosophical ethics of modern times had allowed to lie fallow for generations, is replanted by Schopenhauer.

Ethics is pity. All life is suffering. The will to live that has attained to knowledge is, therefore, seized with deep pity for all creatures. It experiences not only the woe of mankind but that of all creatures with it. What is called in ordinary ethics "love" is in its real essence pity. In its overpowering feeling of pity, the will to live is diverted from itself. Its purification begins.

How anxious Kant and Hegel and others are in their ethics to deprive direct pity of its rights because it does not suit their theories! Schopenhauer takes the gag out of its mouth and bids it speak. Those who, like Fichte, Schleiermacher, and others, base ethics on a laboriously thought-out world-scheme, expect man to run every time to the topmost attic of his reflections to fetch down his motives to moral action. According to the sociological utilitarians, he should always first sit down and calculate what is ethical. Schopenhauer bids him do something never yet heard of in philosophical ethics—listen to his own heart. The elemental ethical that by the others has been pushed into the corner can now, thanks to him, take its proper place again.

The others, in order not to get embarrassed with their theories, have to limit ethics exclusively to the conduct of man to man. They anxiously insist that pity for animals is not ethical in itself but has importance only in view of the kindly disposition that must be maintained among men. Schopenhauer tears down these fences and teaches love: to the most insignificant being in creation.

The artificial and curious pleas, too, that the rest produce to put man into an ethical relation to organized society disappear in Schopenhauer. Fichte and Hegel's ethical overvaluation of the state makes him smile. He himself is left free from the necessity of dragging into ethics worldly things that refuse to be fitted in. He can allow the conviction that ethics consists in being different from the world to flame up in dazzling clearness. He is pledged to no concessions since he does not, like the others, represent a morality that has a purposive aim in the world. Because his philosophy is world- and life-denying, he can be an elemental moralist when others have to renounce being that. Nor does he need, like them, to sever all connection with Jesus and religious ethics. He can appeal as often as he likes to the fact that his philosophy establishes only what has always been accepted by the piety of Christianity and of the Indians as the essential element in the moral. It is well known that Schopenhauer judged Christianity to have the Indian spirit and to be probably, in some way or other, of Indian origin.

Elemental morality now once more obtains its right place in a thinking conception of the universe, and this explains the enthusiasm that Schopenhauer arouses when he at last gets known. That it was possible to ignore for nearly forty years the very significant matter that he gave to the world remains one of the most remarkable facts in the history of European thought. The optimistic worldview passed at that time for so self-evident that the man who laid hands upon it, even in the directly illuminating thoughts upon ethics to which Schopenhauer gave utterance, could not obtain a hearing. At a later period, also, many attach themselves to Schopenhauer only because of his ethical maxims, with their natural and attractive appeal, and refuse to accept his consistent worldview of world- and life-negation. It is a right feeling that guides them.

Schopenhauer's outlook on the universe, like that of the Brahmans, because it reveals itself as consistent world- and life-denial, is in the last resort not ethical but supra-ethical. Even though through several chapters of his ethics he can speak in more elemental fashion than Spinoza, Fichte, Schleiermacher, and Hegel, he is nevertheless in reality no more ethical than they are. He ends, as they do, in the frozen sea of the supra-ethical point of view, but at the South Pole instead of at the North. The price that he pays for being able to outbid them in elemental ethics is his philosophy of world- and life-negation. But the price is a ruinous one.

With Schopenhauer, as with the Indians, ethics is only a phase of world- and life-negation. It is nothing in itself but merely what it is in the frame provided by that worldview. And everywhere there peeps through his ethically tinted world- and life-negation world- and life-negation as such. Like a ghostly sun in the sky it devours ethics, just as the real sun devours a mass of clouds from which men are vainly hoping to get a refreshing shower of rain.

On the assumption of world- and life-negation, all ethical action is illusory. Schopenhauer's pity is merely deliberative. Of pity that brings help he can have no real knowledge any more than can the Indian thinkers. Like all will to action in the world, such pity has no sense. It has no power to lighten the misery of the rest of creation, since that misery lies in the will to live, which is irretrievably full of suffering. The one thing, therefore, that pity can do is to enlighten the will to live everywhere about the delusion in which it is held captive, and bring it to the apathy and peace offered by world- and life-negation. Schopenhauer's pity, like that of the Brahmans and the Buddha, is, at bottom, merely theoretical. It can use as its own the words of the religion of love, but it stands at a far lower level. As is the case with the thinkers of India, the ideal of inactivity obstructs the way to the real ethics of love.

The ethics also of self-perfecting is present in Schopenhauer more in word than in reality. The attainment of inward freedom from the world is really ethical only if the personality is thereby enabled to work as a more direct force in the world, but this thought is not to be found either in Schopenhauer or in the Indians. World- and life-negation is, with them, an end in itself, and it continues to assert itself when its ethical character has ceased. Higher than ethics, says Schopenhauer, stands asceticism. Everything that helps deaden the will to live, is to him significant. Men and women who renounce love and the hope of offspring so that there may be less life in the world are to him in the right. Those who deliberately choose religious suicide, and after employing every conceivable device for deadening the will to live allow the lamp of life to be extinguished, as the Brahmans do, by withholding all nourishment from the body, these similarly act as truly enlightened men. Only suicide as the outcome of despair is to be rejected. That is, of course, not a result of the true life-denial but is, on the contrary, the act of a life-affirming will, which is simply discontented with the conditions in which it finds itself.

With Schopenhauer, then, the ethical reaches only so far as world- and life-negation has willed and so far as it is in a position to be declared ethical. The ethical is only an introduction to and a preparation for liberation from the world. It is, at bottom, by an intellectual act that the suspension of the will to live is consummated. If I have won my way through to understanding that the whole phenomenal world is delusion and misery, and that my will to live has no need to take the world or itself seriously, then I am saved. How far and to what extent I then take part in the game of life with the consciousness that I am but a player has no importance.

Schopenhauer does not think out the pessimistic worldview in the great and calm manner of the wise men of India. He behaves under its influence like a nervous and sickly European. While they, on the basis of the liberating knowledge they have reached, advance with majestic gait from the ethical to the supra-ethical, and leave good and evil behind them, as things over which they have equally triumphed, he reveals himself as a miserable Western skeptic. Incapable of living out the worldview that he preaches, he clings to life as to money, appreciates the pleasures of the table as well as those of love, and has more contempt than pity for mankind. As though to justify himself in this, in *The World as Will and Representation*, where he has just been speaking about the deadening of the will to live, he rebels against the notion that anyone who teaches a saintly course of life must also live like a saint. "It is indeed," so runs the famous passage, "a strange demand to make of a moralist that he shall recommend no other virtue than those that he himself possesses. To sum up in a series of conceptions the whole essence of the world, in abstract terms, in general terms, and with clearness, and to offer it thus as a reflected copy in permanent rational conceptions that are always ready to hand: that and nothing else is philosophy."

With these sentences Schopenhauer's philosophy commits suicide. Hegel has a right to say that philosophy is only reflective, not imperative, thinking, for his own philosophy does not claim to be anything more. But *The World as Will and Representation* protests with illuminating language and in a tone of urgent entreaty against the will to live. It ought, therefore, to be the life creed of the author.

The fact that Schopenhauer can, for a moment, so far forget himself as to express himself skeptically about ethics has its own deep-reaching explanation. It belongs to the essence of world- and life-negation, which he wishes to proclaim as ethics, that it cannot be thought out consistently to a conclusion and cannot be consistently put into practice. Even with the Brahmans and the Buddha, it keeps itself alive by inadmissible concessions to world- and life-affirmation. But with Schopenhauer it goes so far in that direction that he can no longer make any attempt to bring theory and practice into harmony but must resolutely live in an atmosphere of mendacity.

He does succeed in making the ethical radiance that world- and life-negation can assume flash up in brilliant colors. But of really producing ethics from world- and life-negation, he is as little capable as the Indians.

Friedrich Nietzsche (1844–1900) in the early period of his activity is under the spell of Schopenhauer. One of his *Untimely Meditations* bears the title: "Schopenhauer as Educator." Later on he goes through a development that leads him to recognize as the ideal a scientifically deepened positivism and utilitarianism. He is his real self first when, starting with *The Gay Science,* he tries to establish his worldview of the higher life-affirmation and thereby becomes anti-Schopenhauer, anti-Christian, and anti-utilitarian.

His criticism of current philosophical and religious ethics is passionate and malicious. But it goes deep. He casts at them two reproaches: that they have made a pact with non-veracity and that they do not allow a human being to become a personality. In this he says only what had long been due. Skeptics had already made public many such complaints. But he speaks as one who is searching for the truth and is concerned about the spiritual future of mankind, thus giving such complaints a new tone and a wider range. Whereas the current philosophy believed that it had in the main solved the ethical problem and was united with biological and sociological utilitarianism in the conviction that in the department of individual ethics there were no more discoveries to be made, Nietzsche overthrows the whole game and shows that all ethics rests upon the morals of the individual. The question about the essential nature of good and evil that was generally accepted as settled, he puts forward again in elemental fashion. The truth that ethics in its real nature is a process of self-perfecting shines out in his works, as in Kant's, although in a different light. Hence, his place is in the first rank of the ethical thinkers of mankind. Those who were torn from their false certainty when his impassioned writings descended on the lowlands of the thought of the outgoing nineteenth century, as the south wind sweeps down from the high mountains in spring, can never forget the gratitude they owe to this upheaver of thought, with his preaching of veracity and personality.

According to Nietzsche, accepted ethics is deficient in veracity, because the conceptions of good and evil that it puts into circulation do not spring out of man's reflection on the meaning of his life but have been invented in order to keep individuals useful to the majority. The weak proclaim that sympathy and love are good because that is to their advantage. Thus led astray, all men try to force themselves to the opinion that they fulfill the highest destiny of their existence by self-sacrifice and the devotion of their lives to others. But this opinion never becomes a real inward conviction. They live out their lives without any thought of their own as to what makes life valuable. They join the crowd in praising the morality of humility and self-sacrifice as the true morality, but they do not really believe in it. They feel self-assertion to be what is natural and act accordingly, without admitting the fact to themselves. They do not question the general ethical prestige of humility and self-sacrifice; they help maintain it, from fear that individuals stronger than themselves might become dangerous to them if this method of taming men were abandoned.

Current morality, then, is something with which mankind as a whole is deceived by means of traditional views and with which individuals deceive themselves.

With indignant statements like these, Nietzsche is so far in the right that the ethics of humility and self-sacrifice does, as a matter of principle, avoid engaging in a clear and practical discussion with reality. It exists by leaving quite undetermined the degree of life-denial involved. In theory it proclaims life-negation; in practice, however, it allows a life-affirmation that has thereby become unnatural and sickly to prevail. Stripped of all its passion, then, Nietzsche's criticism means that only that system of ethics deserves to be accepted that springs from independent reflection on the meaning of life and arrives at a straightforward understanding with reality.

Individual morality comes before social morality. Not what it means for society, but what it means for the perfecting of the individual, is the first question that has to be put. Does it allow a man to become a personality or not? It is here, says Nietzsche, that current ethics fails. It does not allow men to grow straight up but trains them like stunted trees on espaliers. It puts humility and self-surrender before men as the content of perfection; but for the ethical that consists in man being one with himself and thoroughly sincere, it has no understanding.

What does "noble" mean? shouts Nietzsche with harsh words to his age as being the ethical question that has been forgotten. Those who, when the question re-echoed everywhere, were touched by the truth that was stirring, and the anxiety that was quivering within it, have received from that solitary thinker all that he had to give to the world.

If life-negation brings with it so much that is unnatural and fraught with doubt, it cannot be ethics. Ethics, then, must consist of a higher life-affirmation.

But what is higher life-affirmation? Fichte and the speculative philosophers in general make it consist in this: that the will of man conceives itself within the infinite will, and in consequence of this no longer belongs to the

universe in merely natural fashion but surrenders itself consciously and will-
ingly to it as an energy that acts in intelligent harmony with the infinite will.
Nietzsche sees clearly that, in this way, they have not arrived at any convincing
idea of the content of the higher life-affirmation but are moving in the region of
the abstract. He himself means to remain at all costs elemental, and he, therefore, avoids philosophizing about the universe, showing himself thereby to be
a true moralist like Socrates. He jeers at those who, not content with belittling
mankind, proceed further to profane the reality of the world by declaring that
it exists merely in the human imagination. It is only on the essential nature
of the will to live and the way to use it most completely in experience that he
wishes to reflect.

His original belief was that he could conceive the higher life-affirmation as
the development to a higher spirituality of the will to live. But when he attempted
to develop this idea in the course of his study, it took on another form. Higher
spirituality means, of course, the repressing of natural impulses and natural
claims on life and is thereby in some way or other connected with life-negation.
Higher life-affirmation, therefore, can consist only in the entire content of the
will to live being raised to its highest conceivable power. Man fulfills the meaning of his life by affirming with the clearest consciousness of himself everything
that is within him—even his impulses to secure power and pleasure.

But Nietzsche cannot get rid of the antagonism between the spiritual and
the natural. Just in proportion as he emphasizes the natural does the spiritual
shrink back. Gradually, under the visible influence of the mental disease that is
threatening him, his ideal man becomes the "superman," who asserts himself
triumphantly against all fate and seeks his own ends without any consideration
for the rest of mankind.

From the very outset, Nietzsche is condemned, in his thinking out what
life-affirmation means, to arrive at the higher form of it by a more or less meaningless living out of life to the full. He wants to listen to the highest efforts of
the will to live without putting it in any relation to the universe. But the higher
life-affirmation can be a living thing only when life-affirmation tries to understand itself in world-affirmation. Life-affirmation in itself, in whichever direction it turns, can become only enhanced life-affirmation, never a higher form
of it. Unable to follow any fixed course, it careers wildly in circles like a ship
with its tiller firmly lashed.

Nietzsche, however, instinctively shrinks from fitting life-affirmation into
world-affirmation and bringing it by that method to development into a higher
and ethical life-affirmation. Life-affirmation within world-affirmation means
self-devotion to the world, but with that there follows somehow or other life-
negation within the life-affirmation. But it is just this interplay of the two that

Nietzsche wants to get rid of because it is there that ordinary ethics comes to grief.

He was not the first to put forward in Western thought the theory of living one's own life to the full. Greek sophists and others after them anticipated him in this. There is a great difference, however, between him and his predecessors. They are for living a full life because it brings them enjoyment. He, on the other hand, brings to the theory the much deeper thought that by living one's own life victoriously to the full, life itself is honored, and that by the enhancement of life the meaning of existence is realized. Men of genius and strong individuality, therefore, should be intent on allowing only the greatness that is in them to have free play.

Nietzsche's true predecessors are unknown to him. They have their home, like those of Spinoza, in China. In that country, life-affirmation made the attempt to come to clear ideas about itself. In Lao-tse and his pupils, it is still naively ethical. In Chwang-tse it becomes cheerful resignation, in Lie-tse the will to secret power over things; in Yang-tse it ends in an all-round living of life to the full. Nietzsche is a synthesis, appearing in European mentality, of Lie-tse and Yang-tse. It is only we Europeans who are capable of producing the philosophy of brutality.

Zarathustra is, for him, the symbol of the thoughts that are forming within him: Zarathustra, the hero of veracity who dares to value natural life as a good thing, and Zarathustra, the genius who is far removed from the Jewish–Christian mode of thought.

At bottom, Nietzsche is no more unethical than Schopenhauer. He is misled by the ethical element that is present in life-affirmation into giving the status of ethics to life-affirmation as such. Thereby, he falls into the absurdities that follow from an exclusive affirmation of life, just as Schopenhauer falls into those of an exclusive denial of life. Nietzsche's will to power should cause no more offense than Schopenhauer's will to self-annihilation, as it is explained in the passages in his works that deal with asceticism. It is interesting to note that neither of the two men lives in accordance with his view of life. Schopenhauer is no ascetic but a bon vivant, and Nietzsche does not lord it over his fellow men but lives in seclusion.

Life-affirmation and life-negation are both, for a certain distance, ethical; pursued to a conclusion, they become unethical. This result, which was reached by the optimistic thought of China and the pessimistic thought of India, makes its appearance in Europe in Nietzsche and Schopenhauer because they are the only thinkers on this continent who philosophize in elemental fashion about the will to live and venture to follow the paths of one-sidedness. Each completing the other, they pronounce sentence on the ethics of European philosophy by bringing into daylight again the elemental ethical thoughts contained in life-negation as in life-affirmation, thoughts that philosophy was keeping buried. Arriving as they do at the non-ethical by thinking out to a conclusion, one of them life-negation, the other life-affirmation, they corroborate together the statement that the ethical consists neither of life-negation nor of life-affirmation but is a mysterious combination of the two.

9

Reverence for Life

Schweitzer presents here his theory of reverence for life in the context of his criticism of the direction in which our civilization has been developing and also in the context of his presentation of the history of ethics. He argues that his ethical viewpoint emerges from our recognition of an inner necessity to respect the sacredness of all life. This inner necessity is connected with what Schweitzer believes is "an unlimited responsibility" that we as ethical creatures have toward everything alive. Schweitzer's ethics does not directly concern the specific actions that we undertake but rather deals with our attitudes toward all life.

In this presentation of his view, Schweitzer contrasts the ethics of reverence for life to thoughtlessness, egotistical self-assertion, and the ethics of society. Reverence for life demands constant thoughtfulness because it cannot be expressed in terms of moral precepts valid for all situations but demands that we adjust our attitudes to the problems at hand. It also demands a restriction of egotistical self-assertiveness because it requires that we dedicate ourselves to the service of others. Yet, to serve others does not mean to lose one's own personality. As the greatest "enemy" of the ethics of reverence for life, Schweitzer lists the "ethics of society," which he believes has dominated our civilization. The ethics of society imposes certain "supra-personal" obligations on individuals (e.g., patriotism, the

Selection; "The Ethics of Reverence for Life," Ch. 26 of *Civilization and Ethics*, Part II of *The Philosophy of Civilization;* first translated by C. T. Campion and published as *Civilization and Ethics* (New York: Macmillan, 1929); reprinted with minor changes from *The Philosophy of Civilization* (Amherst, NY: Prometheus Books, 1987), 307–329.

common good, etc.) and demands that, whenever such obligations clash with our personal recognition of what we ought to do, the preference should be given to supra-personal obligations. Schweitzer argues that the ethics of society is pseudo-ethics, for we must serve society without abandoning ourselves to it.

Complicated and laborious are the roads along which ethical thought, which has mistaken its way and taken too high a flight, must be brought back. Its course, however, maps itself out quite simply if, instead of taking apparently convenient shortcuts, it keeps to its right direction from the very beginning. For this three things are necessary: it must have nothing to do with an ethical interpretation of the world; it must become cosmic and mystical—that is to say, it must seek to conceive all the self-devotion that rules in ethics as a manifestation of an inward, spiritual relation to the world; and it must not lapse into abstract thinking, but must remain elemental, understanding self-devotion to the world to be self-devotion of human life to every form of living being with which it can come into relation.

The origin of ethics is that I think out the full meaning of the world-affirmation that, together with the life-affirmation in my will to live, is given by nature and try to make it a reality.

To become ethical means to begin to think sincerely.

Thinking is the argument between willing and knowing that goes on within me. Its course is a naïve one, if the will demands of knowledge to be shown a world that corresponds to the impulses that it carries within itself, and if knowledge attempts to satisfy this requirement. This dialogue, which is doomed to produce no result, must give place to a debate of the right kind, in which the will demands from knowledge only what it really knows.

If knowledge answers solely with what it knows, it is always teaching the will one and the same fact, namely, that in and behind all phenomena there is a will to live. Knowledge, though ever becoming deeper and more comprehensive, can do nothing except take us ever deeper and ever further into the mystery that all that is, is will to live. Progress in science consists only in increasingly accurate description of the phenomena in which life in its innumerable forms appears and passes, letting us discover life where we did not previously expect it and putting us in a position to turn to our own use in this or that way what we have learnt of the course of the will to live in nature. But what life is, no science can tell us.

For our conception of the universe and of life, then, the gain derived from knowledge is only that it makes it harder for us to be thoughtless because it ever more forcibly compels our attention to the mystery of the will to live that we see stirring everywhere. Hence, the difference between learned and unlearned is entirely relative. The unlearned man who, at the sight of a tree in flower, is overpowered by the mystery of the will to live that is stirring all round him knows more than the scientist who studies under the microscope or in physical and chemical activity a thousand forms of the will to live. With all his knowledge of the life course of these manifestations of the will to live he is still not moved by its mystery, while he is seduced into vanity at being able to describe exactly any of its fragments.

All true knowledge passes on into experience. The nature of the manifestations I do not know, but I form a conception of it in analogy to the will to live that is within myself. Thus, my knowledge of the world becomes experience of the world. The knowledge that is becoming experience does not allow me to remain in the face of the world a man who merely knows, but forces upon me an inward relation to the world and fills me with reverence for the mysterious will to live that is in all things. By making me think and wonder, it leads me ever upward to the heights of reverence for life. There, it lets my hand go. It cannot accompany me further. My will to live must now find its way about the world by itself.

It is not by informing me what this or that manifestation of life means in the sum total of the world that knowledge brings me into connection with the world. It goes about with me not in outer circles but in the inner ones. From within outward, it puts me in relation to the world by making my will to live feel everything around it as also will to live.

With Descartes, philosophy starts from the dogma "I think, therefore I exist." With this paltry, arbitrarily chosen beginning, it is landed irretrievably on the road to the abstract. It never finds the right approach to ethics and remains entangled in a dead world- and life view. True philosophy must start from the most immediate and comprehensive fact of consciousness, which says "I am life, which wills to live, in the midst of life, which wills to live." This is not an ingenious dogmatic formula. Day by day, hour by hour, I live and move in it. At every moment of reflection it stands fresh before me. There bursts forth from it again and again, as from roots that can never dry up, a living world- and life view that can deal with all the facts of Being. A mysticism of ethical union with Being grows out of it.

As in my own will to live there is a longing for wider life and for the mysterious exaltation of the will to live, which we call pleasure, with dread of annihilation and of the mysterious depreciation of the will to live, which we call pain; so is it also in the will to live all around me, whether it can express itself before me, or remains dumb.

Ethics consists, therefore, in my experiencing the compulsion to show to all will to live the same reverence as I do to my own. There we have, given us, that basic principle of the moral, which is a necessity of thought. It is good to maintain and to encourage life; it is bad to destroy life or to obstruct it.

As a matter of fact, everything that in the ordinary ethical valuation of the relations of men to each other ranks as good can be brought under the description of material and spiritual maintenance or promotion of human life, and of effort to bring it to its highest value. Conversely, everything that ranks as bad in human relations is, in the last analysis, material or spiritual destruction or obstruction of human life, and negligence in the endeavor to bring it to its highest value. Separate individual categories of good and evil that lie far apart and have apparently no connection at all with one another fit together like the pieces of a jigsaw puzzle, as soon as they are comprehended and deepened in this the most universal definition of good and evil.

The basic principle of the moral, which is a necessity of thought, means, however, not only an ordering and deepening but also a widening of the current views of good and evil. A man is truly ethical only when he obeys the compulsion to help all life that he is able to assist and shrinks from injuring anything that lives. He does not ask how far this or that life deserves one's sympathy as being valuable nor, beyond that, whether and to what degree it is capable of feeling. Life as such is sacred to him. He tears no leaf from a tree, plucks no flower, and takes care to crush no insect. If in summer he is working by lamplight, he prefers to keep his windows shut and breathe a stuffy atmosphere rather than see one insect after another fall with singed wings upon his table.

If he walks on the road after a shower and sees an earthworm that has strayed on to it, he bethinks himself that it must get dried up in the sun if it does not return soon enough to ground into which it can burrow, so he lifts it from the deadly stone surface and puts it on the grass. If he comes across an insect that has fallen into a puddle, he stops a moment in order to hold out a leaf or a stalk on which it can save itself.

He is not afraid of being laughed at as sentimental. It is the fate of every truth to be a subject for laughter until it is generally recognized. Once, it was considered folly to assume that men of color were really men and ought to be treated as such, but the folly has become an accepted truth. Nowadays it is thought to be going too far to declare that constant regard for everything that lives, down to the lowest manifestations of life, is a demand made by rational ethics. The time is coming, however, when people will be astonished that mankind needed so long a time to learn to regard thoughtless injury to life as incompatible with ethics.

Ethics is responsibility without limit toward all that lives.

As a general proposition, the definition of ethics as a relationship within a disposition to reverence for life does not make a very moving impression. But it is the only complete one. Compassion is too narrow to rank as the total essence of the ethical. It denotes, of course, only interest in the suffering will to live. But ethics includes also feeling as one's own all the circumstances and all the aspirations of the will to live, its pleasure, too, and its longing to live itself out to the full, as well as its urge to self-perfecting.

Love means more, since it includes fellowship in suffering, in joy, and in effort, but it shows the ethical only in a simile, although in a simile that is natural and profound. It makes the solidarity produced by ethics analogous to that which nature calls forth on the physical side, for more or less temporary purposes, between two beings that complete each other sexually, or between them and their offspring.

Thought must strive to bring to expression the nature of the ethical in itself. To effect this it arrives at defining ethics as devotion to life inspired by reverence for life. Even if the phrase "reverence for life" sounds so general as to seem somewhat lifeless, what is meant by it is nevertheless something that never lets go of the man into whose thought it has made its way. Sympathy, and love, and every kind of valuable enthusiasm are given within it. With restless living force, reverence for life works upon the mind into which it has entered and throws it into the unrest of a feeling of responsibility that at no place and at no time ceases to affect it. Just as the screw that churns its way through the water drives the ship along, so does reverence for life drive the man.

Arising, as it does, from an inner compulsion, the ethics of reverence for life is not dependent on the extent to which it can be thought out to a satisfying conception of life. It need give no answer to the question of what significance the ethical man's work for the maintenance, promotion, and enhancement of life can be in the total happenings of the course of nature. It does not let itself be misled by the calculation that the maintaining and completing of life that it practices is hardly worth consideration beside the tremendous, unceasing destruction of life that goes on every moment through natural forces. Having the will to action, it can leave on one side all problems regarding the success of its work. The fact, in itself, that in the ethically developed man there has made its appearance in the world a will to live that is filled with reverence for life and devotion to life is full of importance for the world.

In my will to live, the universal will to live experiences itself otherwise than in its other manifestations. In them it shows itself in a process of individualizing that, so far as I can see from the outside, is bent merely on living itself out to the full and in no way on union with any other will to live. The world is a ghastly drama of will to live divided against itself. One existence makes its way at the cost of another; one destroys the other. One will to live merely exerts its will against the other and has no knowledge of it. But in me the will to live has come to know about other wills to live. There is in it a yearning to arrive at unity with itself, to become universal.

Why does the will to live experience itself in this way in me alone? Is it because I have acquired the capacity of reflecting on the totality of Being? What is the goal of this evolution that has begun in me?

To these questions, there is no answer. It remains a painful enigma for me that I must live with reverence for life in a world that is dominated by creative will that is also destructive will, and destructive will that is also creative.

I can do nothing but hold to the fact that the will to live in me manifests itself as will to live that desires to become one with other will to live. That is, for me, the light that shines in the darkness. The ignorance in which the world is wrapped has no existence for me; I have been saved from the world. I am thrown, indeed, by reverence for life into unrest such as the world does not know, but I obtain from it a blessedness that the world cannot give. If in the tender-heartedness produced by being different from the world another person and I help each other in understanding and pardoning, when otherwise will would torment will, the division of the will to live is at an end. If I save an insect from a puddle, life has devoted itself to life, and the division of life against itself is ended. Whenever my life devotes itself in any way to life, my finite will to live experiences union with the infinite will in which all life is one, and I enjoy a feeling of refreshment that prevents me from pining away in the desert of life.

I, therefore, recognize it as the destiny of my existence to be obedient to this higher revelation of the will to live in me. I choose for my activity the removal of this division of the will to live against itself, so far as the influence of my existence can reach. Knowing now the one thing needful, I leave on one side the enigma of the universe and of my existence in it.

The surmisings and the longings of all deep religiousness are contained in the ethics of reverence for life. This religiousness, however, does not build up for itself a complete philosophy but resigns itself to the necessity of leaving its cathedral unfinished. It finishes the chancel only; but in this chancel, piety celebrates a living and never-ceasing divine service.

The ethics of reverence for life shows its truth also in that it includes in itself the various elements of ethics in their natural connection. Hitherto, no system of ethics has been able to present in its parallelism and its interaction the effort after self-perfecting, in which man acts upon himself without outward deeds and activist ethics. The ethics of reverence for life can do this and indeed in such a way that it not only answers academic questions but also produces a deepening of ethical insight.

Ethics is reverence for the will to live within me and without me. From the former comes first the profound life-affirmation of resignation. I apprehend my will to live as not only something that can live itself out in happy occurrences but also something that has experience of itself. If I refuse to let this self-experience disappear in thoughtlessness and persist in feeling it to be valuable, I begin to learn the secret of spiritual self-realization. I win an unsuspected freedom from the various destinies of life. At moments when I had expected to find myself shattered, I find myself exalted in an inexpressible and surprising happiness of freedom from the world, and I experience therein a clarification of my life view. Resignation is the vestibule through which we enter ethics. Only he who in deepened devotion to his own will to live experiences inward freedom from outward occurrences is capable of devoting himself in profound and steady fashion to the life of others.

Just as in reverence for my own will to live I struggle for freedom from the destinies of life, so I struggle, too, for freedom from myself. Not only in face of what happens to me but also with regard to the way in which I concern myself with the world, I practice the higher self-maintenance. Out of reverence for my own existence I place myself under the compulsion of veracity toward myself. Everything I might acquire would be purchased too dearly by action in defiance of my convictions. I fear that if I were untrue to myself, I should be wounding my will to live with a poisoned spear.

The fact that Kant makes, as he does, sincerity toward oneself the central point of his ethics testifies to the depth of his ethical feeling. But because in his search for the essential nature of the ethical he fails to find his way through to reverence for life, he cannot comprehend the connection between veracity toward oneself and activist ethics.

As a matter of fact, the ethics of sincerity toward oneself passes imperceptibly into that of devotion to others. Such sincerity compels me to actions that manifest themselves as self-devotion in such a way that ordinary ethics derives them from devotion.

Why do I forgive anyone? Because I feel sympathy with him, ordinary ethics says. It allows men, when they pardon others, to seem to themselves wonderfully good and allows them to practice a style of pardoning that is not free from humiliation of the other. It thus makes forgiveness a sweetened triumph of self-devotion.

The ethics of reverence for life does away with this crude point of view. All acts of forbearance and of pardon are for it acts forced from one by sincerity toward oneself. I must practice unlimited forgiveness because, if I did not, I should be wanting in sincerity to myself, for it would be acting as if I myself were not guilty in the same way as the other has been guilty toward me.

Because my life is so liberally spotted with falsehood, I must forgive falsehood that has been practiced upon me; because I myself have been in so many cases wanting in love and guilty of hatred, slander, deceit, or arrogance, I must pardon any want of love, and all hatred, slander, deceit, or arrogance that have been directed against myself. I must forgive quietly and unostentatiously; in fact, I do not really pardon at all, for I do not let things develop to any such act of judgment. Nor is this any eccentric proceeding; it is only a necessary widening and refining of ordinary ethics.

We have to carry on the struggle against the evil that is in mankind, not by judging others but by judging ourselves. Struggle with oneself and veracity toward oneself are the means by which we influence others. We quietly draw them into our efforts to attain the deep spiritual self-realization that springs from reverence for one's own life. Power makes no noise. It is there and works. True ethics begins where the use of languages ceases.

The innermost element then, in activist ethics, even if it appears as self-devotion, comes from the compulsion to sincerity toward oneself and obtains therein its true value. The whole ethics of being other than the world flows pure only when it comes from this source. It is not from kindness to others that I am gentle, peaceable, forbearing, and friendly but because by such behavior I prove my own profoundest self-realization to be true. Reverence for life that I apply to my own existence, and reverence for life that keeps me in a temper of devotion to other existence than my own interpenetrate each other.

Because ordinary ethics possesses no basic principle of the ethical, it must engage at once in the discussion of conflicting duties. The ethics of reverence for life has no such need for hurry. It takes its own time to think out in all directions its own principle of the moral. Knowing itself to be firmly established, it then settles its position with regard to these conflicts.

The ethics of reverence for life has to try conclusions with three adversaries: these are thoughtlessness, egoistic self-assertion, and society.

To the first of these, it usually pays insufficient attention because no open conflicts arise between them. This adversary does, nevertheless, obstructs it imperceptibly.

There is, however, a wide field of which our ethics can take possession without any collision with the troops of egoism. Man can accomplish much that is good without having to require of himself any sacrifice. And if there really goes with it a bit of his life, it is so insignificant that he feels it no more than if he were losing a hair or a flake of dead skin.

Over wide stretches of conduct, the inward liberation from the world, the being true to oneself, the being different from the world, yes, and even self-devotion to other life is only a matter of giving attention to this particular relationship. We fall short so much because we do not keep ourselves up to it. We do not stand sufficiently under the pressure of any inward compulsion to be ethical. At all points the steam hisses out of the boiler that is not tightly closed. In ordinary ethics the resulting losses of energy are as high as they are because such ethics has at its disposal no single basic principle of the moral, which acts upon thought. It cannot tighten the lid of the boiler; indeed, it does not ever even examine it. But reverence for life, being something that is ever present to thought, penetrates unceasingly and in all directions a man's observation, reflection, and resolutions. He can keep himself clear of it as little as the water can prevent itself from being colored by the dye stuff that is dropped into it. The struggle with thoughtlessness is started and is always going on.

But what is the position of the ethics of reverence for life in the conflicts that arise between inward compulsion to self-sacrifice and the necessary upholding of the ego?

I, too, am subject to division of my will to live against itself. In a thousand ways, my existence stands in conflict with that of others. The necessity to destroy and to injure life is imposed upon me. If I walk along an unfrequented path, my foot brings destruction and pain upon the tiny creatures that populate it. In order to preserve my own existence, I must defend myself against the existence that injures it. I become a persecutor of the little mouse that inhabits my house, a murderer of the insect that wants to have its nest there, a mass murderer of the bacteria that may endanger my life. I get my food by destroying plants and animals. My happiness is built upon injury done to my fellow men.

How can ethics be maintained in face of the horrible necessity to which I am subjected through the division of my will to live against itself?

Ordinary ethics seeks compromises. It tries to dictate how much of my existence and of my happiness I must sacrifice and how much I may preserve at the cost of the existence and happiness of other lives. With these decisions it produces experimental, relative ethics. It offers as ethical what is in reality not ethical but a mixture of non-ethical necessity and ethics. It thereby brings about a huge confusion and allow the starting of an ever-increasing obscuration of the conception of the ethical.

The ethics of reverence for life knows nothing of a relative ethics. It makes only the maintenance and promotion of life rank as good. All destruction of and injury to life, under whatever circumstances they take place, it condemns as evil. It does not keep in store adjustments between ethics and necessity all ready for use. Again and again, and in ways that are always original, it is trying to come to terms in man with reality. It does not abolish for him all ethical conflicts but compels him to decide for himself in each case how far he can remain ethical and how far he must submit himself to the necessity for destruction of and injury to life, and therewith incur guilt. It is not by receiving instruction about agreement between the ethical and the necessary that a man makes progress in ethics but only by coming to hear more and more plainly the voice of the ethical, by becoming ruled more and more by the longing to preserve and promote life, and by becoming more and more obstinate in resistance to the necessity for destroying or injuring life.

In ethical conflicts man can arrive only at subjective decisions. No one can decide for him at what point, on each occasion, lies the extreme limit of possibility for his persistence in the preservation and furtherance of life. He alone has to judge this issue, by letting himself be guided by a feeling of the highest possible responsibility toward other life.

We must never let ourselves become blunted. We are living in truth when we experience these conflicts more profoundly. The good conscience is an invention of the devil.

What does reverence for life say about the relations between man and the animal world?

Whenever I injure life of any sort, I must be quite clear whether it is necessary. Beyond the unavoidable, I must never go, not even with what seems insignificant. The farmer who has mowed down a thousand flowers in his meadow as fodder for his cows must be careful on his way home not to strike off in wanton pastime the head of a single flower by the roadside, for he thereby commits a wrong against life without being under the pressure of necessity.

Those who experiment with operations or the use of drugs upon animals or inoculate them with diseases so as to be able to bring help to mankind with the results gained must never quiet any misgivings they feel with the general reflection that their cruel proceedings aim at a valuable result. They must first have considered in each individual case whether there is a real necessity to force upon any animal this sacrifice for the sake of mankind. And they must take the most anxious care to mitigate as much as possible the pain inflicted. How much wrong is committed in scientific institutions through neglect of anesthetics, which, to save time or trouble, are not administered! How much, too, through animals being subjected to torture merely to demonstrate to students generally known phenomena! By the very fact that animals have been subjected to experiments and have, by their pain, won such valuable results for suffering humanity, a new and special relation of solidarity has been established between them and us. From that springs for each one of us a compulsion to do to every animal all the good we possibly can. By helping an insect when it is in difficulties, I am only attempting to cancel part of man's ever-new debt to the animal world. Whenever an animal is in any way forced into the service of man, every one of us must be concerned with the sufferings that, for that reason, it has to undergo. None of us must allow to take place any suffering for which he himself is not responsible, if he can hinder it in any way. He must not soothe his conscience with the reflection that he would be mixing himself up in something that does not concern him. No one must shut his eyes and regard as nonexistent the sufferings of which he spares himself the sight. Let no one regard as light the burden of his responsibility. While so much ill treatment of animals goes on, while the moans of thirsty animals in railway trucks sound unheard, while so much brutality prevails in our slaughterhouses, while animals have to suffer in our kitchens painful death from unskilled hands, while animals have to endure intolerable treatment from heartless men, or are left to the cruel play of children we all share the guilt.

We are afraid of making ourselves conspicuous if we let it be noticed how we feel for the sufferings that man brings upon the animals. At the same time, we think that others have become more "rational" than we are and regard what we are excited about as usual and a matter of course. Yet, suddenly, they will let slip a word that shows us that they, too, have not yet learned to acquiesce. And now, though they were strangers, they are quite near us. The mask in which we deceived each other falls off. We know now, from one another, that we feel alike about being unable to escape from the gruesome proceedings that are taking place unceasingly around us. What a making of a new acquaintance!

The ethics of reverence for life guards us from letting each other believe, through our silence, that we no longer experience what, as thinking men, we must experience. It prompts us to keep each other sensitive to what distresses us and to talk and act together, just as the responsibility we feel moves us, and without any feeling of shyness. They make us join in keeping on the lookout for opportunities of bringing some sort of help to animals to make up for the great misery that men inflict on them, and thus to step for a moment out of the incomprehensible horror of existence.

In the matter also of our relation to other men, the ethics of reverence for life throws upon us a responsibility so unlimited as to be terrifying.

Here, again, it offers us no rules about the extent of the self-maintenance that is allowable; again, it bids us in each case to thrash the question out with the absolute ethics of self-devotion. I have to decide, in accordance with the responsibility of which I am conscious, how much of my life, my possessions, my rights, my happiness, my time, and my rest I must devote to others and how much I may keep for myself.

In the question of possessions, the ethics of reverence for life is outspokenly individualist in the sense that wealth acquired or inherited should be placed at the service of the community, not through any measures taken by society, but through the absolutely free decision of the individual. It expects everything from a general increase in the feeling of responsibility. Wealth it regards as the property of society left in the sovereign control of the individual. One man serves society by carrying on a business in which a number of employees earn their living, another by giving away his wealth in order to help his fellows. Between these two extreme kinds of service, let each decide according to the responsibility that he finds determined for him by the circumstances of his life. Let no man judge his neighbor. The one thing that matters is that each shall value what he possesses as means to action. Whether this is accomplished by his keeping and increasing his wealth, or by surrender of it, matters little. Wealth must reach the community in the most varied ways if it is to be of the greatest benefit to all.

Those who possess little to call their own are most in danger of holding what they have in a purely selfish spirit. There is profound truth in the parable of Jesus that makes the servant who had received least the least loyal to his duty.

My rights, too, the ethics of reverence of life does not allow to belong to me. It forbids me to still my conscience with the reflection that, as the more efficient man, by quite legitimate means I am advancing myself at the cost of one who is less efficient than I. In what the law and public opinion allow me, it sets a problem before me. It bids me think of others and make me ponder whether I can allow myself the inward right to pluck all the fruit that my hand can reach. Thus it may happen that, in obedience to consideration for the existence of others, I do what seems to ordinary opinion to be folly. Yes, it may even show itself to be folly by the fact that my renunciation has not been of any use to him for whom it was made. And yet I was right. Reverence for life is the highest court of appeal. What it commands has its own significance, even if it seems foolish or useless. We all look, of course, in one another, for the folly that indicates that we have higher responsibilities making themselves felt in our hearts. Yet it is only in proportion as we all become less rational, in the meaning given it by ordinary calculation, that the ethical disposition develops in us and allows problems to become soluble that have hitherto been insoluble.

Nor will reverence for life grant me my happiness as my own. At the moments when I should like to enjoy myself without restraint, it wakes in me reflection about misery that I see or suspect, and it does not allow me to drive away the uneasiness I feel. Just as the wave cannot exist for itself but is ever a part of the heaving surface of the ocean, so must I never live my life for itself but always in the experience that is going on around me. It is an uncomfortable doctrine that the true ethics whispers into my ear. You are happy, it says; there-fore, you are called upon to give much. Whatever more than others you have received in health, natural gifts, working capacity, success, a beautiful child-hood, harmonious family circumstances, you must not accept as being a matter of course. You must pay a price for them. You must show more than average devotion of life to life.

To the happy the voice of the true ethics is dangerous, if they venture to listen to it. When it calls to them, it never damps down the irrational that glows within it. It assails them to see whether it can get them off their smooth track and turn them into adventurers of self-devotion, people of whom the world has too few.

Reverence for life is an inexorable creditor! If it finds anyone with nothing to pledge but a little time and a little leisure, it lays an attachment on these. But its hard-heartedness is good and sees clearly. The many modern men who as industrial machines are engaged in callings in which they can in no way be active as men among men are exposed to the danger of merely vegetating in an egoistic life. Many of them feel this danger and suffer under the fact that their daily work has so little to do with spiritual and ideal aims and does not allow them to put into it anything of their human nature. Others acquiesce; the thought of having no duties outside their daily work suits them very well.

But that men should be so condemned or so favored as to be released from responsibility for self-devotion as men to men, the ethics of reverence for life will not allow to be legitimate. It demands that every one of us in some way and with some object shall be a human being for human beings. To those who have no opportunity in their daily work of giving themselves in this way, and have nothing else that they can give, it suggests their sacrificing something of their time and leisure, even if, of these, they have but a scant allowance. It says to them, find for yourselves some secondary activity, inconspicuous, perhaps secret. Open your eyes and look for a human being, or some work devoted to human welfare, that needs from someone a little time or friendliness, a little sympathy, or sociability, or labor. There may be a solitary or an embittered fel-low man, an invalid or an inefficient person to whom you can be something. Perhaps it is an old person or a child. Or some good work needs volunteers who can offer a free evening or run errands. Who can enumerate the many ways in which that costly piece of working capital, a human being, can be employed? More of him is wanted everywhere! Search, then, for some investment for your humanity and do not be frightened away if you have to wait or be taken on trial. And be prepared for some disappointments. But in any case, do not be without some secondary work in which you give yourself as a man to men. It is marked out for you, if you only truly will to have it.

Thus does the true ethics speak to those who have only a little time and a little human nature to give. Well will it be with them if they listen and are preserved from becoming stunted natures because they have neglected this devotion of self to others.

But to everyone, in whatever state of life he finds himself, the ethics of reverence for life does this: it forces him without cessation to be concerned at heart with all the human destinies and all the other life destinies that are going through their life course around him and to give himself, as man, to the man who needs a fellow man. It will not allow the scholar to live only for his learning, even if his learning makes him very useful, nor the artist to live only for his art, even if by means of it he gives something to many. The ethics of reverence for life does not allow the very busy man to think that with his professional activities he has fulfilled every demand upon him. It demands from all that they devote a portion of their life to their fellows. In what way and to what extent this is prescribed for him, the individual must gather from the thoughts that arise in him and from the destinies among which his life moves. One man's sacrifice is outwardly insignificant. He can accomplish it while continuing to live a normal life. Another is called to some conspicuous act of self-sacrifice and must, therefore, put aside regard for his own progress. But let neither judge the other. The destinies of men have to be decided in a thousand ways in order that the good may become actual. What he has to bring as an offering is the secret of each individual. But one with another we have all to recognize that our existence reaches its true value only when we experience in ourselves something of the truth of the saying "He that loseth his life shall find it."

The ethical conflicts between society and the individual arise out of the fact that the latter has to bear not only a personal but also a supra-personal responsibility. When only my own person is concerned, I can always be patient, always forgive, always exercise forbearance, always be merciful. But each of us comes into a situation where he is responsible not only for himself but also for a cause and then is forced into decisions that conflict with personal morality.

The craftsman who manages a business, however small, and the musician who conducts public performances cannot be men in the way they would like to be. The one has to dismiss a worker who is incapable or given to drink, in spite of any sympathy he has for him and his family; the other cannot let a singer whose voice is the worse for wear appear any longer, although he knows what distress he thus causes.

The more extensive a man's activities, the oftener he finds himself in the position of having to sacrifice something of his humanity to his supra-personal responsibility. From this conflict customary consideration leads to the decision that the general responsibility does, as a matter of principle, annul the personal. It is in this sense that society addresses the individual. For the soothing of consciences for which this decision is too categorical, it perhaps lays down a few principles that undertake to determine in a way that is valid for everybody how far in any case personal morality can have a say in the matter.

No course remains open to current ethics but to sign this capitulation. It has no means of defending the fortress of personal morality because it has not at its disposal any absolute notions of good and evil. Not so the ethics of reverence for life. It possesses, as we can see, what the other lacks. It, therefore, never surrenders the fortress, even if it is permanently invested. The ethics of reverence for life feels itself in a position to persevere in holding it and by continual sorties to keep the besiegers on the *qui vive*.

Only the most universal and absolute purposiveness in the maintenance and furtherance of life, which is the objective aimed at by reverence for life, is ethical. All other necessity or expediency is not ethical but only a more or less necessary necessity or a more or less expedient expediency. In the conflict between the maintenance of my own existence and the destruction of, or injury to, that of another, I can never unite the ethical and the necessary to form a relative ethical; I must choose between ethical and necessary and, if I choose the latter, must take it upon myself to incur guilt by an act of injury to life. Similarly, I am not at liberty to think that in the conflict between personal and supra-personal responsibility I can balance the ethical and the expedient to make a relative ethical or even annul the ethical with the purposive; I must choose between the two. If, under the pressure of the supra-personal responsibility, I yield to the expedient, I become guilty in some way or other through failure in reverence for life.

The temptation to combine with the ethical into a relative ethical the expedient that is commanded me by the supra-personal responsibility is especially strong because it can be shown, in defense of it, that the person who complies with the demand of this supra-personal responsibility acts unegoistically. It is not to his individual existence or his individual welfare that he sacrifices another existence or welfare, but he sacrifices an individual existence and welfare to what forces itself upon him as expedient in view of the existence or the welfare of a majority. But ethical is more than unegoistic. Only the reverence felt by my will to live for every other will to live is ethical. Whenever I in any way sacrifice or injure life, I am not within the sphere of the ethical, but I become guilty, whether it be egoistically guilty for the sake of maintaining my own existence or welfare, or unegoistically guilty for the sake of maintaining a greater number of other existences or their welfare.

This so easily made mistake of accepting as ethical a violation of reverence for life, if it is based upon unegoistic considerations, is the bridge by, crossing which, ethics enters unawares the territory of the non-ethical. The bridge must be broken down.

Ethics goes only so far as does humanity—humanity meaning consideration for the existence and the happiness of individual human beings. Where humanity ends, pseudo-ethics begins. The day on which this boundary is once and for all universally recognized and marked out so as to be visible to everyone will be one of the most important in the history of mankind. Thenceforward, it can no longer happen that ethics that is not ethics at all is accepted as real ethics and deceives and ruins individuals and peoples.

The system of ethics hitherto current has hindered us from becoming as earnest as we ought to be by the fact that it has utterly deceived us as to the many ways in which each one of us, whether through self-assertion or by actions justified by supra-personal responsibility, becomes guilty again and again. True knowledge consists in being gripped by the secret that everything around us is will to live and in seeing clearly how again and again we incur guilt against life.

Fooled by pseudo-ethics, man stumbles about in his guilt like a drunkard. If he gains knowledge and becomes serious, he seeks the road that least leads him into guilt.

We are all exposed to the temptation of lessening the guilt of inhumanity, which comes from our working under supra-personal responsibility, by withdrawing as far as possible into ourselves. But such freedom from guilt is not honestly obtained. Because ethics starts with world- and life-affirmation, it does not allow us this flight into negation. It forbids us to be like the housewife who leaves the killing of the eel to her cook and compels us to undertake all duties involving supra-personal responsibility that fall to us, even if we should be in a position to decline them for reasons more or less satisfactory.

Each one of us, then, has to engage, insofar as he is brought to it by the circumstances of his life, in work that involves supra-personal responsibility. But we must do this not in the spirit of the collective body but in that of the man who wishes to be ethical. In every individual case, therefore, we struggle to preserve as much humanity as is possible, and in doubtful cases we venture to make a mistake on the side of humanity rather than on that of the object in view. When we have become aware and earnest, we think of what is usually forgotten: that all public activity has to do not only with the facts that are to be made actual in the interest of the collective body but also with the creation of the state of mind that promotes the welfare of that body. The creation of such a spirit and temper is more important than anything directly attained in the facts. Public activity in which the utmost possible effort is not made to preserve humanity ruins the character. He who under the influence of supra-personal responsibility simply sacrifices men and human happiness when it seems right accomplishes something. But he has not reached the highest level. He has only outward not spiritual influence. We have spiritual influence only when others notice that we do not decide coldly in accordance with principles laid down once and for all but in each individual case fight for our sense of humanity. There is too little among us of this kind of struggle. From the most insignificant man who is engaged in the smallest business, right up to the political ruler who holds in his hands the decision for peace or war, we act too much as men who, in any given case, can prepare without effort to be no longer men but merely the executive of general interests. Hence, there is no longer among us any trust in a righteousness lighted up with human feeling. Nor have we any longer any real respect for one another. We all feel ourselves in the power of a mentality of cold, impersonal, and usually unintelligent opportunism, which stiffens itself with appeals to principle and in order to realize the smallest interests is capable of the greatest inhumanity and the greatest folly. We, therefore, see among us one temper of impersonal opportunism confronting another, and all problems are resolved in a purposeless conflict of force against force because there is nowhere at hand such a spirit as will make them soluble.

It is only through our struggles for humanity that forces that work in the direction of the truly rational and expedient can become powerful while the present way of thinking prevails. Hence, the man who works with supra-personal responsibilities has to feel himself answerable not only for the successful result that is to be realized through him but for the general disposition that has to be created.

Thus, we serve society without abandoning ourselves to it. We do not allow it to be our guardian in the matter of ethics. That would be as if the solo violinist allowed his bowing to be regulated by that of the double-bass player. Never for a moment do we lay aside our mistrust of the ideals established by society, and of the convictions that are kept by it in circulation. We always know that society is full of folly and will deceive us in the matter of humanity. It is an unreliable horse and blind into the bargain. Woe to the driver if he falls asleep!

All this sounds too hard. Society serves ethics by giving legal sanction to its most elementary principles and handing on the ethical principles of one generation to the next. That is much, and it claims our gratitude. But society is also something that checks the progress of ethics again and again, by arrogating to itself the dignity of an ethical teacher. To this, however, it has no right. The only ethical teacher is the man who thinks ethically and struggles for ethics. The conceptions of good and evil that are put in circulation by society are paper money, the value of which is to be calculated not by the figures printed upon it, but by its relation to its exchange value in the gold of the ethics of reverence for life. But so measured, the rate of exchange is revealed as that of the paper money of a half-bankrupt state.

The collapse of civilization has come about through ethics being left to society. A renewal of it is possible only if ethics becomes once more the concern of thinking human beings and if individuals seek to assert themselves in society as ethical personalities. In proportion as we secure this, society will become an ethical, instead of the purely natural, entity that it is by origin. Previous generations have made the terrible mistake of idealizing society as ethical. We do our duty to it by judging it critically and trying to make it, so far as possible, more ethical. Being in possession of an absolute standard of the ethical, we no longer allow ourselves to make acceptable as ethics principles of expediency or of the vulgarest opportunism. Nor do we remain any longer at the low level of allowing to be current, as in any way ethical, meaningless ideals of power, of passion, or of nationalism, which are set up by miserable politicians and maintained in some degree of respect by bewildering propaganda. All the principles, dispositions, and ideals that make their appearance among us we measure, in their showy pedantry, with a rule on which the measures are given by the absolute ethics of reverence for life. We allow currency only to what is consistent with the claims of humanity. We bring into honor again regard for life and for the happiness of the individual. Sacred human rights we again hold high; not those that political rulers exalt at banquets and tread underfoot in their actions but the true rights. We call once more for justice, not that which imbecile authorities have elaborated in a legal scholasticism, nor that about which demagogues of all shades of color shout themselves hoarse, but that which is filled to the full with the value of each single human existence. The foundation of law and right is humanity.

Thus, we confront the principles, dispositions, and ideals of the collective body with humanity. At the same time, we shape them in accordance with reason, for only what is ethical is truly rational. Only so far as the current disposition of men is animated by ethical convictions and ideals is it capable of truly purposive activity.

The ethics of reverence for life puts in our hands weapons for fighting false ethics and false ideals, but we have strength to use them only so far as we— each one in his own life—preserve our humanity. Only when those men are numerous who in thought and in action bring humanity to terms with reality will humanity cease to be current as a mere sentimental idea and become what it ought to be, a leaven in the minds of individuals and in the spirit of society.

10

The Ethics of Reverence
for Life

This is Schweitzer's most popular presentation of the ethics of reverence for life. He approaches the issue of ethics of reverence for life by arguing that a valid ethical theory must be reflected in the natural order. Before attempting to show how the ethics of reverence for life fulfils this requirement, he establishes two foundations of his ethical approach: (1) the realization that he is a will to live in the midst of life which wills to live, and (2) the significance of resignation, by which he means the recognition of our dependence upon events beyond our control. With these two postulates accepted, Schweitzer outlines six defining characteristics of his theory. First, this ethics is rational because it is developed as a result of thinking about life. Second, this ethics is absolute in the sense of being contrasted to that which is practicable and achievable. Third, the ethics of reverence for life is universal insofar as it applies to all living beings. Fourth, the ethics of reverence for life has spiritual significance insofar as it seeks to attain harmony with the mysterious Spirit of the universe. Fifth, the ethics of reverence for life is natural, in the sense in which Hume claims that sympathy is natural. Sixth, Schweitzer argues that this sympathy, which lies at the bottom of reverence for life, is part of our psychological makeup. By using several examples, he tries to show that even animals display the rudiments of this sympathy. This disposition, given to us naturally, we need to develop in the direction of highest spirituality.

Complete essay; originally published in 1936 in *Christendom*, vol. 1, No. 2, 225–239; reprinted here from Henry Clark, *The Ethical Mysticism of Albert Schweitzer* (Boston: Beacon, 1962), 180–194.

In the history of world thought, we seem to be met by a confusion of antagonistic systems. But if we look closely, we see that certain essential laws of thought are to be discerned. And as we trace them, we see a definite progress in this bewildering history. In fact, there emerge two main classes of problems. To begin with, we see certain facade problems, important looking, but not really connected with the main structure. Questions as to the reality of the world and the problem of knowledge belong here. Kant tried in vain to solve the essential questions by busying himself with these scientific, facade problems. Admittedly, they are intriguing, but they are not the real, elementary matters.

We are concerned with the other problems, the essential ones. As we know life in ourselves, we want to understand life in the universe, in order to enter into harmony with it. Physically, we are always trying to do this. But that is not the primary matter; for the great issue is that we shall achieve a spiritual harmony. Just to recognize this fact is to have begun to see a part of life clearly.

There is in each of us the will to live, which is based on the mystery of what we call "taking an interest." We cannot live alone. Though man is an egoist, he is never completely so. He *must* always have some interest in life about him. If for no other reason, he must do so in order to make his own life more perfect. Thus it happens that we want to devote ourselves; we want to take our part in perfecting our ideal of progress; we want to give meaning to the life in the world. This is the basis of our striving for harmony with the spiritual element.

The effort for harmony, however, never succeeds. Events cannot be harmonized with our activities. Working purposefully toward certain ends, we assume that the Creative Force in the world is doing likewise. Yet, when we try to define its goal, we cannot do so. It tends toward developing a type of existence, but there is no coordinated, definite end to be observed, even though we think there should be. We like to imagine that man is nature's goal; but facts do not support that belief.

Indeed, when we consider the immensity of the universe, we must confess that man is insignificant. The world began, as it were, yesterday. It may end tomorrow. Life has existed in the universe but a brief second. And certainly man's life can hardly be considered the goal of the universe. Its margin of existence is always precarious. Study of the geologic periods shows that. So does the battle against disease. When one has seen whole populations annihilated by sleeping sickness, as I have, one ceases to imagine that human life is nature's goal. In fact, the Creative Force does not concern itself about preserving life. It simultaneously creates and destroys. Therefore, the will to live is not to be understood within the circle of Creative Force. Philosophy and religion have repeatedly sought the solution by this road; they have projected our will to perfection into nature at large, expecting to see its counterpart there. But in all honesty we must confess that to cling to such a belief is to delude ourselves.

As a result of the failure to find ethics reflected in the natural order, the disillusioned cry has been raised that ethics can, therefore, have no ultimate validity. In the world of human thought and action today, humanitarianism is definitely on the wane. Brutality and trust in force are in the ascendant. What, then, is to become of that vigorous ethics that we inherited from our fathers?

Knowledge may have failed us; but we do not abandon the ideals. Though they are shaken, we do not turn from them to sheer skepticism. In spite of being unable to prove them by rational argumentation, we nevertheless believe that there is a proof and defense for them within themselves. We are, so to speak, immunized against skepticism. Indeed, the classical skepticisms were, after all, puerile. That a truth cannot be proved by argument is no reason that it should be utterly abandoned, so long as it is in itself possessed of value. Kant, trying to escape from skepticism, is a pre-indication of this immunity. In intent, his philosophy is great and eternal. He said that truth is of two kinds: scientific and spiritual. Let us look to the bottom of this; not by Kant's method, however, since he was often content with naïve reflections on very deep questions. We shall avoid his way of seeking abstract solutions and distinctions between material and immaterial. Instead, let us see that truths that are not provable in knowledge are given to us in our will to live.

Kant sought to give equal value to practical and theoretical reason. More, he felt the demand for an absolute ethics. It would, he thought, give new authority to spiritual and religious truth, thus making up for the loss involved in not being able to verify these truths by knowledge. This is the very heart of Kant's gospel, being much more important than anything he taught about space and time. But he did not know where to find the new ethics. He gave only a new, more handsome, and more impressive facade to the old. By his failure to point out the new ethics, he missed the new rationalism. His thought was on too narrow a basis.

The essential thing to realize about ethics is that it is the very manifestation of our will to live. All our thoughts are given in that will to live, and we but give them expression and form in words. To analyze reason fully would be to analyze the will to live. The philosophy that abandons the old rationalism must begin be meditating on itself. Thus, if we ask, "What is the immediate fact of my consciousness? What do I self-consciously know of myself, making abstractions of all else, from childhood to old age? To what do I always return?" we find the simple fact of consciousness is this, *I will to live*. Through every stage of life, this is the one thing I know about myself. I do not say, "I am life," for life continues to be a mystery too great to understand. I know only that I cling to it. I fear its cessation—death. I dread its diminution—pain. I seek its enlargement—joy.

Descartes started on this basis. But he built an artificial structure by presuming that man knows nothing, and doubts all, whether outside himself or within. And in order to end doubt, he fell back on the fact of consciousness: *I think*. Surely, however, that is the stupidest primary assumption in all philosophy. Who can establish the fact that he thinks, except in relation to thinking *something*? And what that something is, is the important matter. When I seek the first fact of consciousness, it is not to know that I think, but to get hold of myself. Descartes would have a man think once, just long enough to establish the certainty of being, and then give over any further need of meditation. Yet meditation is the very thing I must not cease. I *must* ascertain whether my thoughts are in harmony with my will to live.

Bergson's admirable philosophy also starts from such a beginning. But he arrives at the sense of time. The fact of immediate consciousness, however, is much more important than the sense of time. So Bergson misses the real issue.

Instinct, thought, the capacity for divination, all these are fused with the will to live. And when it reflects upon itself, what path does it follow? When my will to live begins to think, it sees life as a mystery in which I remain by thought. I cling to life because of my reverence for life. For, when it begins to think, the will to live realizes that it is free. It is free to leave life. It is free to choose whether or not to live. This fact is of particular significance for us in this modern age, when there are abundant possibilities for abandoning life, painlessly and without agony.

Moreover, we are all closer to the possibility of this choice than we may guess of one another. The question that haunts men and women today is whether life is worth living. Perhaps each of us has had the experience of talking with a friend one day, finding that person bright, happy, apparently in the full joy of life; and then the next day, we find that he has taken his own life! Stoicism has brought us to this point, by driving out the fear of death; for, by inference it suggests that we are free to choose whether to live or not. But if we entertain such a possibility, we do so by ignoring the melody of the will to live, which compels us to face the mystery, the value, the high trust committed to us in life. We may not understand it, but we begin to appreciate its great value. Therefore, when we find those who relinquish life, while we may not condemn them, we do pity them for having ceased to be in possession of themselves. Ultimately, the issue is not whether we do or do not fear death. The real issue is that of reverence for life.

Here, then, is the first spiritual act in man's experience: reverence for life. The consequence of it is that he comes to realize his dependence upon events quite beyond his control. Therefore, he becomes resigned. And this is the second spiritual act: resignation.

What happens is that one realizes that he is but a speck of dust, a plaything of events outside his reach. Nevertheless, he may at the same time discover that he has a certain liberty, as long as he lives. Sometime or another, all of us must have found that happy events have not been able to make us happy, nor unhappy events to make us unhappy. There is within each of us a modulation, an inner exaltation, that lifts us above dependence upon the gifts of events for our joy. Hence, our dependence upon events is not absolute; it is qualified by our spiritual freedom. Therefore, when we speak of resignation, it is not sadness to which we refer, but the triumph of our will to live over whatever happens to us. And to become ourselves, to be spiritually alive, we must have passed beyond this point of resignation.

The great defect of modern philosophy is that it neglects this essential fact. It does not ask man to think deeply on himself. It hounds him into activity, bidding him find escape thus. In that respect, it falls far below the philosophy of Greece, which taught men better the true depth of life.

I have said that resignation is the very basis of ethics. Starting from this position, the will to live comes first to veracity as the primary ground of virtue. If I am faithful to my will to live, I cannot disguise this fact, even though such disguise or evasion might seem to my advantage. Reverence for my will to live leads me to the necessity of being sincere with myself. And out of this fidelity to my own nature grows all my faithfulness. Thus, sincerity is the first ethical quality that appears. However lacking one may be in other respects, sincerity is the one thing that he must possess. Nor is this point of view to be found only among people of complex social life. Primitive cultures show the fact to be equally true there. Resignation to the will to live leads directly to this first virtue: sincerity.

Having reached this point, then, I am in a position to look at the world. I ask knowledge what it can tell me of life. Knowledge replies that what it can tell me is little, yet immense. Whence this universe came, or whither it is bound, or how it happens to be at all, knowledge cannot tell me. Only this: that the will to live is everywhere present, even as in me. I do not need science to tell me this; but it cannot tell me anything more essential. Profound and marvelous as chemistry is, for example, it is like all science in the fact that it can lead me only to the mystery of life, which is essentially in me, however near or far away it may be observed.

What shall be my attitude toward this other life? It can be only of a piece with my attitude toward my own life. If I am a thinking being, I must regard other life than my own with equal reverence. For I shall know that it longs for fullness and development as deeply as I do myself. Therefore, I see that evil is what annihilates, hampers, or hinders life. And this holds good whether I regard it physically or spiritually. Goodness, by the same token, is the saving or helping of life, the enabling of whatever life I can to attain its highest development.

This is the absolute and rational ethics. Whether such-and-such a man arrives at this principle, I may not know. But I know that it is given inherently in the will to live. Whatever is reasonable is good. This we have been told by all the great thinkers. But it reaches its best only in the light of this universal ethics, the ethics of reverence for life, to which we come as we meditate upon the will to live. And since it is important that we recognize to the best of our ability the full significance of this ethics, let us now devote our attention to some commentaries upon it.

Our first commentary: The primary characteristic of this ethics is that it is rational, having been developed as a result of thought upon life.

We may say that anyone who truly explores the depths of thought must arrive at this point. In other words, to be truly rational is to become ethical. (How pleased Socrates would be with us for saying this!) But if it is so simple a matter of rationality, why has it not long since been achieved? It has, indeed, been long on the way, while in every land thought has been seeking to deepen ethics. Actually, whenever love and devotion are glimpsed, reverence for life is not far off, since one grows from the other. But the truth of the matter is that thought fears such an ethics. What it wants is to impose regulations and order that can be duly systematized. This ethics is not subject to such bounding. Therefore, when modern thought considers such an ethics, it fears it and tries to discredit it by calling it irrational. In this way its development has been long delayed.

Again, it may be asked if this sort of meditation is not definitely that of civilized rather than primitive men. The primitive man, it may be argued, knows no such reverence for life. To this I must agree, having associated with primitives in my work in Africa. Nevertheless, it remains true that the primitive who begins to meditate must proceed along the same path. He must start with his own will to live, and that is certain to bring him in this direction. If he does not reach a point as far along the way as we do, that is because we can profit by the meditations of our predecessors. There are many great souls who have blazed sections of the trail for us. Proceeding along that way, I have led you to this conclusion: that rational processes, properly pursued, must lead to the true ethics.

Another commentary: What of this ethics? Is it absolute?

Kant defines absolute ethics as that which is not concerned with whether it can be achieved. The distinction is not one of absolute as opposed to *relative*, but *absolute* as distinct from *practicable* in the ethical field. An absolute ethics calls for the creating of perfection in this life. It cannot be completely achieved, but that fact does not really matter. In this sense, reverence for life is an absolute ethics. It does not lay down specific rules for each possible situation. It simply tells us that we are responsible for the lives about us. It does not set either maximum or minimum limits to what we must do.

In point of fact, every ethics has something of the absolute about it, just as soon as it ceases to be mere social law. It demands of one what is actually beyond his strength. Take the question of man's duty to his neighbor. This ethics cannot be fully carried out without involving the possibility of complete sacrifice of self. Yet, philosophy has never bothered to take due notice of the distinction. It has simply tried to ignore absolute ethics because such ethics cannot be fitted into tabulated rules and regulations. Indeed, the history of world teachings on the subject may be summarized in the motto: "Avoid absolute ethics, and thus keep within the realm of the possible."

We have already noted that Kant did postulate and demand an absolute ethics as the foundation for a spiritual ethics. He knew it must be more profound than what is just and reasonable. But he did not succeed in establishing what it was. All he did was label ordinary ethics "absolute." Consequently, he ended in a muddle of abstraction. As Descartes said, "Think," without telling what to think, so Kant demanded, "Observe absolute ethics," without elucidating what the term involved. The ethics he proposed could not be called absolute in matter of content. Kant's "practical ethics" proved to be simply the good old utilitarian ethics of his own day, adorned with the label, "absolute." He failed by not thinking far enough. To justify the name, absolute ethics must be so not only in authority but in matter of content as well.

Another commentary: Reverence for life is a universal ethics.

We do not say this because of its absolute nature but because of the boundlessness of its domain. Ordinary ethics seeks to find limits within the sphere of human life and relationships. But the absolute ethics of the will to live must reverence every form of life, seeking so far as possible to refrain from destroying any life, regardless of its particular type. It says of no instance of life, "This has no value." It cannot make any such exceptions, for it is built upon reverence for life as such. It knows that the mystery of life is always too profound for us and that its value is beyond our capacity to estimate. We happen to believe that man's life is more important than any other form of which we know. But we cannot prove any such comparison of value from what we know of the world's development. True, in practice, we are forced to choose. At times we have to decide arbitrarily which forms of life, and even which particular individuals, we shall save and which we shall destroy. But the principle of reverence for life is nonetheless universal.

Ordinary ethics has never known what to do with this problem. Not realizing that the domain of ethics must be boundless, it has tried to ignore any absolute ethics. But when its boundlessness is realized, then its absoluteness is more plain. Indian thought recognizes this, but it limits its effectiveness by making ethics negative. The characteristic attitude of Indian thought is less a positive reverence for life than a negative duty to refrain from destroying. This comes about through a failure to appreciate the essentially illusory nature of an ethics of inaction. Nor has European thought been free from that same illusion. The great works on philosophy and ethics in recent years have all tried to avoid absolute ethics by concentrating on a type that should apply only socially. But when reason travels its proper course, it moves in the direction of a universally applicable ethics.

Another commentary: A universal ethics has great spiritual significance.

Ordinary ethics is too narrow and shallow for spiritual development. Our thought seeks ever to attain harmony with the mysterious Spirit of the Universe. To be complete, such harmony must be both active and passive. That is to say, we seek harmony both in deed and in thought. I want to understand my ethical activity as being at the service of the Universal Spirit.

Spinoza, Hegel, and the Stoics show us that the harmony of peace is a passive harmony, to which true philosophy leads us and toward which religion tries to lead us. But this does not suffice, since we want to be at one in activity as well. Philosophy fails us here because of too narrow an ethical basis. It may seek to put me in relation to society and even to humanity at large (although contemporary philosophies are, in some instances, directed only toward the relationship to a nation or a race). In any case, no philosophy puts me in relationship to the universe on an ethical basis. Instead, the attempt is made to take me there by knowledge, through understanding. Fichte and Hegel present such an intellectual philosophy. But it is an impossible path. Such philosophies are bankrupt. Ethics alone can put me in true relationship with the universe by my serving it, cooperating with it; not by trying to understand it. This is why Kant is so profound when he speaks of practical reason. Only by serving every kind of life do I enter the service of that Creative Will whence all life emanates. I do not understand it; but I do know (and it is sufficient to live by) that by serving life, I serve the Creative Will. It is through community of life, not community of thought, that I abide in harmony with that Will. This is the mystical significance of ethics.

Every philosophy has its mystical aspects, and every profound thought is mystical. But mysticism has always stopped with the passive, on an insufficient basis, as regards ethics. Indian, Stoical, medieval, all the great mysticisms, have aimed at achieving union through passivity. Yet every true mysticism has instincts of activity, aspiring to an ethical character. This fact explains the development of Indian mysticism from the detachment of Brahmanism to modern Hindu mysticism. Medieval mysticism, in the same way, comes in its great exponent, [Master] Eckhardt, to the point where it longs to comprehend true ethics. Failing to find the universal ethics, it has commonly been content to exist with none. But in the universal ethics of reverence for life, mystical union with the Universal Spirit is actually and fully achieved. Thus, it is proved to be indeed the true ethics. For it must be plain that an ethics that only commands is incomplete, while one that lets me live in communion with the Creative Will is a true and complete ethics.

In what sense is this a natural ethics, and how does it stand in relation to other explanations of the origin of ethics?

There have been three general classifications of ethical origins. The first is a spiritual interpretation. We find in Plato, Kant, and many others the assertion that ethics comes out of an inherent, insubstantial, given sense of duty, which has its source in our own power of reason. Through it, we are told, we see ourselves bound to the immaterial world. The exponents of this view believed that they had thus given great dignity to ethics. But there are difficulties in the way of accepting this view. It bears little resemblance to our own ethical sense, and we cannot see how it can be carried into our lives in this world in which we live.

The second classification is composed of the intellectual theories of ethics. Here we find such philosophies as those of the Stoics and Lao-tse. This group claims to see ethics in the natural world and concludes, thereby, that whoever is in harmony with the universe is, by that fact, ethical. Now, this is a grand theory, and it is based on a profound realization that one who is truly in such harmony must be ethical. But the fact remains that we do not understand the Spirit of the Universe. Therefore, we cannot draw any ethics from such an understanding. Consequently, these theories of ethics are pallid and lacking in vigor. What they really amount to is a negative quietism, which has been tinged with ethics.

The third classification consists of three kinds of natural ethics. There is, to start with, the suggestion that ethics exists within our very natures, waiting to be developed. It is argued that we are primarily composed of egoism, but that we nevertheless have an inherent selflessness. Altruism, as we know it, is thus simply exalted egoism. Man is assumed to get his greatest fulfillment in society; therefore, he must serve it, sacrificing his own wishes temporarily. But such an explanation is childish.

Next comes the sort of natural ethics that is said to exist in man's nature but is incapable of being developed by the individual himself. Society, so the theory runs, has worked out a system of ethics in order to subject the individual to its will. Centuries of such exalting of society have had beneficial results, but it is mere delusion to imagine that that which has actually been created by society is native to us. But observe how childish this is also. I grant that society has its place in ethics, but the fact remains that I have individual as well as social relationships, and society simply cannot be responsible for the ethics that determines my dealings in the individual sphere.

The third type of natural ethics was expounded by Hume. It admits that ethics is a matter of sentiment but explains that it is given in the nature of man, for the sake of preserving his life. Thus, in the late eighteenth century, came Hume's teaching that ethics is natural, while in the same period came Kant's realization that it must be absolute.

To explain that ethics is a matter of feeling, prompted by our own hearts, Hume called it sympathy. The capacity to understand and live others' lives in our own is, he said, what makes us developed individuals. In this, he was joined by George Adam Smith. They were headed in the right direction, too. If they had properly explored sympathy, they would have reached the universal ethics of reverence for life. But they stopped on the very threshold of their great opportunity because they were dominated by the contemporary dogma that ethics is concerned only with the relationship of man to man. Therefore, they twisted sympathy to mean only a relationship between like kinds. Spencer and Darwin did the same thing in their time, putting ethics on the basis of the herd. This brought them to the explanation of non-egoistic action as arising from herd instinct. What Darwin failed to see is that the herd relationship is more than this superficial sort of instinct. He did, it is true, catch a glimpse of the possibility of sympathy extending beyond the range of man and society. But he concluded that it was just a higher development of the herd instinct!

It is only when we break loose from such traditions that we find sympathy to be natural for any type of life, without any restrictions, so long as we are capable of imagining in such life the characteristic that we find in our own; that is, dread of extinction, fear of pain, and the desire for happiness. In short, the adequate explanation of sympathy is to be found rooted back in reverence for life.

But let us inquire into this sympathy more closely. On what foundations does it exist? What is its natural explanation? To answer these questions, let us ask ourselves how we can live the life of another being in our own lives. In part, we depend upon the knowledge received through our senses. We see others; we hear them; we may touch them or be touched by them. And we may then engage in activities to help them. In other words, there is a natural, physical aspect to the matter that anyone must recognize. But what *compels* all this?

The important thing is that we are part of life. We are born of other lives; we possess the capacities to bring still other lives into existence. In the same way, if we look into a microscope we see cell producing cell. So, nature compels us to recognize the fact of mutual dependence, each life necessarily helping the other lives that are linked to it. In the very fibers of our being, we bear within ourselves the fact of the solidarity of life. Our recognition of it expands with thought. Seeing its presence in ourselves, we realize how closely we are linked with others of our kind. We might like to stop here, but we cannot. Life demands that we see through to the solidarity of all life that we can in any degree recognize as having some similarity to the life that is in us.

No doubt you are beginning to ask whether we can seriously mean that such a privilege extends to other creatures besides man. Are they, too, compelled by ethics? I cannot say that the evidence is always as apparent as it may be in human instances. But this I can say, that wherever we find the love and sacrificial care of parents for offspring (for instance) we find this ethical power. Indeed, any instance of creatures giving aid to one another reveals it. Moreover, there are probably more proofs than we might at first think. Let me tell you of three instances that have been brought to my attention.

The first example was told me by someone from Scotland. It happened in a park where a flock of wild geese had settled to rest on a pond. One of the flock had been captured by a gardener, who had clipped its wings before releasing it. When the geese started to resume their flight, this one tried frantically, but vainly, to lift itself into the air. The others, observing his struggles, flew about in obvious efforts to encourage him; but it was no use. Thereupon, the entire flock settled back on the pond and waited, even though the urge to go on was strong within them. For several days they waited until the damaged feathers had grown sufficiently to permit the goose to fly. Meanwhile, the unethical gardener, having been converted by the ethical geese, gladly watched them as they all finally rose together and resumed their long flight.

My second example is from my hospital in Lambaréné. I have the virtue of caring for all stray monkeys that come to our gate. (If you have had any experience with large numbers of monkeys, you know why I say it is a virtue thus to take care of all comers until they are old enough or strong enough to be turned loose, several together, in the forest—a great occasion for them—and for me!) Sometimes there will come to our monkey colony a wee baby monkey whose mother has been killed, leaving this orphaned infant. I must find one of the older monkeys to adopt and care for the baby. I never have any difficulty about it, except to decide which candidate shall be given the responsibility. Many a time it happens that the seemingly worst-tempered monkeys are most insistent upon having this sudden burden of foster-parenthood given to them.

My third example was given me by a friend in Hanover, who owned a small café. He would daily throw out crumbs for the sparrows in the neighborhood. He noticed that one sparrow was injured, so that it had difficulty getting about. But he was interested to discover that the other sparrows, apparently by mutual agreement, would leave the crumbs that lay nearest to their crippled comrade, so that he could get his share, undisturbed.

So much, then, for this question of the natural origin of the ethics of reverence for life. It does not need to make any pretensions to high titles or noble-sounding theories to explain its existence. Quite simply, it has the courage to admit that it comes about through physiological makeup. It is given physically. But the point is that it arrives at the noblest spirituality. God does not rest content with commanding ethics. He gives it to us in our very hearts.

This, then, is the nature and origin of ethics. We have dared to say that it is born of physical life, out of the linking of life with life. It is, therefore, the result of our recognizing the solidarity of life that nature gives us. And as it grows more profound, it teaches us sympathy with *all* life. Yet, the extremes touch, for this material-born ethics becomes engraved upon our hearts and culminates in spiritual union and harmony with the Creative Will, which is in and through all.

11

The Problem of Ethics
in the Evolution
of Human Thought

This selection is the complete text of Schweitzer's address before l'Académie des Sciences Morales et Politiques on his official installation as a member of the Academy at the Institut de France, on October 20, 1952. This essay is also his last presentation of the ethics of reverence for life. As the title indicates, Schweitzer gives a brief summary of the history of ethical thought, including references to Asian thought and the early Christianity, in order to explain the place of his ethical view in this larger narrative. Unlike his other presentations of the ethics of reverence for life, Schweitzer here insists on three related ideas: (1) the development of the ideal of self-perfection, as derived from Socrates, Plato, and Aristotle; (2) the idea of the brotherhood of all human beings, as developed by the Stoics; and (3) the spiritual aspect of reverence for life, as derived from Jesus. With regard to this last point, Schweitzer insists that we cannot experience God directly but can get in touch with God by submitting ourselves to the mystery of life and by devoting ourselves to all the living creatures that we have the opportunity and the ability to serve. Through reverence for life we come to worship God in a way that is simple, profound, and alive.

In the space of a single lecture, I can give only a very summary account of the problem of ethics in the evolution of human thought. I shall, therefore, confine myself to the broad outlines of that evolution,

Complete essay; originally published in French in 1952; this translation, by John Russell, was published as an appendix in Jacques Feschotte, *Albert Schweitzer: An Introduction* (Boston: Beacon, 1955), 114–130.

and in doing so shall attempt to make them as clear as possible. What we call "ethics" and "morality," in terms borrowed respectively from Greek and Latin, may broadly be said to be concerned with the problem of how to behave well toward ourselves and toward others. We feel obliged to think not only of our own well-being but of that of other people and of society in general.

The first stage in the development of ethics began with the idea that this "thinking of others" should be put on an ever-broader basis. Primitive man thinks of others only within the narrowest limits. He confines himself to those whom he sees as distantly related to himself by blood: the members of his tribe, that is to say, whom he regards as constituents of the same large family. I speak from experience in this. My patients at Lambaréné illustrate the point. Sometimes I ask a savage of that sort to render certain little services to a fellow patient who cannot look after himself. He will at once ask whether the other man is a member of his tribe. And if the answer is "no," he will frankly reply: "This not brother for me." Neither persuasion nor threats will induce him to commit the unimaginable action and put himself out for a stranger. It is I who must give in.

But as men think more and more about themselves and about their behavior to others, they come to realize that other men, as such, are their kith and their kin. And slowly, with the evolution of ethics, they see the circle of their responsibilities grow wider and wider until it includes every human being with whom they have any sort of association.

It is on this level of understanding that we find the Chinese thinkers: Lao-tse, born in 604 BC; Kung-tse (Confucius), 551–479 BC; Meng-tse, 372–289 BC; Chwang-tse, in the fourth century BC; and the Hebrew prophets Amos, Hosea, and Isaiah, in the eighth century BC. The idea that we each of us have a responsibility toward every other human being was put forward by Jesus and Paul and is an integral part of Christian ethics.

For the great thinkers of India, be they Brahmans, or Buddhists, or Hindus, the idea of the universal brotherhood of man is part of the metaphysical idea of existence. But it is not easy for them to incorporate it in their ethical systems— for the existence of castes, in India, has erected barriers between man and man that have been sanctified by tradition and cannot now be abolished.

Nor, in the seventh century BC, could Zoroaster encompass the notion of the brotherhood of man. He had to distinguish between those who believed in Ormuzd, the god of goodness and light, and the unbelievers, who remained under the aegis of the demons. He insisted that the believers, in their struggle to bring about the reign of Ormuzd, should consider the unbelievers as their enemies and treat them accordingly. To understand the situation, we must remember that the believers were Bactrian tribesmen, who had adopted a sedentary

mode of life and wanted to live as honest and peaceable farmers; the unbelievers were tribes who had remained nomadic, lived in the desert, and supported
themselves by pillage.

Plato, Aristotle, and the other thinkers of the classical period of Greek philosophy thought only in terms of the Greek—the Greek freeman, moreover,
who was not concerned to earn his own living. Those who did not belong to
that aristocracy they regarded as inferior beings and unworthy of serious attention. Only in the second period of Greek thought—that in which Stoicism and
Epicureanism flowered simultaneously—did both schools become willing to
accept the idea of human equality and of the intrinsic interest of human beings
as such. The most remarkable champion of this new conception was the Stoic
Panaetius, who lived in the second century (180–110) BC. It is Panaetius who is
the prophet of humanism.

The idea of the brotherhood of man never became popular in ancient
times. But there is great importance for the future in the fact that philosophers
should have acclaimed it as eminently rational. We must admit, though, that
the idea that a human being, as such, has a right to our interest has never
enjoyed the full authority to which it might lay claim. Right up to our own
time it has been menaced, as it is today, by the importance that we ascribe to
differences of race, or religious belief, or nationality. It is these differences that
make us look upon our kinsman as a stranger deserving of indifference, if not,
indeed, of contempt.

Anyone who analyzes the development of ethics must take into account the
influence that is exerted upon ethics by the particular conception of the world
to which it is related. There is, of course, a fundamental difference between
these various conceptions. This difference lies in the particular way of looking
upon the world itself. Some thinkers believe that we should take an affirmative
view of the world—interest ourselves, that is to say, in its affairs and in the part
we ourselves play in them. Others take a negative view and advise us to take
no interest at all in the world or in our own existence within it. Of these two
attitudes, the affirmative is nearer to nature; the negative view does violence to
it. The one invites us to be at home in the world and to take a vigorous part in
its affairs; the other urges us to live in it as strangers and to choose non-activity
as the basis of our life here. Ethics, as such, belongs to the affirmative faction. It
springs from the need to act, and to act for good. Consequently, the affirmation
of the world is favorable to the development of ethics; the negative attitude, on
the other hand, must thwart that development. In the first case, ethics can offer
itself for what it is; in the second, it must give up the idea of doing so.

The thinkers of India deny the world. So do the Christians of antiquity and
of the Middle Ages. The Chinese sages, the Hebrew prophets, Zoroaster, and

the European thinkers of the Renaissance and modern times are all champions of affirmation.

The Indian thinkers denied the world because they were convinced that true existence is immaterial, immutable, and eternal, and that the existence of the material world is artificial, deceptive, and ephemeral. The world that we like to consider real is merely, in their eyes, a mirage of the immaterial world in time and space. It is a mistake for us to interest ourselves in this phantasmagoria and in the part we play in it. Non-activity is the only form of behavior that is compatible with knowledge of the true nature of existence. Of course, non-activity has an ethical quality, in a certain degree. A man who renounces the things of this world renounces with them the egoism that material interests and vulgar covetousness would otherwise inspire in him. Moreover, non-activity implies nonviolence. It saves a man from the danger of harming others by acts of violence.

Nonviolence is extolled by the philosophers of Brahmanism, Sankhya, and Jainism. Like the Buddha, they consider it the high point of ethics. It is, however, imperfect and incomplete. It allows a man to be egoistic to the point of thinking of nothing but his own salvation. This he hopes to secure by a mode of life that conforms to a true knowledge of the nature of existence. It exacts this not in the name of compassion but in the name of a metaphysical theory; and though it asks him to abstain from evil, it does not require him to act in accordance with the wish to do good.

Only an ethical system that is allied to the affirmation of the world can be natural and complete. If the Indian thinkers take it into their heads to yield to the promptings of an ethics more generous than that of *ahimsā*, they can do so only by making concessions to the affirmative point of view—and to the principle of activity. When the Buddha takes a stand against the coldness of the Brahman doctrine and preaches the virtues of pity, he can hardly resist the temptation to break free of the principle of non-activity. More than once he gives in to it and cannot help committing acts of charity or recommending his disciples to do the same. Under the cover of ethics, for century after century in India the affirmation of the world carries on an underground struggle against the principle of non-activity. In the Hindu religion, which is a religious reaction against the exactions of Brahmanism, this affirmation actually gets recognized as the equal of non-activity. The entente between them is proclaimed and specified in the *Bhagavad-Gita*, a didactic poem that is incorporated in the great epic of the *Mahabharata*.

The *Bhagavad-Gita* admits the Brahman conception of the world. It recognizes that the material world has only a deceptive reality and cannot claim to engage our interest. It is merely, the poem says, an amusing spectacle that God has mounted for his own diversion. It is only as a spectator, therefore, that man is authorized to take part in it. But he has the right to suppose that he is to continue playing his part in the entertainment. He is justified in doing so by the fact that he knows why he is doing it. The man who goes about his work in the world with no other intention than that of doing God's will pursues the truth every bit as effectively as he who opts for non-activity. Undiscerning activity, on the other hand—activity that is prompted by interest in the world and the wish to achieve some object, however trivial—such activity is wrong and cannot be justified.

No ethics worthy of the name can be satisfied by the concept of the world as a diversion that God has put up for his amusement. True ethics asserts the necessity of action. The theory did, however, allow ethics to keep going in India at a time when its existence was threatened by Brahmanism.

Contemporary thinkers in India make great concessions to the principle of activity and affirm that it is also to be found in the *Upanishads*. That is quite true. The explanation is that in ancient times, as we learn from the *Veda* hymns, the Aryans of India led a life that was filled with a naïve delight in living. The Brahman doctrine of the denial of the world appears only alongside the doctrine of affirmation in the *Upanishads*—sacred texts that date from the beginning of the first millennium before Christ.

The Christianity of antiquity and the Middle Ages preaches the denial of the world but does not, as a consequence, enjoin non-activity. This peculiarity derives from the fact that its denial of the world is quite different from that preached by the Indians. Christianity declared that the world as we know it is not a phantasmagoria but an imperfect world that is destined to be transformed into the perfect world: that of the Kingdom of God. The idea of the Kingdom of God was created by the Hebrew prophets of the eighth century BC. It is also at the heart of the religion founded by Zoroaster in the seventh century BC.

Jesus announced the imminent transformation of the material world into the world of the Kingdom of God. He exhorted mankind to seek that perfection that would enable them to enjoy a new existence in the new world. He preached the abandonment of the things of this world. To do good was the whole duty of man. Man was allowed, in fact, to be indifferent to the world, but not to his duty toward other men. Action keeps all its rights, in the Christian ethics, and all its obligations, too. That is where it differs from the ethics of the Buddha, with which it has in common the idea of compassion. Animated as it is by the spirit of activity, Christian ethics retains an affinity with the affirmation of the world.

The early Christians regarded the transformation of the world into the Kingdom of God as near at hand; but it has never occurred. Therefore, during antiquity and the Middle Ages, Christians despaired of this world and yet had none of those hopes that had buoyed the early Christians. It would have been natural had they come round to the affirmation of the world. Their ethics of activity made it quite possible. But in antiquity and the Middle Ages, there did not exist that passionate affirmation of the world that alone would have served the purpose. This passionate affirmation came into being at the time of the Renaissance. Christianity joined forces with it during the sixteenth and seventeenth centuries. Along with the ideal of self-perfection that it derived from Jesus, its ethics now embraced the Renaissance ideal: that of creating new and better conditions, material and spiritual alike, in which human beings could live together in society. Thenceforward, Christian ethics had a specific end in view and could attain to its fullest development. The civilization in which we live, and that we now have to sustain and perfect, was born of the union between Christianity and the enthusiastic affirmation of the world, which we owe to the Renaissance. The ethical conceptions of both Zoroaster and the Chinese sages were affiliated, from the very beginning, with the affirmation of the world. They, too, carry within themselves energies that could bring forth a civilization based on ethics.

After attaining a certain level, ethics tends to develop in depth. This tendency manifests itself in the compulsive search for the fundamental principle of good. Ethics no longer finds complete satisfaction in defining, enumerating, and enjoining various virtues and various duties. It seeks to analyze the link that unites them in their diversity, and to discover how it is that they all flow from a single conception of good. It was in this way that the great Chinese sages came to proclaim goodwill toward all fellow men as the root of virtue. Even before Jesus, Hebrew ethics concerned itself with the problem of the one great commandment: the Law that was to contain all law. In accord with the traditions of Hebrew theology, Jesus raised love to the rank of the supreme commandment.

In the first century of the Christian era, certain Stoics followed the path laid down by Panaetius, the creator of the idea of humanism. They, too, came to consider love as the virtue of virtues. These men were Seneca, Epictetus, and the emperor Marcus Aurelius. Fundamentally, their ethics was that of the great Chinese sages. They had in common with them not only the principle of love but—what is really important—the conviction that it stems from reason and is fundamentally reasonable.

During the first and second centuries of our era, Greco-Roman philosophy came, therefore, to profess the same ethical ideal as Christianity. There seemed every possibility of an entente between Christianity and the ancient world.

Nothing came of it. The ethics of Stoicism never became popular. Moreover, the Stoics considered Christianity as the worst of superstitions. Was it not based on a "divine revelation" that had occurred in the person of Jesus Christ? Did not Christians await the miraculous coming of a new world? Christianity, for its part, despised philosophy as mere terrestrial wisdom. They were also divided by the fact that philosophy kept to the idea of the affirmation of the world, and the Christians to its denial. No agreement was possible.

And yet, centuries later, they did reach an understanding. In the sixteenth and seventeenth centuries, Christianity became familiar with the passionate affirmation of the world, which the Renaissance had bequeathed to European thought. It also made the acquaintance of the ethics of Stoicism and was amazed to find that Jesus' principle of love was there put forward as one of the truths of reason. Among the thinkers who recognized their double allegiance—to Christianity and to Stoicism—were Erasmus and Hugo Grotius.

Under the influence of Christianity, philosophical ethics acquired an element of passion that it had not previously possessed. Under the influence of philosophy, Christian ethics began to reflect upon what it owed to itself and what it had to accomplish in the world. Consequently, there arose a spirit that would no longer tolerate the injustice, the cruelty, and the harmful superstitions that it had previously allowed. Torture was abolished and, with it, the scourge of sorcery trials. Inhuman laws gave place to others more clement. Reforms unprecedented in human history were conceived and carried out in the first excitement of the discovery that the principle of love is ordained by reason.

Certain eighteenth-century philosophers—among them, Hartley, Baron d'Holbach, Helvétius, and Bentham—thought that the argument of sheer utility was sufficient to demonstrate the rational necessity of altruism. The Chinese and the Stoics had also advanced this argument, but they had used others as well. The eighteenth-century thesis was that altruism is merely an enlightened form of egoism, and a conclusion drawn from the fact that the well-being of individuals, and of society as a whole, can be assured only by a system of mutual devotion. This superficial view was contested by Kant, among others, and by the Scottish philosopher David Hume. Kant, wishing to defend the dignity of ethics, went so far as to say that its utility should not be taken into consideration at all. Manifest as it may be, it should not, he said, be accepted as an ethical motive. The doctrine of the categorical imperative asserts that the commands of ethics are absolute. It is our conscience that reveals to us what is right and what is wrong, and we have only to obey. We carry within us a moral law that gives us the certainty of belonging not only to the world as we know it in time and space but also to the world as such—the world, that is to say, of the spirit.

Hume, on the other hand, proceeds empirically in his attack upon the utilitarian thesis. Analyzing the motives of ethics, he concludes that it is sentiment, above all, that governs them. Nature, he argues, has endowed us with the faculty of sympathy, and it is this that allows us, and in fact compels us, to enter into the joys, the apprehensions, and the sufferings of others. We are, he says, like strings that vibrate in unison with those of the orchestra. It is this sympathy that leads us to devote ourselves to others and to wish to contribute to their well-being and to that of society. Philosophy since Hume—if we leave Nietzsche out of account—has never seriously questioned that ethics is above all a matter of compassion.

But where does this leave ethics? Can it limit and define our obligations toward our fellow men? Can it reconcile egoism and altruism, as the utilitarian theory attempted to do?

Hume barely considers the question. Nor has any later philosopher felt bound to consider the consequences of the principle of devotion-from-compassion. One might almost think that they sensed that these consequences might prove disquieting. And disquieting they are. The ethics of devotion-from-compassion no longer has the character of a law, as we should wish it to have. It no longer embodies cut-and-dried commandments. It is fundamentally subjective and leaves to each one of us an individual responsibility of deciding to what point our devotion should go.

Not only are there no longer any precise commandments: ethics has come to concern itself less and less with what is possible (the province, after all, of all law). It is constantly obliging us to attempt what is impossible and to extend our devotion to the point at which our very existence is compromised. In the hideous times that we have lived through, there were many such situations; and many, too, were the people who sacrificed themselves for others. Even in everyday life, and although the ethics of devotion may not demand of us this last sacrifice, it often requires us to ignore our own interests and to relinquish our advantages in favor of others. Too often, alas, we manage to stifle our conscience and, with it, our sense of responsibility. There are many conflicts, moreover, in which the ethics of devotion abandons us to ourselves. How often can a great industrialist congratulate himself on having given a post not to the man who was best qualified but to the man who most needed it? Woe betide such people if they decide, after one or two experiments of this sort, that the argument from compassion may always be overruled.

One last conclusion must be drawn from the principle of devotion: it no longer allows us to concern ourselves only with other human beings. We must behave in exactly the same way toward all living creatures, of whatever kind, whose fate may, in some respect, be our concern. They, too, are our kith and our kin, inasmuch as they too crave happiness, know the meaning of fear and suffering, and dread annihilation. To a man who has kept his feelings intact, it is quite natural to have pity for all living creatures. Philosophy likewise should decide to acknowledge that our behavior toward them must be an integral part of the ethics that it teaches. The reason is quite simple. Philosophy is rightly apprehensive that this immense enlargement of the sphere of our responsibilities will deprive ethics of whatever chance it still has of framing its commandments in a reasonable and satisfying way.

The man who is concerned for the fate of all living creatures is faced with problems even more numerous and more harassing than those that confront the man whose devotion extends only to his fellow human beings. In our relations with animals, we are continually obliged to harm, if not actually to kill, them. The peasant cannot rear all the newborn animals in his flock. He can keep only those that he can feed and that will eventually repay what they have cost him. In many cases we have to sacrifice certain lives in order to save others. A man who rescues a strayed bird may have to kill insects or fish to keep it alive. Such actions are entirely arbitrary. What right has he to sacrifice a multitude of lives in order to save the life of a single bird? And if he kills off what he considers to be dangerous animals in order to protect more peaceable ones, then there, too, he is in the realm of the arbitrary.

Each one of us, therefore, must judge whether it is really necessary for us to kill and to cause pain. We must resign ourselves to our guilt because our guilt is forced upon us. We must seek forgiveness by letting slip no opportunity of being of use to a living creature.

How great an advance it would be if men could only remember the kindness that they owe to such creatures and if they could refrain from harming them through thoughtlessness! If we have any self-respect, where our civilization is concerned, we must struggle against those feelings and those traditions—and they are many—that do violence to humanity. I cannot refrain in this connection from naming two practices that should no longer be tolerated in our civilization: bullfighting, where the bull is put to death, and stag hunting.

Ethics is complete only when it exacts compassion toward every living thing.

There has been another great change in the position of ethics: it can no longer expect to be supported by a conception of the world that, in itself, justifies ethics.

In every age ethics has been supposed to conform to the true nature of the universal will, which is made manifest in creation. It was in conformity with this will that ethics issued its commands. Not only was religion based upon this conviction; the rationalist philosophies of the seventeenth and eighteenth centuries also took it as their base.

But the ethical conception of the world is based upon its own optimistic interpretation of that world. Ethics endows the universal will with qualities and intentions that give satisfaction to its own way of feeling and judging. But during the nineteenth century, research—which after all can be guided only by regard for the truth—was compelled to admit that ethics can expect nothing and gain nothing from a true knowledge of the world. The progress of science consists in an ever more precise observation of the processes of nature. It is this that allows us to make use of the energies that manifest themselves in the universe. But at the same time, these researches oblige us, in an ever-greater degree, to relinquish all hope of understanding its intentions. The world offers us the disconcerting spectacle of the will to life in conflict with itself. One existence maintains itself at the expense of the other. In the world as it is, we see horror mingled with magnificence, absurdity with logic, and suffering with joy.

How can the ethics of devotion be kept going without the support of a notion of the world that justifies it? It seems destined to founder in skepticism. This is not, however, the fate to which it is foredoomed. In its infancy, ethics had to appeal to a conception of the world that would satisfy it. Once it realizes that devotion is its basic principle, it becomes fully aware of its nature—and, in doing so, becomes its own master. We, too, by meditating on the world, and on ourselves, can come to understand the origins and the foundation of ethics. What we lack is complete and satisfactory knowledge of the world. We are reduced to the simple observation that everything in it is life, like itself, and that all life is mystery. True knowledge of the world consists in being penetrated by the mystery of existence and of life. The discoveries of scientific research merely make this mystery yet more mysterious. The penetration of which I speak corresponds to what the mystics call "learned ignorance"—ignorance, that is to say, that at least grasped at what is essential.

The immediate datum of our consciousness, to which we revert whenever we want to understand ourselves and our situation in the world, is this: I am life, which wants to live, and all around me is life that wants to live. Myself permeated by the will to life, I affirm my life: not simply that I want to go on living but that I feel my life as a mystery and a standard of value. When I think about life, I feel obliged to respect all the will to life around me and to feel in it a mysterious value that is the equal of my own. The fundamental idea of good, therefore, is that it consists in preserving life, in favoring it and wishing to raise it to its highest point; and evil consists in the destruction of life, in the injury of life, or in the frustration of its development.

The principle of this veneration of life corresponds to that of love, as it has been discovered by religion and philosophy in their search for the fundamental notion of good.

The term "reverence for life" is broader and, for that reason, less vital than that of love, but it bears within it the same energies. This essentially philosophical notion of good has also the advantage of being more complete than that of love. Love includes only our obligations toward other beings. It does not include our obligations toward ourselves. One cannot, for instance, deduce from it the necessity of telling the truth: yet this, together with compassion, is the prime characteristic of the ethical personality. Reverence for one's own life should compel man, whatever the circumstances may be, to avoid all dissimulation and, in general, to become *himself* in the deepest and noblest sense.

Through reverence for life we enter into a spiritual relationship with the world. Philosophy has tried, and tried in vain, to build up some grandiose system that will bring us into contact with the absolute. The absolute is so abstract in character that we cannot communicate with it. It is not given to us to put ourselves at the service of the infinite and inscrutable creative will, which is at the basis of all existence. We can understand neither its nature nor its intentions. But we can be in touch with that will, in a spiritual sense, by submitting ourselves to the mystery of life and devoting ourselves to all the living creatures that we have the opportunity and the ability to serve. An ethics that enjoins us to concern ourselves only with human beings and human society cannot have this same significance. Only a universal ethics, which embraces every living creature, can put us in touch with the universe and with the will that is there manifest. In the world, the will to life is in conflict with itself. In us—by a mystery that we do not understand—it wishes to be at peace with itself. In the world, it is manifest; in us, it is revealed. It is our spiritual destiny to be other than the world. By conforming to it, we live our existence instead of merely submitting to it. Through reverence for life, we come to worship God in a way that is simple, profound, and alive.

PART III

"My Life Is My Argument": The Application of the Ethics of Reverence for Life

12

Bach and Aesthetics

For Schweitzer, one of the world's most renowned organists, music is never a mere pastime but a message of faith and love. He discovers a similar attitude in Bach: "For Bach, music is above all the most effective way of glorifying God." In this famous book on Bach, Schweitzer wants to make a contribution to aesthetics, not to the history of music. He intends to show the unity of art and to prove that "art for art's sake can be only an abstraction; art is the transmission of ideas." At the very beginning of the book, Schweitzer first divides artists into "subjective" and "objective." In the case of the former, their art has its source in the personality of the artist (e.g., Wagner and Nietzsche). Bach belongs to the order of objective artists, "who are wholly of their own time, and work only with the forms and ideas that their time proffers them." Schweitzer compares Bach to Kant, whose work displays the same impersonal character. This kind of genius is "not an individual, but a collective soul."

Schweitzer also maintains that there is an intimate connection between various forms of art, specifically of music, poetry, and painting. For him, Goethe is a poet who is really a painter, while Nietzsche is a poet who is a musician. Wagner is a musician and a poet, while Bach's art is deeply pictorial. In Bach's music, the beauty of nature is seen rather than felt. Sometimes, claims Schweitzer, Bach's pictorial interest overbalanced

Selection from *J. S. Bach*, trans. Ernest Newman (London: A. & C. Black, 1923), vol. 1, Ch. 1: "The Roots of Bach's Art," 1–4, and from "The Symbolism of Bach," originally published as *J. S. Bach, le musicien–poete*, by Albert Schweitzer. Leipzig: Breitkopf & Härtel, 1908, 325–341; reprinted here from *Music in the Life of Albert Schweitzer*, ed. Charles R. Joy (New York: Harper and Row, 1951), 123–135.

his musical interest, and he then exceeded the limits of pure music. Schweitzer does
not see any problem is these interconnections of various forms of art. The problem is
rather that we apply arbitrary categories in order to classify artists according to the
means they externally use. A closer look at the great works of art unmistakably dis-
plays a coexistence of different artistic gifts in the same personality.

Some artists are subjective, some objective. The art of the former has its source
in their personality; their work is almost independent of the epoch in which
they live. A law unto themselves, they place themselves in opposition to their
epoch and originate new forms for the expression of their ideas. Of this type
was Richard Wagner.

Bach belongs to the order of objective artists. These are wholly of their own
time, and work only with the forms and the ideas that their time proffers them.
They exercise no criticism upon the media of artistic expression that they find
lying ready to their hand and feel no inner compulsion to open out new paths.
Their art not coming solely from the stimulus of their outer experience, we
need not seek the roots of their work in the fortunes of its creator. In them the
artistic personality exists independently of the human, the latter remaining in
the background as if it were something almost accidental. Bach's works would
have been the same even if his existence had run quite another course. Did we
know more of his life than is now the case, and were we in possession of all
the letters he had ever written, we should still be no better informed as to the
inward sources of his works than we are now.

The art of the objective artist is not impersonal but supra-personal. It is as
if he felt only one impulse—to express again what he already finds in existence
but to express it definitively, in unique perfection. It is not he who lives—it
is the spirit of the time that lives in him. All the artistic endeavors, desires,
creations, aspirations, and errors of his own and of previous generations are
concentrated and worked out to their conclusion in him.

In this respect the greatest German musician has his analogue only in the
greatest of German philosophers. Kant's work has the same impersonal character. He is merely the brain in which the philosophical ideas and problems of
his day come to fruition. Moreover, he uses unconcernedly the scholastic forms
and terminology of the time, just as Bach took up the musical forms offered to
him by his epoch without examining them.

Bach, indeed, is clearly not a single but a universal personality. He profited
by the musical development of three or four generations. When we pursue
the history of this family, which occupies so unique a position in the art life
of Germany, we have the feeling that everything that is happening there must
culminate in something consummate. We feel it to be a matter of course that

some day shall come a Bach in whom all those other Bachs shall find a post-humous existence, one in whom the fragment of German music that has been embodied in this family shall find its completion. Johann Sebastian Bach—to speak the language of Kant—is a historical postulate.

Whatever path we traverse through the poetry and the music of the Middle Ages, we are always led to him.

The grandest creations of the chorale from the twelfth to the eighteenth century adorn his cantatas and Passions. Handel and the others make no use of the superb treasures of chorale melody. They want to be free of the past. Bach feels otherwise; he makes the chorale the foundation of his work.

If we pursue, again, the history of the harmonization of the chorale, we are once more led up to him. What the masters of polyphonic music—Eccard, Praetorius, and the others—strove after, he accomplishes. They could harmonize the melody only; his music at the same time reproduces the text.

So it is, again, with the chorale preludes and the chorale fantasias. Pachelbel, Börn, and Buxtehude, the masters in this field, created the forms. But it was not given to them to quicken the forms with the spirit. If all their struggles toward the ideal were not to be in vain, a greater man had to come who should make his chorale fantasias musical poems.

Out of the motet, under the influence of Italian and French instrumental music, came the cantata. From Schütz onward, for a whole century, the sacred concert struggles for its free and independent place in the church. People feel that this new music is cutting the ground of the old church service from under their feet. It forces itself further and further out of the frame of the service, aiming at becoming an independent religious drama and aspiring toward a form like that of the opera. The oratorio is being prepared. At this juncture Bach appears and creates cantatas that endure. A generation later it would have been too late. As regards their form, his cantatas do not differ from the hundreds upon hundreds of others written at that time and now forgotten. They have the same external defects; they live, however, by their spirit. Out of the ardent will to create of generations that could not themselves give birth to anything durable, there has come for once a will equal to the ideal that hovered before the two previous generations and that triumphs in spite of all the errors of its epoch, purely by the grandeur of its thought.

At the end of the seventeenth century, the musical Passion drama demands admission into the church. The contest rages, for and against. Bach puts an end to it by writing two Passions that, on their poetical and formal sides, derive wholly from the typical works of that time but are transfigured and made immortal by the spirit that breathes through them.

Bach is thus a terminal point. Nothing comes from him; everything merely leads up to him. To give his true biography is to exhibit the nature and the unfolding of German art, which comes to completion in him and is exhausted in him—to comprehend it in all its strivings and its failures. This genius was not an individual but a collective soul. Centuries and generations have labored at this work, before the grandeur of which we halt in veneration. To anyone who has gone through the history of this epoch and knows what the end of it was, it is the history of that culminating spirit, as it was before it objectivated itself in a single personality.

Bach was a poet; and this poet was at the same time a painter.

This is not at all a paradox. We have the habit of classifying an artist according to the means he uses to interpret his inner life: a musician if he uses sounds, a painter if he uses colors, a poet if he uses words. But we must admit that these categories, established by external criteria, are very arbitrary. The soul of an artist is a complex whole in which mingle, in proportions infinitely variable, the gifts of the poet, the painter, the musician. Nothing compels us to set forth as a principle that the sort of thing that issues from a man must always express an internal dream of the same order: that, for instance, one can transcribe a dream of a musical nature with the help of sound. There is no impossibility in conceiving a poet's dream expressed in color, or a musician's dream taking the form of words, and so forth. The instances of such transcriptions abound.

Schiller was a musician. In conceiving his works he had auditive sensations. In a letter to Körner (May 25, 1792), he expressed himself thus: "The music of a poem is more often present in my soul, when I sit down at my table to write, than the exact idea of the contents, about which I am often hardly in agreement with myself." Goethe himself was a painter to the extent that he was for a long time haunted by the idea that that perhaps was his true vocation. He studied design with assiduity and suffered from not being able to render things as he saw them. We know how he sought to consult fate, in the course of a journey on foot that took him from Wetzlar toward the Rhine, in order to put an end to these uncertainties and to decide upon his future. "I was following the right bank of the Lahn," he says in his autobiographical *Poetry and Truth*, "and I saw at some distance below me the river shining in the rays of the sun, and partly hidden by a lush growth of willows. Then my old desire to be able to paint such things worthily awakened in me. By chance I held in my left hand a fine pocketknife; and at the very moment I heard resounding in my soul an imperious command to hurl this knife immediately into the stream. If I saw it fall into the water, my artistic aspirations would be realized; if the fall of the knife were hidden by the overhanging branches, I should have to renounce my wishes and my efforts. I had hardly thought of it when this fancy was executed, for without any regard for the utility of the knife, which had a number of parts, I threw it immediately with all my strength and with my left hand into the river. Unfortunately, this time I also experienced the deceitful ambiguity of oracles, of which the ancients have already so bitterly complained. The plunge of the knife was hidden from me by the last branches of the willows, but the water was thrown up by the shock like a powerful fountain and was perfectly visible to me. I did not interpret the incident to my advantage; and the doubt it awakened in my mind had subsequently this unhappy consequence, that I applied myself to the study of design in a more desultory and negligent manner. Thus I myself gave the oracle the chance to fulfill itself."

Goethe became a poet, therefore, while he remained a painter: his work is composed of portraits and landscapes. Visual evocation—in this lie the originality and the secret of his narrative talent. His letters from Switzerland are sketches; and in his letters from Italy, he congratulates himself "on having always had the gift of seeing the world with the eyes of a painter, whose pictures were present to his mind." In his gondola trips, Venice seemed to him like a succession of pictures from the Venetian school. His characters are portraits; in Faust, it is himself that he paints. All the idyllic scenes in this vast drama, naïve, tragic, burlesque, fantastic, allegoric, are so many backdrops on which the portrait of Goethe stands out at different moments of his life. Even music he perceived in a visual form: in listening to Bach he saw tall people in their finery descending with solemn steps a great staircase.

Is there any reason for recalling the classic case of Taine, this painter in literature? Gottfried Keller, author of *Romeo and Juliet in the Village*, began in the same way with painting. Conversely, Böcklin is a poet who has gone astray among the painters. His poetic imagination carries him away to mythological distances and calls forth before his painter's eyes, in the form of concrete images, this world of elementary forces dreamed of by the pantheistic poets. From that moment on what does the poet care for lines or colors? Pictorial composition, exactness of design—he holds them cheap; the essential thing for him is ever more and more to express his ideas. Nothing is more significant in this respect than Böcklin's last work, that formless but dramatic picture in the museum at Basel of the pestilence.

Nietzsche was a musician. He even made some attempts at musical composition and submitted his drafts to Wagner. They are still more mediocre than the designs of Goethe. But at one time he thought he had the gifts of a composer. He did possess them, in effect: it was he who created in literature the symphonic style. His method of composing a literary work is that of a writer of symphonies; study from this point of view his *Beyond Good and Evil,* and you will find even little fugues like those in the symphonies of Beethoven. To read a work without rhythm was for him an ordeal. "Even our good musicians write badly," he cried peevishly. Is not this affinity strange between Nietzsche, the musician among the thinkers, and Wagner, the thinker among the musicians? Their fate was to meet only to separate, to love each other only to hate each other. Nevertheless, of all the Wagnerians, Nietzsche is the only one who understood the soul of the master of Bayreuth. It was he who found this formula, so perfectly true, to characterize the artistic spirit of Wagner: "Wagner as a musician should be classified among the painters; as a poet among the musicians; as an artist, in a more general sense, among the actors."

It is from this coexistence of different artistic instincts in the same personality that we must start to establish those reciprocal relations that unite the arts. In aesthetics we have too long delighted in formulating definitions borrowed from the nature of the different arts and then in piling up on this arbitrary base theories and controversies. From this there have usually resulted axioms and judgments whose solidity was only illusory. What has not been said or written about descriptive music! For some it is nothing less than the final goal of all music; for others it represents the degeneracy of pure music: affirmations diametrically opposed, neither of which may be called false but which contain only parts of the truth. How to resolve this antinomy? By studying the question, we would say, from the point of view of the psychology of history.

Every art teaches us psychology, manifesting "descriptive" tendencies insofar as it wishes to express more than its own proper medium of expression will permit. Painting wants to express the feelings of the poet; poetry wants to evoke plastic visions; music wishes to paint and to express ideas. It is as if the soul of "the other artist" wants also to speak. Pure art is only an abstraction. Every work of art, to be understood, should suggest a complex representation, in which are mingled and harmonized sensations of every kind. He who, before a picture of a landscape filled with heather, does not hear the vague music of the humming of bees, does not know how to see; just as the man for whom music evokes no vision knows not how to hear. The logic of art is the logic of the association of ideas; and the artistic impression is all the greater when the complex associations of ideas, conscious and subconscious, are communicated through the medium of the work, in a way more intense and more complete. Art is the transmission of the association of ideas.

The painters do not simply copy nature, they reproduce it, so that we may share the surprise and the emotion that they themselves, seeing her as poets, experienced in her presence. And what do they teach us, if not to look at nature everywhere with the eyes of the poet?

Descriptive music is, then, legitimate, since painting and poetry are like the unconscious elements without which the language of sounds could not be conceived. There is a painter in every musician. Listen to him, and this second nature will immediately appear to you. To express the simplest idea, the musicians could not get along without pictures and metaphors. Their language is a kind of word painting, from which arises the attraction of their writings, so original, so picturesque, often also so odd and incoherent. Nothing could be more interesting than their letters in this regard: they show their minds ceaselessly agitated by visual images.

The descriptive tendency appears already in the works of the primitives. It is a very naïve, imitative tendency; they wish to reproduce the song of the birds, laughter, lamentation, the sound of a spring or a cascade; even more, they pretend to represent entire scenes and end with musical narrations where the climaxes in a composition are supposed to correspond to those of a story. It is precisely in the two generations before Bach that we see the simultaneous appearance in Italy, Germany, and France of this rudimentary descriptive music. So it is in characteristic pieces of Froberger and the French harpsichordists, with which Bach was acquainted; in the orchestral descriptions of the Hamburg masters, the Keisers, the Matthesons, and the Telemanns; and especially in the biblical sonatas of Kuhnau, which are a kind of classic expression of this tendency.

This primitive descriptive music has not come to an end; on the contrary, it reappears with all its pretensions in our program music. In the hands of Liszt and his disciples, great and small, who travel in this direction, the symphony becomes a symphonic poem (*Symphonische Dichtung*). The climaxes cannot be explained by themselves; they necessitate a commentator to announce what the music is going to represent. Make no mistake: however great the means it employs and the clarity of expression it attains, this descriptive music is, nonetheless, primitive and marginal in art, just because it cannot be explained by itself. And when it is practiced by musicians of the second order, it is in vain that they multiply the explanations and comments on each measure; this primitive character becomes only more accentuated. Such were the old painters, who used to represent the utterance of their characters by garlands of words issuing from their mouths, instead of being content with gestures and expressions.

The story of primitive descriptive music is, therefore, divided into two periods: ancient and modern. Here and there we are in the presence of normal tendencies, which in view of the way they appear and develop have resulted only in a false art.

In pictorial art we notice an analogous anomaly: biblical painting. Seduced by episodes known to everybody, the painters, ancient and modern, allow themselves to be carried beyond the natural limits of pictorial narration. They think to represent such and such an episode in sacred history by assembling on the same canvas the people who figure in it; they never think of asking if the action in the episode could be concentrated in a single scene and be interpreted in a concrete way by the attitude of characters, as the logic of every pictorial composition requires. Like the biblical scenes in Kuhnau's cantatas, their works can be explained only by their implications. A man with a knife, a child with bound hands, a head that appears through the clouds, a ram in the bushes: all these brought together on a single canvas represent the story of Abraham's sacrifice. A woman and a man sitting beside a well, a dozen men coming two by two along the road, in the background people leaving a village: this is Jesus and the Samaritan woman.

Biblical painting provides an abundance of examples of this false pictorial narration, which in truth is only pretty imagery. However finished the execution, it does not make us forget the complete absence of composition. In reality, there are only a very few biblical scenes that lend themselves to painting; the others are not such as to fulfill the desired conditions.

The only man who really showed discernment in his choice of subjects, and who never made a false biblical painting, is Michelangelo. Let us compare with his powerful evocations of sacred history the simple illustrations that Veronese has given us. Admirable and enchanting as *The Marriage at Cana* is in form, should we not think this was an ordinary banquet if it were not for a kind of tacit understanding between the painter and the public?

Biblical painting and historical painting are the two aspects of false description in the history of painting, and these two chapters in the history of plastic art have their parallel in the history of music. The two supreme representatives of the descriptive genre are, in plastic art, Michelangelo; in music, Bach.

Bach was a poet, but he lacked the gift of expression. His language was without distinction, and his poetic taste was no more developed than that of his contemporaries. Would he otherwise have accepted so gladly the libretti of Picander?

Nonetheless, he was a poet in his soul, in that he looked in a text first of all for the poetry it contained. What a difference there was between him and Mozart! Mozart is purely a musician; he takes a given text and clothes it in a beautiful melody. Bach, on the other hand, digs in it; he explores it thoroughly, until he has found the idea that, in his eyes, represents the heart of it and which he will have to illustrate in music. He has a horror of neutral music, superimposed on a text with nothing in common with it except the rhythm and a wholly general feeling. Often, it is true, when he finds himself in the presence of a text that has no salient idea, he is forced to make the best of a bad situation, but before resigning himself to it he does his utmost to discover some germ of music in the text itself. The musical phrase he applies to it is already born from the natural rhythm of the words. In this he goes beyond Wagner. In Handel we often perceive a latent antagonism between the words of the poetic text and the musical phrase superimposed on it. For instance, he sometimes divides long periods into several phrases, which cease from that point to form a whole. In Bach, on the other hand, the musical period is modeled on the phrasing of the text; it springs from it naturally. The longest phrase is rendered by one of those magnificent musical periods of which he has the secret. From passages without any structure, which at first sight seem unsuited to any declamation, he draws the most beautiful musical phrases, and with such a natural skill that one is surprised he did not suspect this phrasing before.

His greatest concern was to give the text the luster that music requires. It does not matter much to him that he amplifies the feeling expressed by these words; contentment readily becomes exuberant joy, and sadness extreme anguish. Often he seizes upon a single word that for him gathers up all the musical substance of the text, and in his composition gives it an importance it actually does not have. This is evident in the text of the cantata "*Es ist ein trotzig and versagtes Ding*" (It is an insolent and discouraging thing), No. 176, where he has given musical expression only to the word "*trotzig*" (insolent), though the whole passage has rather to do with contrition. Often he presents the text in a false light, but he always brings into the foreground the idea that lends itself to musical expression. The composition brings this out, as in *repoussé* work.

His dramatic instinct is not less developed. The plan of the *St. Matthew Passion,* so admirably conceived from the dramatic point of view, is his own invention. In every text he seeks the contrasts, the opposing elements, the gradations, to be brought out by the music. In the little collection of chorales (*Orgelbüchlein*), he brings out most clearly the importance he attaches to the contrasts: he arranges the chorales there in such a way that one sets another in relief. In the same way, in the mystical cantatas he opposes the fear of death (*Todesfurcht*) to the joyous nostalgia for death (*Freudige Todessehnsucht*). He often enriches a text by commenting upon it with a chorale theme that one hears in the orchestra. To the text "*Ich steh mit einem Fuss im Grabe*" (I am standing with one foot in the grave) is added the chorale, "Lord, deal with me according to Thy mercy" (Cantata No. 156); in a recitative from the cantata "*Wachet, betet*" (Watch and pray), No. 70, the trumpet suddenly sounds the chorale of the last judgment, "*Es ist gewisslich an der Zeit*" (Surely it is the time); in the cantata "*Sehet, wir gehen hinauf nach Jerusalem*" (Come, we are going up to Jerusalem), No. 159, rises the Passion chorale, "*O Haupt voll Blut and Wunden*" (O Head, covered with blood and wounds).

But that which occupies the most prominent place in Bach's work is pictorial poetry. Above everything else he seeks the picture, and in this respect he is very different from Wagner, who is rather a lyric dramatist. Bach himself is nearer to Berlioz, and nearer still to Michelangelo. If it had been possible for him to see a picture by Michelangelo, doubtless he would have found in him something of his own soul.

But his contemporaries remained unaware of his painter's soul. His pupils and his sons did not perceive his pictorial instincts any more than they suspected that his true greatness was as a musical poet. So, too, with Forkel, Mossevius, von Winterfeld, Bitter, and Spitta. Spitta, whose profound acquaintance with the works of Bach put him in a position to see things clearly, has a fear of carrying his researches in that direction. When he cannot do otherwise, he confesses that such and such a page contains descriptive music, and is always sure to add that it is there purely by accident, to which one would be wrong to attach any importance. These examples are curiosities for him, nothing more. On every occasion he insists that the music of Bach is above such puerilities, that it is pure music, the only kind that is classic. This apprehension leads him astray. The fear that one day someone would find descriptive music in Bach, and that this discovery would injure his reputation as a classic writer, prevents Spitta from recognizing the role it plays in his compositions.

Let us watch Bach at his work. However bad the text, he is satisfied with it if it contains a picture. When he discovers a pictorial idea it takes the place of the whole text; he seizes on it even at the risk of going contrary to the dominant idea of the text. Preoccupied as he is exclusively with the pictorial element, he does not perceive the weakness and the flaws in the libretto.

Nature itself he perceives, so to speak, in a pictorial fashion. The poetry of nature in his work is not at all lyrical, as it is with Wagner: it is seen rather than felt; it is the tornadoes, the clouds that advance along the horizon, the falling leaves, the restless waves.

His symbolism also is visual, like that of a painter; that is how he expresses ideas that are completely abstract. In the cantata No. 77, for the thirteenth Sunday after Trinity, he deals with the verse from the Gospels, "Thou shalt love the Lord thy God with all thy heart, and with all thy soul, and with all thy strength, and with all thy mind, and thou shalt love thy neighbor as thyself" (Luke 10:27), Christ's reply to the scribe who asked him what was the greatest of all the commandments. These commandments, great and little, are then represented by the melody from the chorale *Dies sind die heilgen zehn Gebote* (These are the holy ten commandments), which the organ basses sound forth in minims and the trumpets in crotchets, while the choir renders the words of the Savior, who proclaims the new law of love.

Was Bach clearly conscious of this pictorial instinct? He hardly seems to have been. We have not found among his confidences to his pupils any allusion that allows us to say so. The title of the *Orgelbüchlein* announces that the pieces contained there are model chorales; but he does not say that they are typical just because they are descriptive. And besides, are not all the parodies he made of his own works, that suppress in this way the pictorial intent of his music, there to show that his descriptive instinct was unconscious? Then where in the genius is the dividing line between the conscious and the unconscious? Is he not one and the other at the same time? This is true of Bach: he is not conscious of the importance of descriptive music in his work; but in his way of seeing the subjects to be treated, and in his choice of the means, he is thoroughly clairvoyant.

The great mistake of all the primitives consists in wishing to translate into music everything they find in a text. Bach avoids this danger. He is well aware that the climaxes of a text should be, if one is to risk retracing them with sound, both simple and strongly accented. Hence, the times when he uses this means are very rare.

Moreover, when he follows the indications of a text, he does not insist upon it in the pretentious fashion of the primitives. We must admire the way in which, in the recitatives of the *St. Matthew Passion,* he underlines one word in this way, and another word in that. These are light musical inflections, destined to pass unobserved. It is the same with the cantatas and with the chorales. On the other hand, when a new motif appears in the text, the music changes immediately, since for Bach a new picture requires a new theme. In some choruses two or even three themes occur successively, because the text demands them. So in the cantata "*Siehe, ich will viel Fischer aussenden*" (Behold, I will send out many fishermen), No. 88, based on the text in Jeremiah: "Behold, I will send for many fishers, saith the Lord, and they shall fish them; and after will I send for many hunters, and they shall hunt them." The music of the first part paints a picture of waves, because the word "fisher" brings to Bach's mind a lake; in the second half (*Allegro quasi presto*), it is hunters climbing over the mountains: we hear fanfares. Many of the airs show the same peculiarity: the theme of the middle part corresponds to an image other than that of the principal part.

What is there to say except that the music of Bach is descriptive only as far as its themes are always determined by an association of pictorial ideas? This association is sometimes energetically asserted and sometimes almost unconscious. There are themes whose pictorial origin would not at first be suspected, if it were not for the fact that in other works is to be found an entire series of analogous themes whose origin is not at all doubtful. There are then more accented themes that explain the origin of the others. When one brings together the Bach themes, one discovers a series of associations of pictorial ideas that are regularly repeated when the text requires them. This regularity in the association of ideas will not be found in Beethoven, or in Berlioz, or in Wagner. The only one who could be compared with Bach is Schubert. The accompaniment to his *Songs* depends on a descriptive language whose elements are identical with the language of Bach—without, however, attaining to his precision. Schubert hardly knew the works of the Leipzig cantor, but, desiring to translate into music the poetry of the *Songs*, he had to agree with the man who had translated into music the poetry of the chorales.

The musical language of Bach is the most elaborate and most precise in existence. It has, after a fashion, its roots and derivations like any other language.

There is an entire series of elementary themes proceeding from visual images, each of which produces a whole family of diversified themes, in accordance with the different shades of the idea to be translated into music. From the same root we often find in the different works twenty or twenty-five variants; for to express the same idea, Bach returns constantly to the same fundamental formula. Thus, we encounter the walking themes (*Schrittmotive*), expressing firmness and hesitation; the syncopated themes of weariness, themes of quiet, represented by calm undulations; Satan themes, expressed in a sort of fantastic violence; themes of serene peace; themes consisting of two slurred notes, expressing suffering nobly borne; chromatic themes in five or six notes, which express acute pain; and finally, the great category of themes of joy.

There exist fifteen or twenty of these categories, in which one can catalogue all the expressive motifs characteristic of Bach. The richness of his language consists not in the abundance of different themes but in the different inflections that the same theme takes in accordance with the occasion. Without this variety of nuances, one might even find fault with his language because of a certain monotony. It is indeed the linguistic monotony of all great thinkers, who find only one expression for the same idea because it is the only true one.

But Bach's language permits him to define his ideas in a surprising fashion. He has a variety of nuances at his disposal to describe pain or joy, which one would seek in vain among other musicians. When the elements of his language are once known, even the compositions that are not associated with any text, like the preludes and the fugues of *The Well-Tempered Clavichord*, become vocal, and announce, after a fashion, a concrete idea. If we have to do with music written for words, we can, without looking at the text, and with the help of the themes alone, define the characteristic ideas.

But the strangest fact of all is that the language of Bach is in no way the fruit of a long experience. The different motifs that express pain are already found in the *Lamento* of the *Cappricio*, which he wrote between the ages of eighteen and twenty. When he composed the *Orgelbüchlein*, which dates from the Weimar epoch, he was about thirty. But at this time all his typically expressive motifs are already formed and fixed and are not afterward subjected to any change. While trying to represent in music a whole series of chorales, he found himself forced to seek ways of expressing himself simply and clearly. He gives up description through musical development and adopts the procedure of expressing everything by the theme. At the same time, he fixes the principal formulas of his musical language.

These little chorales are, therefore, Bach's musical dictionary. One has to begin with them if one is to understand what he wants to say in the cantatas and the Passions.

But in his effort for precision in language, he sometimes transgresses the natural limits of music. It is not to be denied that we find in his works many disappointing pages. It is because a goodly number of his themes proceed from vision rather than from musical imagination, properly so called. In trying to reproduce a visual image, he permits himself to be carried away into the creation of themes that are admirably characteristic but that have nothing left of the musical phrase. In his youthful works such examples were rare because his melodic instinct was still stronger than his descriptive instinct. But later the instances of this ultra-pictorial music become frequent. Among the great chorales of 1736, some, such as the chorales about the Last Supper (VI, No. 30) and about the baptism (VI, No. 17), have already passed beyond the limits of music. It is the same with all the airs constructed on the theme that pictures the steps of a stumbling man. It is so with the cantata *Ich glaube Herr, hilf meinem Unglauben* (Lord, I believe, help thou mine unbelief), No. 109, which is almost impossible to listen to, because it describes a faith that swoons with themes of this kind. Did Bach, when he played or directed these pieces himself, know how to make them agreeable by the perfection of his execution? Did he have some secret of interpretation that we have not yet discovered?

However that may be, the fact is indisputable: his pictorial interest sometimes overbalanced his musical interest. Bach then exceeded the limits of pure music. But his mistake is not comparable to that of the great and little primitives in descriptive music, who sinned through ignorance of the technical resources of the art; his error has its source in the unusual loftiness of his inspiration. Goethe, in composing *Faust*, thought he was writing a piece appropriate for presentation in the theater; but the work became so great and so profound that it can hardly stand dramatic representation. With Bach, also, the intensity of a thought he desires to express without reticence and in all sincerity is sometimes so great that it injures the purely musical beauty. Mistakes were possible for him, but his errors were those only a genius is capable of making.

13

Goethe the Philosopher

Schweitzer always believed that we can find some of the deepest philosophi-
cal insights outside of the strictly philosophical texts and theories. In this
essay Schweitzer first analyzes Goethe's dissatisfaction with the systematic
philosophy of his age and then outlines Goethe's own philosophy of nature
and ethics. Some of what Schweitzer ascribes to Goethe represents his own
standpoints. In Goethe's name he sets three criteria of a meaningful philo-
sophical view: (1) Does it approach nature without preconceived theories?
(2) Does it include a profound and enlightened ethical idea? (3) Does it
have the courage, when it arrives at the ultimate problems raised by research
and thought, to admit that there are mysteries that cannot be plumbed, or
does it rather presume to offer a system that explains everything? Schweitzer
analyzes Goethe's philosophical views in comparison to those of Spinoza,
Kant, Fichte, Schelling, and Hegel. The German philosophers fail both the
first and the third criteria, while Spinoza fails the third one. Schweitzer
then explains Goethe's complex pantheistic mysticism and its relationship to
Christianity. Goethe's moral ideal consists in deepening of the inner life and
its expression in moral action. The primary value of such action is not out-
side the action itself—a moral agent should not expect happiness from life
or positive results of his or her activities. The good is the work of our inner
necessity, and the chief value of good is measured

Complete essay; originally published in the French magazine *Europe* (vol. 27, No. 112, April 15,
1932), in "A Special Number Dedicated to Goethe on the One Hundredth Anniversary of His Death";
translated by Charles R. Joy and reprinted here from Albert Schweitzer, *Goethe: Four Studies* (Boston:
Beacon, 1949), 63–83.

in striving toward the goodness. Together with Goethe, Schweitzer subscribes to the ancient wisdom that "whoever would act should resemble the unreasonable sower of the gospel parable who casts the seed without caring how it will spring up or where it will spring up."

All his life long, Goethe refused to be a systematic philosopher. In one of his poems, he boasts of having achieved splendid results because he never lost his way "thinking about thought."

His dislike of philosophy—so he tells us in *Truth and Poetry*—goes back to his student days. The rationalistic philosophy of the eighteenth century, with which he became acquainted at Leipzig (1765–1768) and at Strasbourg (1770–1772), offers him nothing that he does not already know and irritates him with its doctrinaire quality. He finds fault with it for its scholastic discoloration, especially in its logic and its metaphysics. In *Faust* he expresses freely the feeling that he cherishes.

This philosophy is alien to him also because it pretends to explain everything. By this very fact, he thinks, it proves that it is not giving a true account of the grandeur of nature's mysteries. For example, the materialism advocated by Baron d'Holbach in his *System of Nature*, which appeared in 1770, during Goethe's stay at Strasbourg, and which brags of being the quintessence of rationalistic philosophy in giving the simplest explanations of the physical and spiritual world, seems to him to be a dull and decrepit philosophy.

Voltaire, for whom, in general, he has great respect, displeases him because, in fighting against the narrowness of the prevailing religion, he ridicules the church, the guardian of religious tradition, even while trying to conserve certain fundamental religious truths. For Goethe, the moral and religious tradition preserved in the Bible is something sacred. He knows well enough that not everything in it is of the same religious or ethical value, but he does not want to have profane hands laid on it. He insists that men should recognize the existence of mysteries in religion, as in nature, and that men should approach them with respect.

The position taken by Goethe at Strasbourg toward the French and German philosophy of his time remains decisive throughout his life, as he tells us in *Truth and Poetry*. Every time he confronts some new philosophy, he studies it from three principal points of view: (1) Does it touch the reality of nature without preconceived theories, and does it bring men into direct contact with nature? (2) Has it a profound and enlightened ethical idea? (3) Does it have the courage, when it arrives at the ultimate problems raised by research and thought, to admit that there are mysteries that cannot be plumbed, or does it rather presume to offer a system that explains everything? Every philosophy

that gives a satisfying response to these three fundamental demands he recognizes as plausible.

Whenever he feels that he is dealing with eminent thinkers, he endeavors
to penetrate as deeply as possible into their world of ideas, and he is more likely
to exaggerate the inspiration he gets from them than to underestimate it.

He tries hard also not to let himself be dominated by the distrust that he
cherishes instinctively against the philosophers. In a letter to Jacobi, written on
November 23, 1801, he defines his position in happy terms:

> To every man, who stands upon his experience, and who is and
> remains always a "philosopher without knowing it" in any striking
> results he may reach, I concede the right to be somehow apprehen-
> sive about philosophy, and especially about the philosophy of our age.
> But let not his apprehension degenerate into aversion; rather, let it
> take the form of calm and prudent inclination.

Let us now examine, one after the other, the philosophical systems with which
Goethe came into contact and the way in which he reacted to each of them.

Let no one imagine for a moment that Goethe has broken completely with
the rationalistic philosophy of the eighteenth century. He sees clearly that the
social, economic, and intellectual progress that takes place under his eyes is
due to the rational, ethical ideal proclaimed by this philosophy. It is only its
idea of the world, on which it pretends to base its ideal, that seems to him
inadequate.

Basically, Goethe recognizes the same end as Kant: to give a safer and
deeper foundation to the ethical and spiritual values contained in the contemporary rationalistic philosophy. Kant tries to do this by elaborating a new theory
of knowledge, Goethe by examining more profoundly nature itself and the relations of men to it. Kant makes a detour; Goethe goes straight to the point.

To Herder, whom Goethe met for the first time in 1770 at Strasbourg, the
young Goethe owed very much. He found in him something that he had never
before witnessed: a philosopher who had rid himself of all dogmatism, striving
to penetrate into reality by the strength of his feeling. Herder revealed to him
also certain perceptions concerning the problems of man's spiritual development of which Goethe had had up to that time no idea. Later the two men took
divergent roads, for their natures were quite dissimilar, and Herder could not
understand how Goethe could hope to comprehend nature by purely scientific
labors.

Rousseau enchants Goethe and his Strasbourg friends by preaching a
return to nature which accords with their own personal ideas. As early as 1791,

in his *Metamorphosis of Plants*, Goethe respectfully recalls the "solitary stroller who loved plants" and whose footsteps he had followed in his study of botany.

The Encyclopedists, far from being a healthy influence upon him, plunge him into confusion instead by the very plethora of the things they have assembled.

About Diderot he expresses a curious opinion in *Truth and Poetry*: "In everything for which the French reproach him he is a typical German."

Upon his return from Strasbourg to Frankfurt, he plunges for the first time into the study of Spinoza (this is in 1774) and discovers in him a masterful teacher who satisfies his deepest aspirations. In the *Metamorphosis of Plants*, he declares that Shakespeare, Linnaeus, and Spinoza are the three men who have exercised the strongest influence upon him. The reason Goethe is so strongly attracted to Spinoza is that he finds in him for the first time ideas clearly formulated that he himself had long felt confusedly and chaotically: that God is not outside nature but within it and identical with it, that the purpose of ethics is to bring a man to perfection without doing violence to his own nature, that happiness consists in achieving an inner peace. This contact with Spinoza clarifies his own ideas and purifies his soul. One may well wonder what would have happened to the young Goethe if, at the critical moment in his life, Spinoza's *Ethics* had not won him to its severe discipline.

Nevertheless, in his memory of Spinoza, reverent and grateful as it is in *Truth and Poetry*, Goethe is fully aware that he has retained his independence. Here is the way he expresses it: "I cannot clearly distinguish between the thoughts which came to me from reading of the *Ethics* and those which I contributed to it." And further on: "Besides, one must not fail to recognize the fact that it is only between opposite natures that the closest ties are really established."

Indeed, it is the Stoic ideas of Spinoza that influence Goethe; the attraction they have for him is so strong that he ignores the rigid, geometrical logic in which they are expressed.

In reality, Goethe is a disciple of Spinoza only insofar as he is a Stoic.

His admiration for Spinoza brought him into contact with Friedrich Heinrich Jacobi, who was one of the first to call attention once more to the thinker then almost forgotten. Goethe went to visit him in Düsseldorf in 1774 and at once felt for him, for the first time, something that he called an intimate friendship. But later, when Jacobi turned away from Spinoza and published his book *Concerning Things Divine* (1811), in which he insisted upon a sharp distinction between pantheism and theism and postulated the existence of a transcendent and personal God, the friendship of the two men cooled.

In 1784, at Weimar, Goethe took up the *Ethics* of Spinoza again with Frau von Stein. His agreement with Spinoza kept him a bit apart from the philosophic trends of that era.

It is interesting to note the judgment that Schiller, during a brief sojourn at Weimar, described Goethe, who was then in Italy, and his circle of admirers, as having:

> a proud disdain of all speculation, an attachment to nature carried to the point of affectation, a resignation to the fact that one can count only upon the five senses, in short a certain infantile simplicity in the use of reason characterizes him, him and all of his coterie in this place. They prefer to collect plants and study minerals rather than to lose their way in vain, speculative demonstrations. (Letter from Schiller to Körner, August 12, 1787)

What a splendid mixture of praise and mockery!

Upon his return from Italy in 1788, Goethe has to take a stand in relation to Kant. Reinhold, one of the enthusiastic admirers of the Königsberg philosopher, has won all of Jena to the *Critique of Pure Reason,* which appeared in 1781. "For some time," Wieland writes in a letter of February 18, 1789, "Goethe has been studying Kant's book, the *Critique of Pure Reason,* with great concentration." His conversion to Kant is not, however, very far advanced when, in 1794, he makes the acquaintance of Schiller and establishes a friendship with him, which he has long avoided because of his belief that Schiller is too revolutionary. Schiller, steeped in Kant, bends all his energies to win Goethe to the Königsberg gospel. It is just to please him that Goethe in all good faith seeks to get rid of what he calls in one place his "impenitent realism." It is in vain; he always falls back into it. He cannot agree to have no further relations, immediate and frank, with nature. The great formal edifice of the *Critique of Pure Reason* seems to him, as he said in an 1813 discourse in memory of Wieland, "a dungeon which restrains our free and joyous excursions into the field of experience."

Goethe shows great reserve about Kant's discoveries in the domain of the theory of knowledge but, on the other hand, acknowledges the everlasting merit of having discarded all those ideas that founded morality upon utility and of having demonstrated the independence and the sovereignty of ethics.

He praises Kant also for having sustained in his *Critique of Judgment,* which appeared in 1790, the truth that nature, like art, is not determined by final causes and that they are both creative. In this way Kant works with him to raze the restricting walls that hem in the conception of the world elaborated by the rationalism of the eighteenth century and to restore to nature all of its rights.

But Goethe is unable to pardon the Königsberg thinker for having supported, in his *Religion within the Limits of Reason Alone,* the idea that there is in human nature something fundamentally evil. He sees in this a concession unworthy of the great thinker to the doctrine of original sin, which is so repugnant to him.

This does not prevent him from chanting the praises of Kant when Victor Cousin comes to visit him on October 20, 1817, and from declaring to Eckermann on April 11, 1827, that he considers Kant to be the most eminent of modern philosophers.

Goethe goes so far as to say to the Genevese Soret in 1830: "For in spite of everything, I am also a Kantian." But caution prompts him to add hastily that he accepts only certain affirmations of the Kantian philosophy and that, at other points, he holds a very different opinion.

He comes into contact with the representatives of the post-Kantian philosophy through his position as curator of the University of Jena, where the three most important of them taught: Fichte from 1794 to 1799, Schelling from 1798 to 1803, and Hegel from 1801 to 1806.

Goethe has hardly any sympathy for Fichte, with his intense nature, and he does not do credit to his real worth; he even regrets that Fichte was called to Jena to succeed Reinhold. When Fichte sends him his great work, *Foundation of the Entire Science of Knowledge,* he replies in a very diplomatic way: "As for me I would be most grateful to you if you would reconcile me to the philosophers that I cannot get along without and with whom I can never come to terms" (June 24, 1794).

His relations with Schelling and Hegel were of an entirely different kind. In both of them he finds again his fundamental, mystical conception that the world is a manifestation of the infinite spirit and that the soul of the world becomes self-conscious in the human spirit. But this primary idea rests upon an entirely different base with them than with him. With them it comes from logical speculation upon the harmonies of nature and of the infinite; with him it comes from a contemplation that plunges into the mysteries of nature. Tyrannically, they force nature to conform to their system: this is what creates a chasm between them that no bridge will ever span. Still he tries to penetrate as far as possible into their thinking.

Goethe separates from Schelling when the latter abandons the idea of the absolute identity of God and nature, as Jacobi had recently done, and places the revelation of God as given by religion on a higher plane than that given by nature.

Goethe has great sympathy for Hegel; he appreciates his scientific and historic knowledge. Hegel, for his part, defends Goethe's theories about light and shows great comprehension for Goethe's researches in natural science.

On February 4, 1829, Goethe declares to Eckermann: "Hegel is certainly an eminent man, and the things he says are excellent if one transposes them into his own language."

At a tea given by Goethe on October 18, 1827, in honor of Hegel, who was then staying in Weimar, the guest praises dialectics as the infallible method for discovering truth, to which his host replies by remarking that it also serves to make the false true, and the true false. Then Goethe goes on to praise the study of nature, where one deals with the true infinite and eternal, which no subtlety of logic can change.

Goethe always sees clearly that speculative philosophy, however important and interesting its ideas might be, is untenable, and that it must at last give place to a philosophy of nature that objectively scrutinizes reality. In this expectant attitude, which he alone among his contemporaries holds, he is right.

To summarize: Goethe borrows nothing from any of the philosophies with which he is in contact. Thanks, however, to his conscientious study of the thought of others, he attains an ever-clearer grasp of his own ideas.

Nowhere has Goethe given a general résumé of his conception of the world. But the ideas contained in his works, or scattered through his letters and his conversations, fall into place in a simple and unified philosophy.

Goethe's philosophy is a philosophy of nature based upon an elementary view of reality. The dominant idea of it is this: only that knowledge is true that adds nothing to nature, either by thought or imagination, and that recognizes as valid only what comes from a research that is free from prejudices and preconceptions, from a firm and pure determination to find the truth, from a meditation that goes deeply into the heart of nature.

The knowledge that this research will give us of God, of the world, and of man, whether it is great or small, will be sufficient to validate our life. Of this Goethe is persuaded.

If thought in all simplicity and truth sticks closely to nature, it cannot admit that there is any existence outside of nature. It must, therefore, stop thinking of God as a being directing nature from outside. It will not be able to conceive of him except as existing and working within nature. To recognize the identity of God and nature is then, according to Goethe, the point of departure for all subsequent thinking.

Therefore, all things are in God and God is in all things.

Goethe professes this pantheistic mysticism in his poetic writings under forms that are ever new and diverse. At bottom this is nothing but the fundamental conviction that always remains the same in European mysticism, whether ancient, medieval, or modern, whenever it passes beyond the obscure stage of feeling and seeks to rise into the sphere of thinking. The mysticism of Goethe has this in common with that of Giordano Bruno (and this is what distinguishes it from that of the Stoics, the medieval mystics, and Spinoza): it is allied with the veneration and the vital contemplation of nature. Its distinguishing characteristic is this, that far from ignoring the natural sciences or setting itself above them by some speculative effort, it wishes to be the consequence of them. From that comes its importance and its austere flavor.

The spirit that animates the philosophy of Goethe is revealed in striking fashion in words spoken to Soret in Goethe's old age: "Nature is always true, always serious, always severe; it is always right and mistakes and errors are always the work of men. It disdains the incapable, it gives itself up and reveals its secrets only to that person who is honest and pure and capable" (February 13, 1829).

Goethe professes this mysticism "of being one with God-Nature" in a time devoid of all mystic sense. In the eyes of the rationalist of the eighteenth century, the interrelations among God, man, and the world are as follows: God directs in the best possible way a world he has created as the best possible world, and, on this world stage, man practices obedience to God. This entirely esoteric idea has its origin in Christianity. The conception of God that Christianity has begotten is the result of a historic process that has raised the ethical God of the people of Israel—the God who exists outside the world—to the rank of a God who is sovereign of the universe. And the great religious problem that Christianity faces is to know how to harmonize the esoteric conception of God that results from the contemplation of nature with the exoteric idea that comes from history, without destroying it in the process.

Christianity, feeling itself threatened by every idea of God that comes from the contemplation of nature, has instinctively assumed a defensive attitude toward all forms of mysticism and pantheism. That is why it thinks of Stoicism, even though its ethics are so close to its own, as its mortal enemy. Therefore, in asserting the identity of God and nature, Goethe has to resign himself to being regarded as a pagan by his time.

Of course, he can invoke the discourse of the Apostle Paul to the Athenians. Paul, according to the account in the book of the Acts of the Apostles, cites the verse of the Greek poet Aratus, who was under the influence of Stoicism: "In him we live and move and have our being; for we are also his offspring." In this way he seems to give the mysticism of "being one with God-Nature" a rightful place in Christianity. In fact, the admirable poems of Goethe about God, the world, and man make constant allusions to these words of Stoic mysticism cited in the Acts of the Apostles. However, these words are only an erratic element in New Testament and Christian thought. It is even very problematical whether Paul actually spoke them at Athens. In his Epistles we do not find any trace of pantheistic mysticism.

Goethe's thought opens, then, a new phase of the endless strife in which the naturalistic ideas of God and the Christian ideas of God come to grips.

How does Goethe introduce the element of ethics into his nature philosophy? The great problem in every philosophy of nature is, in fact, to pass from nature to ethics. Goethe proceeds very much more simply than all of the other pantheists. The latter—for instance, the classical Stoics and Lao-tse—affirm, without being able to prove it, that life in harmony with nature has in itself a moral character; or—as in the Stoicism of Epictetus and Confucius—they even clothe nature with a moral character that it does not have at all. Or, indeed, they found their ethics, as Spinoza does, upon considerations that, at bottom, are alien to their natural philosophy and that they attach to it afterward. Goethe admits simply at the very outset that the ethical factor is given by nature. Divinity is revealed in nature by primordial phenomena, which are not only physical but also ethical (Goethe to Soret, February 13, 1829). Conceptions that take form in the course of the spiritual development of humanity are also manifestations of nature to the degree that the history of humanity is a part of the evolution of nature. The ethics of love as it is revealed in the thought of the prophets of Israel and of Jesus, and of humanity in general, are among these primordial phenomena of the moral order. Goethe, then, thinks that we know by experience, in the deepest and largest sense of this word, that God, who is identical with nature, is, in some mysterious way quite unfathomable by us, not only creative force but also moral will. In no other way could the ethical element show itself in the thought of humanity.

So Goethe can concede that we do not encounter any ethical element in nature outside ourselves and nevertheless insist that the ethical element is a natural phenomenon. The possibility of being noble, good, and helpful distinguishes man from all other beings. "For unfeeling in nature," he says in the poem entitled "The Divine":

Noble let man be,
Helpful and good!
For that alone
Sets him quite apart

From every being
Which we can know.

For unfeeling
Is all nature.

In being moral, man conforms to his own nature. To be in God-Nature means, for Goethe, to be immersed in love.

This is the way in which Goethe solves the problem of problems in philosophy and reaches a philosophy that is based on nature and still admits the ethical element. It is thus that he reconciles pantheism and Christianity.

The worldview that he attains in this manner contains in his judgment all that is necessary for living. As for all the other questions to which his thirst for knowledge would like an answer, he can be satisfied with a presentiment or can wait with resignation until such time as they disclose their secret to him.

From that time on his motto will be: "In the domain of the finite, push your research in every direction and grasp the accessible even to the primordial phenomena; as for the inaccessible, venerate it with modesty." That is what he meant when he said to Eckermann: "Man did not come into the world to solve the problem of the universe, but to find out where the problem begins, and consequently to keep himself within the bounds of the accessible" (October 15, 1825).

Having discovered just by the direct contemplation of nature the essential and the indispensable in his idea of the world, Goethe can renounce what is generally understood to be metaphysics. What is usually taught about the supra-sensible world, he describes as words without basis or meaning. "God has punished you in giving you metaphysics," he writes to Jacobi on May 8, 1786; "as for me he has blessed me by giving me physics."

"If you would make progress toward the infinite," he says in a fine maxim, "be contented in following all the roads of the finite." And again:

What is eternity?
Why art thou so tormented?
Enter thyself!
And if in consciousness thou find'st the endless not,
Then is there naught to aid thee.

All that we ought to know and can know about the supernatural is that everything that is natural has a spiritual foundation, that nothing is spiritual alone or material alone: "There are things of which I can speak to no one except God."

As for the eternal life, Goethe believes that man does not need to know any more about it than what he learns from the identity of God and nature—namely, that every ephemeral being is only a manifestation of an eternal being.

If his feeling demands a more perfect representation of what his eternal life will be, he loves to imagine that he will continue to be in some way or other an active being. This is what he means when he says to Eckermann: "The thought of death leaves me completely undisturbed, for I am firmly persuaded that our spirit is absolutely indestructible in its nature, and will be active from eternity to eternity."

We learn how he tries to imagine existence after death by a conversation he had, on the day of Wieland's funeral, with Falk, for whom he had a great esteem because Falk had founded a home for abandoned children. Still greatly moved by the loss of his venerated friend, Goethe unburdens himself in an unusual way. In picturing eternal existence, he resorts in this interview to Leibniz's doctrine of monads, although, curiously enough, he never refers to Leibniz, to whom he is much nearer than to Spinoza. The monads, he explains to Falk, are indestructible, no matter what element or what part of the universe they may belong to. Upon the death of a man, dissolution takes place, in the sense that the principal monad frees from its service the other monads that united with it during its terrestrial existence to form the corporeal being. These monads then return to the elements to which they belong. Then the principal monad becomes once more the center of a new system of monads, a creative force under a new form. Goethe is sure that he has already existed in this way thousands of times and that he will have to return to the world thousands of times again. But man, he thinks, will not necessarily live again in a human form. Why, he wonders, in this conversation, should I not admit that the indestructible element in Wieland might come to life again in the form of a brilliant star?

What would Leibniz have said to this way of using his doctrine of the monads?

Goethe, therefore, supposes that "we are not all immortal in the same way" (to Eckermann, September 1, 1829).

It will be noticed that Goethe's idea of the persistence of personality differs from the Hindu doctrine of reincarnation. On the other hand, it is found again in a similar form in certain Chinese thinkers. However, Goethe is always clearly aware that every way of picturing the eternal life is full of contradictions. Moreover, he prefers not to raise the question of "how" in any way. He even goes so far as to declare on one occasion to Eckermann: "To meditate upon our eternal existence is a good occupation for men of fashion and for idle women. But the sensible man lets the world to come rest, and shows himself active and useful in this present world" (February 25, 1824).

What he really thinks about it, he has said to Chancellor von Muller, April 29, 1818:

No matter how strongly man may be attracted by the earth and its thousands of diverse phenomena, nonetheless he lifts his searching and nostalgic eyes to the heavens spread out above his head in infinite space, because he feels clearly and profoundly in his heart that he is a citizen of that spiritual realm in which we believe. We cannot help believing in it. We cannot stop believing in it.

In the same way, Goethe considers himself excused by his philosophy of nature from every effort to explain that the world means something to man, and that man's ethical life has a meaning for the world. It is here that the fundamental difference between him and all the philosophy of his day resides. In the last analysis, the rationalistic philosophy, as well as Kant and the speculative philosophy, recognizes no other purpose except to give such a meaning to the world that man himself may find a meaning for his own existence. This end forces them to construct complete systems of philosophy that greatly exceed the content of our experiences. Goethe, on the other hand, can content himself with saying: "Nature has no system; she has and is that life force which from some unknown center with one unbroken and continuous effort leads toward an indeterminable goal." He never tires of insisting that in nature nothing is an end in respect to some other end but that "every creature is an end to itself." In his mind, nature's design, so far as we can speak of a design, is realized to the extent to which each creature achieves fully its own life. "In nature nothing occurs which is not in close relation to the whole" (*Experience as an Intermediary between Object and Subject*, 1792).

Therefore, man does not need to understand the significance of the universe in order to give meaning to his life and his moral activity. It is by an inner necessity that man must be moral, for this necessity is a part of his being.

Goethe's ethics, therefore, like those of Kant, rest upon a categorical imperative. But the moral activity that springs from an inner necessity is much more simply based for him than it is for Kant.

According to Goethe, becoming moral consists not in a man's introducing moral thoughts into his nature but rather in providing a continuous effort toward "ennoblement," in the course of which he strives to free himself from the non-moral elements of his nature and to let all that is good within him achieve its full flowering.

This idea of "ennoblement" dominates all of Goethe's ethics. It is he, not Nietzsche, who is the first to recognize that the great ethical problem is to reconcile the ennoblement of man—that is, the realization of his own nature—with his duty to achieve goodness. He solves the problem by affirming that man never truly realizes himself except through becoming genuinely good.

This idea of Goethe's—that the noble and the good, in the traditional sense of the word, merge—will still retain all its vitalizing force in the thinking of humanity when the revolt of Nietzsche against the traditional idea of the good, and his superman, about which there has been so much ado, will be considered as nothing but an episode in the philosophical history of the nineteenth century.

Goethe seeks to achieve this ennoblement in his own person. His greatest desire in life, he confesses, is to achieve an ideal ever more pure and clear. He labors, with the greatest seriousness, to make the sincerity and the nobility that nature has given him the dominant traits of his character. Ceaselessly, he tries to realize his motto: "Live in peace with the world." This love of truth, of purity, of peace, is responsible for the grandeur and the serenity of his soul.

In a letter to Schelling, he feels himself justified in affirming that he has never permitted himself to utter the least complaint against all the hostility, overt or secret, of which he has been the object.

One criticism often made of the ethics of Goethe is that it lacks enthusiasm. This is true: the fire of passion seems strangely faint within it; nonetheless, a marvelous clarity emanates from it. What is lacking in vitality in his ethics of love is made up for by profundity.

Goethe is an ardent adversary of his contemporary, the English moralist Bentham. The latter, in his fanatical utilitarianism, insists that every individual should try everywhere and in everything to see that his activity conduces to the greatest possible good for the greatest number of people. Goethe, in ill humor, characterizes Bentham as an "old fool" and says that by this postulate he does offense to the individual human life and throws disorder into the life of society. "Do not compel me," Goethe says to Soret in 1830, "to take the greatest good to the community as a controlling test for my profoundly personal existence." The greatest good to the greatest number cannot, in Goethe's eyes, be realized by abolishing the natural bonds between the individual and society. The maximum of love and, consequently, the maximum of well-being, will not be attained unless each individual develops within himself, in the most perfect and personal way, the love that nature has put into his heart. In thus taking issue with the utilitarianism of which Bentham is one of the devoted supporters, Goethe reminds us of how Lao-tse rejected the moral utilitarianism of Confucius.

All of Goethe's ethics is contained in these words: "Be true to yourself as to others."

This ethics does not exclude an active love—it implies it. "Let your aspiration be filled with love, and let your life be action," he said in *Wilhelm Meister's Travels.*

All of Goethe's life gave proof of the active love he bore in his heart. He believed his special mission was to sympathize with and to provide for all moral or spiritual distress that he encountered. He was forced to do this, he said at one time, by "a tyrannical habit." He did not withhold his aid from anyone who might have need of it. How beautiful are the words he spoke to Jacobi in 1781: "We should all pity one another."

On December 10, 1781, he wrote to Frau von Stein: "I pray that God will make me each day more economical that I may be generous with all I have, money or goods, life or death." And even before this, on March 12 of the same year, he wrote to her: "I pray the Graces to give me inner kindness and to conserve it in the full measure of my desire."

Vogel, the doctor who cared for Goethe in his old age, tells us that he was able to help a number of sick people with money that Goethe put at his disposal "for people who needed something more than just alms." But the benefactor forbade him to disclose his name.

The ethical thinking of Goethe is completely expressed in the fact that Wilhelm Meister, the character that most reveals his personality, is moved, by his inner experiences and by the circumstances of his life, to devote himself to others and to offer his services as a surgeon to emigrants.

What Goethe, therefore, sets forth as his moral ideal is the deepening of his inner life and its expression in moral action.

Moreover, any true ethics very naturally implies resignation, according to Goethe. In the realization that it is by an inner necessity that man works to achieve the good, he should find joy and the courage to be active. He should not expect happiness from his life or claim to see the result of his activity. He must not let himself quit when the unreasonable gets the better of the reasonable: "Whoever would act should resemble the unreasonable sower of the gospel parable who casts the seed without caring how it will spring up or where it will spring up" (letter from Goethe to Schiller).

As for himself, this is what he writes to Plessing in 1782: "All that I can say to you is that even in the midst of happiness I live in a state of constant renunciation, and that every day with all my troubles and my work I see that it is not my will that is done, but the will of a higher Power, whose thoughts are not my thoughts."

Goethe insists strongly upon the ethical character of his conception of the world and of civilization. The words that he writes to Eckermann on March 11, 1832, eleven days before his death, are like his moral testament:

Whatever progress spiritual culture may make, whatever development and deepening the sciences may achieve in an ever broader

search, whatever expansion the human spirit may win for itself,
never will we surpass the grandeur and the moral culture of Christianity, as they shine resplendently in the Gospels.

Such is Goethe's philosophy of nature. It is far from being isolated in history; it
is one of the expressions of the simple philosophy of nature, which reappears
under ever-diverse forms in the European and Chinese thinkers and always
leads to a new perfecting of its ethical ideas.

If he had set this forth systematically, it would have probably had some
influence over his epoch. It would perhaps have helped prevent European
thought, after the bankruptcy of speculative philosophy, from finding itself so
crippled in the face of the natural sciences.

But he enshrined it in his poetry, whence it blossoms for the generations
to come in flowers of ever more luminous splendor.

It is to Goethe's philosophy that we may most happily apply what he wrote
to Zelter on November 1, 1829, when he was speaking of what a man might
bequeath from his experience and his thought to posterity. This is how he
expressed it:

If one wants to leave to future generations something from which
they may profit, it should be his confessions. He should set himself
before them as a personality with his cherished thoughts and his pri-
vate opinions. His descendants will be able, if they wish, to find there
what is good for them or what is part of the eternal truth.

14

Gandhi and the Force of Nonviolence

Schweitzer argues that for Gandhi the central question is that of social and ethical education of the entire population. The ultimate goal of that education is to change the political and economic conditions that are the root of poverty. Schweitzer points out that, despite being known as the most influential proponent of nonviolence, the most important thing for Gandhi is not only that nonviolent force should be employed but that all worldly purposive action should be undertaking with the greatest possible deliberate avoidance of violence. Gandhi's greatest practical discovery is that, when ethical and spiritual considerations dominate our lives, they cannot but influence the hearts of our opponents. Gandhi has been the most important teacher of the profound truth that only activity in ethical spirit can really accomplish anything of lasting value in our world.

The philosophy of Mahatma Gandhi is a world in itself.

Born at Porbandar in 1869, Gandhi is a member of the Vaisya caste, the caste of merchants and agriculturists. After attending Indian schools up to his eighteenth year, he came to London to study Law. In 1893 an Indian firm sent him to South Africa to settle a lawsuit, and there he became acquainted with the conditions under which the Indian immigrants were living. He settled in the country as a lawyer and, up to 1914, was the leader of his countrymen in their struggles for their rights. As his method of warfare he chose passive

Selection from *Indian Thought and Its Development*, trans. Mrs. Charles E. B. Russell (Boston: Beacon, 1936), Ch. 15: "Modern Indian Thought," 225–238.

resistance, and it proved successful. In the Boer War (1899), he joined up with other Indians as a volunteer in the Ambulance Service. When the Great War broke out, he was in London and took part in the formation of an ambulance column of Indian volunteers. But at the end of the year 1914, he was obliged to return to India on account of his health, and there he began to study the economic and political problems of his home country. The cause he made his own was the liberation of the Indian laborers who had emigrated to the colonies from the regulation, which had the force of law, that they must be bound by a five years' contract. He fought also for the abolition of abuses on the indigo plantations in Northern India. He became the representative of the rights of the operatives in spinning factories in Ahmedabad, who were at variance with their masters, and of the peasants of the Khaira district, who had got into debt through the failure of their harvest, when they were in conflict with the taxation authorities. By threatening or organizing passive resistance, he always succeeded in gaining recognition for the demands he represented.

When the war was over (1919), he had recourse to similar methods to prevent the passing of exceptional laws against political agitators (the so-called Rowlatt Bills) but discovered that passive resistance in the Panjab led to violent revolutionary movements that were suppressed by the authorities with great severity. He was also disappointed that the British government did nothing after the war to preserve the throne of the sultan at Constantinople, whom the Indian Mohammedans regarded as their religious overlord. In his endeavor to bring about an agreement between the Hindus and Mohammedans, he had made the claims of the latter his own.

In 1920, in common with the Hindu and Mohammedan popular leaders, he formed the momentous resolve to give up cooperation with the British government. In the course of the passive resistance movement to champion the idea of the independence of the Indian people and promote the boycott of imported factory-made materials in favor of the resuscitation of Indian hand-spinning and hand-weaving, serious disturbances occurred in Bombay and Chauri Chaura. As the originator of civil resistance to the authority of the state, Gandhi was condemned to six years' imprisonment, but after some time (1924) he was pardoned. In the years that followed, the enmity that had broken out afresh between Hindus and Mohammedans caused him great grief.

In recent years, withdrawn from politics, he has devoted himself mainly to the question of the social and ethical education of the people. In the forefront of the reforms that must be achieved, he places the removal of the existing prejudices against members of the lowest castes, the so-called Untouchables, who number some fifty million; the abolition of child marriage; the recognition of the principle that women should have equal rights with men; and the complete control of alcohol and poisonous drugs.

Never before has any Indian taken so much interest in concrete realities as has Gandhi. Others were, for the most part, contented to demand a charitable attitude to the poor. But he—and in this his thought is just like that of a modern European—wants to change the economic conditions that are at the root of poverty.

Ninety percent of the population of India lives in villages. During the dry season, which lasts for about six months of the year, work on the land is at a standstill. Formerly, the people made use of this time for spinning and weaving. But since materials manufactured outside India as well as in Indian factories have governed the market, these home industries have been ruined. It is because the villagers have lost their former income from these secondary occupations that there is so much poverty in country districts. And the idleness involved has disastrous results.

Gandhi preaches a healthy feeling for reality when he tries to make it possible for the villagers to take up their hand-spinning and hand-weaving once more and tells them that it is their duty to do so. He rightly sees that here we have the preliminaries of a competition between hand-work and machine-work and that the development of the situation must be guided as far as possible in the interest of the people.

Gandhi is no blind enemy of machines. Insofar as they are necessary, he gives them their due. But he will not agree to their ruining a manual industry that, in itself, is capable of survival. He has great appreciation for the sewing machine, but he still rejects the motorcar although, as promoting intercourse between one village and another, it is in many respects the natural ally of home industries.

His program of village reform also includes the provision of better dwellings and better hygienic conditions and the introduction of rational methods of farming.

The first impulse to the high esteem in which he holds bodily labor and the way of life of the agriculturist and artisan came to him from Ruskin's *Unto This Last,* which he read while he was living in South Africa. He confesses that this book caused an immediate change in his view of life.

Gandhi's feeling for reality is seen also in his relations to the *ahimsā* commandment. He is not satisfied with praising it but examines it critically. He is concerned at the fact that, in spite of the authority of this commandment, there is in India such a lack of pity both for animals and for mankind. He ventures to say, "I hardly think that the fate of animals is so sad in any other country in the world as it is in our own poor India. We cannot make the English responsible for this; nor can we excuse ourselves by pleading our poverty. Criminal neglect is the only cause of the deplorable condition of our cattle."

The fact that the *ahimsā* commandment has not educated the people to a really compassionate attitude he attributes to its having been followed more in the letter than in the spirit. People have thought they were obeying it sufficiently by avoiding killing and causing of pain, while, in reality, the commandment is fulfilled only by the complete practice of compassion.

It is not clear to Gandhi that it belongs to the original nature of the *ahimsā* commandment only to demand abstinence from killing and hurting, and not the complete exercise of compassion. He took upon himself to go beyond the letter of the law against killing, and this, moreover, in a case where he came into conflict with the Hindu reverence for horned cattle. He ended the sufferings of a calf in its prolonged death agony by giving it poison. By this act he caused his Hindu adherents no less offense than when, for the first time, he received untouchables at his settlement (*ashram*).

Thus, in Gandhi's ethical life affirmation, *ahimsā* is freed from the principle of non-activity in which it originated and becomes a commandment to exercise full compassion. It becomes a different thing from what it was in the thought of ancient India.

And through his feelings for reality, Gandhi also arrives at the admission that the commandment not to kill and not to injure cannot be carried out in entirety because man cannot maintain life without committing acts of violence. So, with a heavy heart, he gives permission to kill dangerous snakes and allows the farmer to defend himself against the monkeys that threaten his harvest.

It is one of the most important of Gandhi's acts that he compels Indian ethics openly to come to grips with reality.

So great is his interest in what is worldly that he also has sympathy with sports and games. He demands that, in the schools, as much time should be given to bodily exercises as to the training of the mind, and laments that in his boyhood there were no games, so that he had to be contented with long walks up hill and down dale. So, in one corner, his world- and life-affirmation is marked "Made in England."

But with this feeling for and interest in what is real, there is united in him a purely immaterial idea of what activity is. For him it is an established principle that material problems can be solved only by the spirit. He is convinced that since all that happens in human affairs is conditioned by mind, things can be improved only by bringing about a different state of mind. So, in all that we undertake, we must be careful to make our own mind influence other minds. According to him, the only real forces at our disposal are the spirit of freedom from hatred and the spirit of love. He regards the belief that worldly ends must be pursued by worldly methods as the fatal error responsible for the misery that prevails on this earth.

Gandhi continues what the Buddha began. In the Buddha the spirit of love set itself the task of creating different spiritual conditions in the world; in Gandhi it undertakes to transform *all* worldly conditions.

And according to Gandhi, political activity as well must be governed by the spirit of *ahimsā*. "For me," he wrote in a letter, "there are no politics that are not at the same time a religion."

But is the passive resistance of which Gandhi makes such abundant use to realize his objects really a non-worldly method, derived from the spirit of *ahimsā*, of championing the cause of good in the world against its opponents? Only partly so.

In themselves, *ahimsā* and passive resistance are two quite different things. Only *ahimsā* is non-worldly; passive resistance is worldly.

The ancient Indian *ahimsā* is an expression of world- and life-negation. It sets before it no aims that are to be realized in the world but is simply the most profound effort to attain to the state of keeping completely pure from the world.

But Gandhi places *ahimsā* at the service of world- and life-affirmation directed to activity in the world. With him *ahimsā* engages in activity within the world, and in this way it ceases to be what in essence it is.

Passive resistance is a nonviolent use of force. The idea is that, by circumstances brought about without violence, pressure is brought to bear on the opponent and he is forced to yield. Being an attack that is more difficult to parry than an active attack, passive resistance may be the more successful method. But there is also a danger that this concealed application of force may cause more bitterness than would an open use of violence. In any case, the difference between passive and active resistance is only quite relative.

When Gandhi enlists *ahimsā* in the service of passive resistance, he unites the non-worldly and the worldly. He has not been spared the painful experience that, in such circumstances, the worldly may prove stronger than the non-worldly.

One can even question whether this has not often been the case with himself. Most often he has applied the principle of passive resistance without leaving his opponent the necessary time to come to meet him halfway. There is, in his character, a vehemence that prevents him from patiently letting his confidence rest in the purely spiritual operation of an idea. He has never succeeded in altogether controlling the agitator within his breast.

He is confident that by the non-worldly he can completely spiritualize and ennoble what is worldly, and he really seriously believes that he can practice passive resistance entirely in the spirit of freedom from hatred and of love.

Again and again he points out to his followers that the justification, the reason and the success of what they join him in undertaking for the good of the people is dependent on whether their minds are completely purified. And again and again he emphasizes his conviction that passive resistance, exercised in the spirit of *ahimsā*, must not only be concerned with the achievement of this purpose or that, but that its real aim must be to bring about a mutual understanding founded on love. The nonviolent violence of passive resistance must merely form the riverbed for the floodwaters of the spirit of love.

Thus, then, does Gandhi try to solve the problem of whether, along with action by ethical and spiritual means, action by worldly means can also be justified. He sets up the first as a principle and at the same time retains a minimum of worldly procedure, the exercise, namely, of nonviolent force; and this he places at the service of the ethical and the spiritual.

It must remain a question whether the restriction to nonviolent force and the combination of this (as being the procedure regarded as the least worldly) with the ethical and spiritual method is the right solution of the problem. All mixing up of what is different in essence is an unnatural and dangerous proceeding.

There can also come under consideration a solution that refuses such a limitation of the use of force and in this way upholds the separation between the worldly and the ethical and spiritual. The method is as follows. In combination with the ethical and spiritual means, recourse will be had to worldly purposive procedure. But when the use of force seems unavoidable, then as little force as possible will be employed. And it will be used in such a way that it is regarded only as a last expedient and will be exercised not in a worldly but in an ethical spirit. The important thing is not that only nonviolent force should be employed but that all worldly purposive action should be undertaken with the greatest possible avoidance of violence and that ethical considerations should so dominate ourselves as to influence also the hearts of our opponents. In as far as possible restricting worldly procedure; in explaining and justifying it; in making it effective in the right way, through the ethical disposition that lies behind it: in *such* an application of force in the spirit of nonviolence lies the solution of the problem. But even if one doubts whether Gandhi's method is right in itself and whether the way he has carried out his experiment can give satisfaction, one must nevertheless recognize his extraordinary service in having opened up the problem of activity and pointed to the profound truth that only activity in an ethical spirit can really accomplish anything.

The fact that Gandhi has united the idea of *ahimsā* to the idea of activity directed on the world has the importance not merely of an event in the thought of India but in that of humanity. Through him the attention of ethics is again directed to a fact that had been too much neglected; namely, that the use of force does not become ethically permissible because it has an ethical aim but that, in addition, it must be applied in a completely ethical disposition.

In a conversation with his friend, the Reverend J. J. Doke, a Baptist minister of Johannesburg, Gandhi said that he got the idea of passive resistance in the spirit of *ahimsā* from the sayings of Jesus, "But I say unto you, that ye resist not evil," and "Love your enemies . . . pray for them which despitefully use you and persecute you; that ye may be the children of your Father which is in heaven." And then his idea developed under the influence of the *Bhagavad-Gita* and Tolstoy's *Kingdom of God Is within You.*

It is hard to explain the fact that Gandhi's attitude to war is not completely determined by *ahimsā*. That he served in the Boer War as a volunteer in the Ambulance Corps and would have done the same in the Great War, if he had not been compelled by his health to give up the project, can be understood by his anxiety to alleviate the misery of war; but that in India he tried to enlist volunteers for service as combatants is absolutely irreconcilable with *ahimsā*. He allowed himself to be led astray by the consideration that by such help given in her time of need, England might be induced to recognize the rights of the Indian people. But *ahimsā* is a principle high uplifted above all politics.

And from the standpoint of *ahimsā*, it is strange that Gandhi regards it as so important that his people should retain the right to arm themselves.

Great as is Gandhi's interest in reality, world- and life-negation nevertheless plays a part in his mode of thought.

Gandhi is concerned with the welfare of the people, but at the same time he disavows the ideal of achieving national prosperity. He wishes property to be restricted to what is absolutely necessary for the maintenance of life. Even those who have the means shall not allow themselves to lead a life adjusted to higher pretensions. Through this ideal of the smallest possible needs and smallest possible possessions, Gandhi expects that civilization will be cured of its ills. The fact that he is in agreement with Tolstoy about this is to him a proof that he is championing the right.

World- and life-negation is very strongly expressed in his *Confession of Faith* (1909), which treats of true civilization. In this he adjudges to quack medicine superiority over modern medical science. "The salvation of India," so runs one passage, "lies in its forgetting all it has learnt during the last fifty years. Railways, telegraphs, hospitals, lawyers, doctors and the rest must one and all disappear, and the so-called upper classes must learn conscientiously, piously, and thoughtfully to lead the life of the simple peasant because they recognize that this is the life that bestows real happiness upon us."

Later, in prison, while suffering the tortures of appendicitis, he resolved to accept the aid that the modern scientific art of healing he had so severely condemned could bring him. He allowed an operation to be performed. But he cannot get rid of the thought that, in this, he had acted contrary to his real conviction. "I admit," he wrote in a letter to a Brahmin ascetic who had taken him to task about this apostasy, "that it was a weakness of soul to submit to the surgical operation. Had I been altogether free from self-seeking, I should have resigned myself to the inevitable; but I was mastered by the wish to go on living in this body of mine."

Of late, he has nevertheless allowed that modern medicine and modern hospitals may be in some measure justified.

His world- and life-negation comes to full expression when he not only demands the taming of the desires but sets up the ideal of celibacy.

He knows from experience the misery of child-marriage. His family brought about his marriage when he was thirteen years of age. His wife has proved a faithful and patient life companion. Four sons were born of the marriage.

Gandhi supports celibacy on two grounds. The first is his view that only the man who has renounced all desires possesses the spirituality necessary for true activity. He wrote once, "Whoever wishes to dedicate himself to the service of his country or to perceive something of the glory of the truly religious life must lead a life of chastity, whether he be married or unmarried." The second reason lies in his belief in reincarnation. To a question as to his attitude to marriage, he replied, "The goal of life is redemption. As a Hindu I believe that this redemption—we call it *moksha*—consists in deliverance from re-birth; it is then that we burst the fetters of the flesh, it is then that we become one with God. Now marriage is a hindrance on the way to the highest goal in so far namely as it draws the bonds of the flesh still tighter. Celibacy on the other hand is a powerful aid, for it makes it possible for us to lead a life of complete devotion to God."

But in spite of this strong world- and life-negation, Gandhi can no longer make his own the old ideal that is part and parcel of it—the ideal of a life withdrawn from the world. His friend the Brahmin ascetic, who advised him to retire to a cave and live for meditation alone, received the reply, "I am striving to reach the Kingdom of Heaven which is called the liberation of the soul. In order to reach this I need not seek refuge in a cave. I carry my cave with me."

By a magnificent paradox Gandhi brings the idea of activity and the idea of world- and life-negation into relationship in such a way that he can regard activity in the world as the highest form of renunciation of the world. In a letter to the Brahmin ascetic, he says, "My service to my people is part of the discipline to which I subject myself in order to free my soul from the bonds of the flesh. . . . For me the path to salvation leads through unceasing tribulation in the service of my fellow-countrymen and humanity."

So, in Gandhi's spirit, modern Indian ethical world- and life-affirmation and a world- and life-negation that goes back to the Buddha dwell side by side.

15

The Problem of Peace in the World of Today

Schweitzer was awarded the Nobel Prize for Peace in 1952, but the enormous amount of work in his hospital in Africa prevented him from coming to Europe to receive the award until the end of 1954. In his Nobel Prize address, Schweitzer outlines his own understanding of the political and moral situation in the world, with special attention to the inadequacy of peace established at the end of both world wars. Because of the growing threat of nuclear weapons, he offers a criticism of war on moral grounds by calling war "an evil far graver than in former times." Schweitzer praises Kant for his humanitarian ideas but argues that "perpetual peace" cannot be achieved by political changes and by the establishment of new institutions (such as the League of Nations or the United Nations). The issue of peace is fundamentally an ethical issue, an issue that demands that we turn away from nationalisms of various kinds and pursue a universal humanitarian ideal. Only the pursuit of such an ideal, together with further development of individual spirituality, can create an atmosphere of trust and the foundation for a lasting and genuine peace.

For the subject of my lecture, a redoubtable honor imposed by the award of the Nobel Peace Prize, I have chosen the problem of peace as it is today. In so doing, I believe that I have acted in the spirit of

Complete essay; this is Schweitzer's Nobel Peace Prize address, delivered in Oslo, Norway, on November 4, 1954; reprinted here from the official Web site of the Nobel Prize Organization (http://nobleprize.org/nobel_prizes/peace/laureates/1952/schweitzer-lecture-e.html).

the founder of this prize, who devoted himself to the study of the problem as it existed in his own day and age, and who expected his foundation to encourage consideration of ways to serve the cause of peace.

I shall begin with an account of the situation at the end of the two wars through which we have recently passed.

The statesmen who were responsible for shaping the world of today through the negotiations that followed each of these two wars found the cards stacked against them. Their aim was not so much to create situations that might give rise to widespread and prosperous development as it was to establish the results of victory on a permanent basis. Even if their judgment had been unerring, they could not have used it as a guide. They were obliged to regard themselves as the executors of the will of the conquering peoples. They could not aspire to establishing relations between peoples on a just and proper basis; all their efforts were taken up by the necessity of preventing the most unreasonable of the demands made by the victors from becoming reality; they had, moreover, to convince the conquering nations to compromise with each other whenever their respective views and interests conflicted.

The true source of what is untenable in our present situation—and the victors are beginning to suffer from it as well as the vanquished—lies in the fact that not enough thought was given to the realities of historical fact and, consequently, to what is just and beneficial.

The historical problem of Europe is conditioned by the fact that, in past centuries, particularly in the so-called era of the great invasions, the peoples from the East penetrated farther and farther into the West and Southwest, taking possession of the land. So it came about that the later immigrants intermingled with the earlier, already established immigrants.

A partial fusion of these peoples took place during this time, and new relatively homogeneous political societies were formed within the new frontiers. In western and central Europe, this evolution led to a situation that may be said to have crystallized and become definitive in its main features in the course of the nineteenth century.

In the East and Southeast, on the other hand, the evolution did not reach this stage; it stopped with the coexistence of nationalities that failed to merge. Each could lay some claim to rightful ownership of the land. One might claim territorial rights by virtue of longer possession or superiority of numbers, while another might point to its contribution in developing the land. The only practical solution would have been for the two groups to agree to live together in the same territory and in a single political society, in accordance with a compromise acceptable to both. It would have been necessary, however, for this state of affairs to have been reached before the second third of the nineteenth century.

For, from then on, there was increasingly vigorous development of national consciousness, which brought with it serious consequences. This development no longer allowed peoples to be guided by historical realities and by reason.

The First World War, then, had its origins in the conditions that prevailed in eastern and southeastern Europe. The new order created after both world wars bears in its turn the seeds of a future conflict.

Any new postwar structure is bound to contain the seeds of conflict unless it takes account of historical fact and is designed to provide a just and objective solution to problems in the light of that fact. Only such a solution can be really permanent.

Historical reality is trampled underfoot if, when two peoples have rival historical claims to the same country, the claims of only one are recognized. The titles that two nations hold to disputed parts of Europe never have more than a relative value since the peoples of both are, in effect, immigrants.

Similarly, we are guilty of contempt for history if, in establishing a new order, we fail to take economic realities into consideration when fixing frontiers. Such is the case if we draw a boundary so as to deprive a port of its natural hinterland or raise a barrier between a region rich in raw materials and another particularly suited to exploiting them. By such measures we create states that cannot survive economically.

The most flagrant violation of historical rights, and indeed of human rights, consists in depriving certain peoples of their right to the land on which they live, thus forcing them to move to other territories. At the end of the Second World War, the victorious powers decided to impose this fate on hundreds of thousands of people, and under the most harsh conditions. From this we can judge how little aware they were of any mission to work toward a reorganization that would be reasonably equitable and that would guarantee a propitious future.

Our situation ever since the Second World War has been characterized essentially by the fact that no peace treaty has yet been signed. It was only through agreements of a truce-like nature that the war came to an end; and it is, indeed, because of our inability to effect a reorganization, however elemental, that we are obliged to be content with these truces that, dictated by the needs of the moment, can have no foreseeable future.

This then is the present situation. How do we perceive the problem of peace now?

In quite a new light—different to the same extent that modern war is different from war in the past. War now employs weapons of death and destruction incomparably more effective than those of the past and is consequently a worse evil than ever before. Heretofore, war could be regarded as an evil to which men must resign themselves because it served progress and was even necessary to it. One could argue that, thanks to war, the peoples with the strongest virtues survived, thus determining the course of history.

It could be claimed, for example, that the victory of Cyrus over the Babylonians created an empire in the Near East with a civilization higher than that which it supplanted, and that Alexander the Great's victory, in its turn, opened the way, from the Nile to the Indus, for Greek civilization. The reverse, however, sometimes occurred when war led to the replacement of a superior civilization by an inferior one, as it did, for instance, in the seventh century and at the beginning of the eighth, when the Arabs gained mastery over Persia, Asia Minor, Palestine, North Africa, and Spain, countries that had hitherto flourished under a Greco-Roman civilization.

It would seem then that, in the past, war could operate just as well in favor of progress as against it. It is with much less conviction that we can claim modern war to be an agent of progress. The evil that it embodies weighs more heavily on us than ever before.

It is pertinent to recall that the generation preceding 1914 approved the enormous stockpiling of armaments. The argument was that a military decision would be reached with rapidity and that very brief wars could be expected. This opinion was accepted without contradiction.

Because they anticipated the progressive humanization of the methods of war, people also believed that the evils resulting from future conflicts would be relatively slight. This supposition grew out of the obligations accepted by nations under the terms of the Geneva Convention of 1864, following the efforts of the Red Cross. Mutual guarantees were exchanged concerning care for the wounded, the humane treatment of prisoners of war, and the welfare of the civilian population. This convention did indeed achieve some significant results, for which hundreds of thousands of combatants and civilians were to be thankful in the wars to come. But, compared to the miseries of war, which have grown beyond all proportion with the introduction of modern weapons of death and destruction, they are trivial indeed. Truly, there can be no question of humanization of war.

The concept of the brief war and that of the humanization of its methods, propounded as they were on the eve of war in 1914, led people to take the war less seriously than they should have. They regarded it as a storm that was to clear the political air and as an event that was to end the arms race that was ruining nations.

While some lightheartedly supported the war on account of the profits they expected to gain from it, others did so from a more noble motive: this war must be the war to end all wars. Many a brave man set out for battle in the belief that he was fighting for a day when war would no longer exist.

In this conflict, just as in that of 1939, these two concepts proved to be completely wrong. Slaughter and destruction continued year after year and were carried on in the most inhumane way. In contrast to the war of 1870, the duel was not between two isolated nations but between two great groups of nations, so that a large share of mankind became embroiled, thus compounding the tragedy.

Since we now know what a terrible evil war is, we must spare no effort to prevent its recurrence. To this reason must also be added an ethical one: in the course of the last two wars, we have been guilty of acts of inhumanity that make one shudder, and in any future war we would certainly be guilty of even worse. This must not happen!

Let us dare to face the situation. Man has become superman. He is a superman because he not only has at his disposal innate physical forces, but also commands, thanks to scientific and technological advances, the latent forces of nature that he can now put to his own use. To kill at a distance, man used to rely solely on his own physical strength; he used it to bend the bow and to release the arrow. The superman has progressed to the stage where, thanks to a device designed for the purpose, he can use the energy released by the combustion of a given combination of chemical products. This enables him to employ a much more effective projectile and to propel it over far greater distances.

However, the superman suffers from a fatal flaw. He has failed to rise to the level of superhuman reason that should match that of his superhuman strength. He requires such reason to put this vast power to solely reasonable and useful ends and not to destructive and murderous ones. Because he lacks it, the conquests of science and technology become a mortal danger to him rather than a blessing.

In this context is it not significant that the first great scientific discovery, the harnessing of the force resulting from the combustion of gunpowder, was seen at first only as a means of killing at a distance?

The conquest of the air, thanks to the internal-combustion engine, marked a decisive advance for humanity. Yet, men grasped at once the opportunity it offered to kill and destroy from the skies. This invention underlined a fact that had hitherto been steadfastly denied: the more the superman gains in strength, the poorer he becomes. To avoid exposing himself completely to the destruction unleashed from the skies, he is obliged to seek refuge underground, like a hunted animal. At the same time, he must resign himself to abetting the unprecedented destruction of cultural values.

A new stage was reached with the discovery and subsequent utilization of the vast forces liberated by the splitting of the atom. After a time, it was found that the destructive potential of a bomb armed with such was incalculable and that even large-scale tests could unleash catastrophes threatening the very existence of the human race. Only now has the full horror of our position become obvious. No longer can we evade the question of the future of mankind.

But the essential fact, which we should acknowledge in our conscience, and which we should have acknowledged a long time ago, is that we are becoming inhuman to the extent that we become supermen. We have learned to tolerate the facts of war: that men are killed en masse—some twenty million in the Second World War—that whole cities and their inhabitants are annihilated by the atomic bomb, that men are turned into living torches by incendiary bombs. We learn of these things from the radio or newspapers, and we judge them according to whether they signify success for the group of peoples to which we belong, or for our enemies. When we do admit to ourselves that such acts are the results of inhuman conduct, our admission is accompanied by the thought that the very fact of war itself leaves us no option but to accept them. In resigning ourselves to our fate without a struggle, we are guilty of inhumanity.

What really matters is that we should all of us realize that we are guilty of inhumanity. The horror of this realization should shake us out of our lethargy so that we can direct our hopes and our intentions to the coming of an era in which war will have no place.

This hope and this will can have but one aim: to attain, through a change in spirit, that superior reason that will dissuade us from misusing the power at our disposal.

The first to have the courage to advance purely ethical arguments against war and to stress the necessity for reason governed by an ethical will was the great humanist Erasmus of Rotterdam in his *Querela pacis* (The Complaint of Peace), which appeared in 1517. In this book he depicts Peace onstage, seeking an audience.

Erasmus found few adherents to his way of thinking. To expect the affirmation of an ethical necessity to point the way to peace was considered a utopian ideal. Kant shared this opinion. In his essay "Toward Perpetual Peace," which appeared in 1795, and in other publications in which he touches upon the problem of peace, he states his belief that peace will come only with the increasing authority of an international code of law, in accordance with which an international court of arbitration would settle disputes between nations. This authority, he maintains, should be based entirely on the increasing respect that, in time, and for purely practical motives, men will hold for the law as such. Kant is unremitting in his insistence that the idea of a league of nations cannot be hoped for as the outcome of ethical argument but only as the result of the perfecting of law. He believes that this process of perfecting will come of itself. In his opinion, "nature, that great artist" will lead men, very gradually, it is true, and over a very long period of time, through the march of history and the misery of wars, to agree on an international code of law that will guarantee perpetual peace.

A plan for a league of nations having powers of arbitration was first formulated with some precision by Sully, the friend and minister of Henry IV. It was given detailed treatment by the Abbé Castel de Saint-Pierre in three works, the most important of which bears the title *Projet de paix perpétuelle entre les souverains chrétiens* (Plan for Perpetual Peace between Christian Sovereigns). Kant was aware of the views it developed, probably from an extract that Rousseau published in 1761.

Today we can judge the efficacy of international institutions by the experience we have had with the League of Nations in Geneva and with the United Nations. Such institutions can render important services by offering to mediate conflicts at their very inception, by taking the initiative in setting up international projects, and by other actions of a similar nature, depending on the circumstances. One of the League of Nations' most important achievements was the creation in 1922 of an internationally valid passport for the benefit of those who became stateless as a consequence of war. What a position those people would have been in if this travel document had not been devised through Nansen's initiative! What would have been the fate of displaced persons after 1945 if the United Nations had not existed!

Nevertheless, these two institutions have been unable to bring about peace. Their efforts were doomed to fail since they were obliged to undertake them in a world in which there was no prevailing spirit directed toward peace. And being only legal institutions, they were unable to create such a spirit. The ethical spirit alone has the power to generate it. Kant deceived himself in thinking that he could dispense with it in his search for peace. We must follow the road on which he turned his back.

What is more, we just cannot wait the extremely long time he deemed necessary for this movement toward peace to mature. War today means annihilation, a fact that Kant did not foresee. Decisive steps must be taken to ensure peace, and decisive results obtained without delay. Only through the spirit can all this be done.

Is the spirit capable of achieving what we in our distress must expect of it?

Let us not underestimate its power, the evidence of which can be seen throughout the history of mankind. The spirit created this humanitarianism that is the origin of all progress toward some form of higher existence. Inspired by humanitarianism, we are true to ourselves and capable of creating. Inspired by a contrary spirit, we are unfaithful to ourselves and fall prey to all manner of error.

The height to which the spirit can ascend was revealed in the seventeenth and eighteenth centuries. It led those peoples of Europe who possessed it out of the Middle Ages, putting an end to superstition, witch hunts, torture, and a multitude of other forms of cruelty or traditional folly. It replaced the old with the new in an evolutionary way that never ceases to astonish those who observe it. All that we have ever possessed of true civilization, and indeed all that we still possess, can be traced to a manifestation of this spirit.

Later, its power waned because the spirit failed to find support for its ethical character in a world preoccupied with scientific pursuits. It has been replaced by a spirit less sure of the course humanity should take and more content with lesser ideals. Today, if we are to avoid our own downfall, we must commit ourselves to this spirit once again. It must bring forth a new miracle just as it did in the Middle Ages, an even greater miracle than the first.

The spirit is not dead; it lives in isolation. It has overcome the difficulty of having to exist in a world out of harmony with its ethical character. It has come to realize that it can find no home other than in the basic nature of man. The independence acquired through its acceptance of this realization is an additional asset.

It is convinced that compassion, in which ethics takes root, does not assume its true proportions until it embraces not only man but every living being. To the old ethics, which lacked this depth and force of conviction, has been added the ethics of reverence for life, and its validity is steadily gaining in recognition.

Once more we dare to appeal to the whole man, to his capacity to think and feel, exhorting him to know himself and to be true to himself. We reaffirm our trust in the profound qualities of his nature. And our living experiences are proving us right.

In 1950, there appeared a book entitled *Témoignages d'humanité* (Documents of Humanity), published by some professors from the University of Göttingen who had been brought together by the frightful mass expulsion of the eastern Germans in 1945. The refugees tell in simple words of the help they received in their distress from men belonging to the enemy nations, men who might well have been moved to hate them. Rarely have I been so gripped by a book as I was by this one. It is a wonderful tonic for anyone who has lost faith in humanity.

Whether peace comes or not depends on the direction in which the mentality of individuals develops and then, in turn, on that of their nations. This truth holds more meaning for us today than it did in the past. Erasmus, Sully, the Abbé Castel de Saint-Pierre, and the others who, in their time, were engrossed in the problem of peace dealt with princes and not with peoples. Their efforts tended to be concentrated on the establishment of a supra-national authority vested with the power of arbitrating any difficulties that might arise between princes. Kant, in his essay on perpetual peace, was the first to foresee an age when peoples would govern themselves and when they, no less than the sovereigns, would be concerned with the problem of peace. He thought of this evolution as progress. In his opinion, peoples would be more inclined than princes to maintain peace because it is they who bear the miseries of war.

The time has come, certainly, when governments must look on themselves as the executors of the will of the people. But Kant's reliance on the people's innate love for peace has not been justified. Because the will of the people, being the will of the crowd, has not avoided the danger of instability and the risk of emotional distraction from the path of true reason, it has failed to demonstrate a vital sense of responsibility. Nationalism of the worst sort was displayed in the last two wars, and it may be regarded today as the greatest obstacle to mutual understanding between peoples.

Such nationalism can be repulsed only through the rebirth of a humanitarian ideal among men that will make their allegiance to their country a natural one, inspired by genuine ideals.

Spurious nationalism is rampant in countries across the seas, too, especially among those peoples who formerly lived under white domination and who have recently gained their independence. They are in danger of allowing nationalism to become their one and only ideal. Indeed, peace, which had prevailed until now in many areas, is today in jeopardy.

These peoples, too, can overcome their naive nationalism only by adopting a humanitarian ideal. But how is such a change to be brought about? Only when the spirit becomes a living force within us and leads us to a civilization based on the humanitarian ideal will it act, through us, upon these peoples. All men, even the semicivilized and the primitive are, as beings capable of compassion, able to develop a humanitarian spirit. It abides within them like tinder ready to be lit, waiting only for a spark.

The idea that the reign of peace must come one day has been given expression by a number of peoples who have attained a certain level of civilization. In Palestine it appeared for the first time in the words of the prophet Amos in the eighth century BC and it continues to live in the Jewish and Christian religions as the belief in the Kingdom of God. It figures in the doctrine taught by the great Chinese thinkers: Confucius and Lao-tse in the sixth century BC, Mi-tse in the fifth, and Meng-tse in the fourth. It reappears in Tolstoy and in other contemporary European thinkers. People have labeled it a utopia. But the situation today is such that it must become reality in one way or another; otherwise, mankind will perish.

I am well aware that what I have had to say on the problem of peace is not essentially new. It is my profound conviction that the solution lies in our rejecting war for an ethical reason; namely, that war makes us guilty of the crime of inhumanity. Erasmus of Rotterdam and several others after him have already proclaimed this as the truth around which we should rally.

The only originality I claim is that for me this truth goes hand in hand with the intellectual certainty that the human spirit is capable of creating, in our time, a new mentality, an ethical mentality. Inspired by this certainty, I, too, proclaim this truth in the hope that my testimony may help prevent its rejection as an admirable sentiment but a practical impossibility. Many a truth has lain unnoticed for a long time, ignored simply because no one perceived its potential for becoming reality.

Only when an ideal of peace is born in the minds of the peoples will the institutions set up to maintain this peace effectively fulfill the function expected of them.

Even today, we live in an age characterized by the absence of peace; even today, nations can feel themselves threatened by other nations; even today, we must concede to each nation the right to stand ready to defend itself with the terrible weapons now at its disposal.

Such is the predicament in which we seek the first sign of the spirit in which we must place our trust. This sign can be none other than an effort on the part of peoples to atone as far as possible for the wrongs they inflicted upon each other during the last war. Hundreds of thousands of prisoners and deportees are waiting to return to their homes; others, unjustly condemned by a foreign power, await their acquittal; innumerable other injustices still await reparation.

In the name of all who toil in the cause of peace, I beg the peoples to take the first step along this new highway. Not one of them will lose a fraction of the power necessary for their own defense.

If we take this step to liquidate the injustices of the war that we have just experienced, we will instill a little confidence in all people. For any enterprise, confidence is the capital without which no effective work can be carried on. It creates in every sphere of activity conditions favoring fruitful growth. In such an atmosphere of confidence thus created we can begin to seek an equitable settlement of the problems caused by the two wars.

I believe that I have expressed the thoughts and hopes of millions of men who, in our part of the world, live in fear of war to come. May my words convey their intended meaning if they penetrate to the other part of the world—the other side of the trench—to those who live there in the same fear.

THE PROBLEM OF PEACE IN THE WORLD OF TODAY   227

May the men who hold the destiny of peoples in their hands studiously avoid anything that might cause the present situation to deteriorate and become even more dangerous. May they take to heart the words of the Apostle Paul: "If it be possible, as much as lieth in you, live peaceably with all men." These words are valid not only for individuals but for nations as well. May these nations, in their efforts to maintain peace, do their utmost to give the spirit time to grow and to act.

16

My Life Is My Argument

One of Schweitzer's most often quoted sayings is "My life is my argu-
ment." By this he refers not only to the unity of his thought but also
to the interconnectedness of his action and aspiration. Added to his
autobiography in 1931, this essay outlines two leading insights of his life:
(1) the realization that the world is inexplicably mysterious and full of
suffering, and (2) the conviction that he had been born in a period of
spiritual decline of humanity. Besides leading him to the ethics of rever-
ence for life, these two insights also convince him that ultimate moral
responsibility consists of sharing our gifts with others and of caring for
them. Schweitzer admits that his pursuit of reverence for life and service
to others has been a mixed blessing. His efforts, together with those of
many others guided by the humanitarian ideal, seemed not to bring the
desired results. After two world wars, the world appeared to be racing
toward an all-out nuclear confrontation. Despite his pessimism because
of the apparent absence of any moral purpose in the course of world
events, Schweitzer remains optimistic: because of his confidence in the
power of truth and spirit, he continues to believe in the future of human-
ity. Schweitzer concludes his autobiography with the following words: "I
look forward to the future with calmness and humility so that I may be
prepared for renunciation if it be required of me. Whether we are active

Originally published as an epilogue to Schweitzer's *My Life and Thought*, trans. C. T. Cam-
pion (London: George Allen and Unwin, 1933); reprinted here from Schweitzer, *Out of My Life and
Thought: An Autobiography*, trans. Antje Bultmann Lemke (Baltimore: John's Hopkins University
Press, 1998), 223–245.

or suffering, we must find the courage of those who have struggled to achieve the peace that passeth all understanding."

Two observations have cast their shadows over my life. One is the realization that the world is inexplicably mysterious and full of suffering, the other that I have been born in a period of spiritual decline for mankind.

I myself found the basis and the direction for my life at the moment I discovered the principle of reverence for life, which contains life's ethical affirmation. I, therefore, want to work in this world to help people think more deeply and more independently. I am in complete disagreement with the spirit of our age because it is filled with contempt for thought. We have come to doubt whether thinking will ever be capable of answering questions about the universe and our relationship to it in a way that would give meaning and substance to our lives.

Today, in addition to that neglect of thought, there is also a mistrust of it. The organized political, social, and religious associations of our time are at work convincing the individual not to develop his convictions through his own thinking but to assimilate the ideas they present to him. Any man who thinks for himself is, to them, inconvenient and even ominous. He does not offer sufficient guarantees that he will merge into the organization.

Corporate bodies do not look for their strength in ideas and in the values of the people for whom they are responsible. They try to achieve the greatest possible power, offensive as well as defensive.

Hence, the spirit of the age, instead of deploring the fact that thought seems to be unequal to its task, rejoices in it and gives it no credit for what, in spite of its imperfections, it has already accomplished. Against all evidence, it refuses to admit that human progress up until today has come about through the efforts of thought. It will not recognize that thought may in the future accomplish what it has not yet achieved. The spirit of the age ignores such considerations. Its only concern is to discredit individual thought in every way possible.

Man today is exposed throughout his life to influences that try to rob him of all confidence in his own thinking. He lives in an atmosphere of intellectual dependence, which surrounds him and manifests itself in everything he hears or reads. It is in the people whom he meets every day; it is in the political parties and associations that have claimed him as their own; it pervades all the circumstances of his life.

From every side and in the most varied ways, it is hammered into him that the truths and convictions that he needs for life must be taken away from the associations that have rights over him. The spirit of the age never lets him find himself. Over and over again, convictions are forced upon him just as he is exposed, in big cities, to glaring neon signs of companies that are rich enough to install them and enjoin him at every step to give preference to one or another shoe polish or soup mix.

By the spirit of the age, the man of today is forced into skepticism about his own thinking, so that he may become receptive to what he receives from authority. He cannot resist this influence because he is overworked, distracted, and incapable of concentrating. Moreover, the material dependence that is his lot has an effect on his mind, so he finally believes that he is not qualified to come to his own conclusions.

His self-confidence is also affected by the prodigious developments in knowledge. He cannot comprehend or assimilate the new discoveries. He is forced to accept them as givens, although he does not understand them. As a result of this attitude toward scientific truth, he begins to doubt his own judgment in other spheres of thought.

Thus, the circumstances of the age do their best to deliver us to the spirit of the age. The seed of skepticism has germinated. In fact, modern man no longer has any confidence in himself. Behind a self-assured exterior he conceals an inner lack of confidence. In spite of his great technological achievements and material possessions, he is an altogether stunted being because he makes no use of his capacity for thinking. It will always remain incomprehensible that our generation, which has shown itself so great by its discoveries and inventions, could fall so low in the realms of thought.

In a period that ridicules as antiquated and without value whatever seems akin to rational or independent thought, and which even mocks the inalienable human rights proclaimed in the eighteenth century, I declare myself to be one who places all his confidence in rational thinking. I venture to tell our generation that it is not at the end of rationalism just because past rationalism first gave way to romanticism and later to a pretended realism that reigned in intellectual as well as material life. When we have passed through all the follies of the so-called universal realpolitik, and because of it suffered spiritual misery, there will be no other choice but to turn to a new rationalism more profound and more effective than that of the past. To renounce thinking is to declare mental bankruptcy.

When we give up the conviction that we can arrive at the truth through thinking, skepticism appears. Those who work toward greater skepticism in our age expect that by denouncing all hope of self-discovered truth, men will come to accept as true whatever is forced upon them by authority and by propaganda.

But their calculations are mistaken. Whoever opens the sluices to let a flood of skepticism pour over the land cannot assume that later he can stem the flood. Only a few of those who give up the search for truth will be so docile as to submit once and for all to official doctrine. The mass of people will remain skeptical. They lose all desire for truth, finding themselves quite comfortable in a life without thought, driven now here, now there, from one opinion to another.

But merely accepting authoritarian truth, even if that truth has some virtue, does not bring skepticism to an end. To blindly accept a truth one has never reflected upon retards the advance of reason. Our world rots in deceit. Our very attempt to manipulate truth itself brings us to the brink of disaster.

Truth based on a skepticism that has become belief has not the spiritual qualities of truth that originated in thought. It is superficial and inflexible. It exerts an influence over man, but it cannot reach his inner being. Living truth is only that which has its origin in thought.

Just as a tree bears the same fruit year after year and at the same time fruit that is new each year, so must all permanently valuable ideas be continually created anew in thought. But our age pretends to make a sterile tree bear fruit by tying fruits of truth onto its branches.

Only when we gain confidence that we can find the truth through our own individual thought will we be able to arrive at living truth. Independent thought, provided it is profound, never degenerates into subjectivity. What is true in our tradition will be brought to light through deep thought, and it can become the force of reason in us. The will to sincerity must be as strong as the will to truth. Only an age that has the courage of conviction can possess truth that works as a force of spirit and of reason.

Sincerity is the foundation of the life of the mind and spirit. With its disdain for thinking, our generation has lost its feeling for sincerity. It can, therefore, be helped only by reviving the voice of thought.

Because I have this certainty, I oppose the spirit of the age and accept with confidence the responsibility for contributing to the rekindling of the fire of thought.

The concept of reverence for life is, by its very nature, especially well qualified to take up the struggle against skepticism. It is elemental.

Elemental thinking starts from fundamental questions about the relationship of man to the universe, about the meaning of life, and about the nature of what is good. It is directly linked to the thought that motivates all people. It penetrates our thought, enlarges and deepens it, and makes it more profound.

We find such elemental thinking in Stoicism. When as a student I began to study the history of philosophy, I found it difficult to tear myself away from Stoicism and to make my way through the utterly different thinking that succeeded it. It is true that the results of Stoic thought did not satisfy me, but I had the feeling that this simple kind of philosophizing was the right one. I could not understand how people had come to abandon it.

Stoicism seemed to me great in that it goes straight for its goal, is universally intelligible and at the same time profound. It makes the best of what it recognizes as truth, even if it is not completely satisfying. It puts life into that truth by seriously devoting itself to it. It possesses the spirit of sincerity and urges men to gather their thoughts and to become more inward. It arouses in them a sense of responsibility. It also seemed to me that the fundamental tenet of Stoicism is correct; namely, that man must bring himself into a spiritual relation with the world and become one with it. In its essence, Stoicism is a natural philosophy that ends in mysticism.

Just as I felt Stoicism to be elemental, so I felt that the thought of Lao-tse was the same when I became acquainted with his *Tao Te Ching*. For him, too, it is important that man come, by simple thought, into a spiritual relation with the world and prove his unity with it by his life.

There is, therefore, an essential relationship between Greek Stoicism and Chinese philosophy. The difference between them is that the first had its origin in well-developed, logical thinking, the second in intuitive thinking that was undeveloped yet marvelously profound.

This elemental thinking, however, which emerges in European as in Far Eastern philosophy, has not been able to maintain the position of leadership that it should occupy within systems of thought. It is unsuccessful because its conclusions do not satisfy our needs.

Stoic thought neglects the impulse that leads to ethical acts that manifest themselves in the will to live as it evolved with the intellectual and spiritual development of man. Hence, Greek Stoicism goes no further than the ideal of resignation, Lao-tse no further than the benign passivity that to us Europeans seems so curious and paradoxical.

The history of philosophy documents that the thoughts of ethical affirmation of life, which are natural to man, cannot be content with the results of simple logical thinking about man and his relationship to the universe. They cannot integrate themselves. Logical thought is forced to take detours via which it hopes to arrive at its goal. The detours logic has to take lead primarily to an interpretation of the universe in which ethical action has meaning and purpose.

In the late Stoicism of Epictetus, of Marcus Aurelius, and of Seneca, in the rationalism of the eighteenth century, and in that of Kung-tse (Confucius), Meng-tse (Mencius), Mi-tse (Micius), and other Chinese thinkers, philosophy starts from the fundamental problem of the relationship of man to the universe and reaches an ethical affirmation of life and of the world. This philosophy traces the course of world events back to a world will with ethical aims, and claims man for service to it.

In the thinking of Brahmanism and of the Buddha, in the Indian systems generally, and in the philosophy of Schopenhauer, the opposite explanation of the world is put forward; namely, that the life that runs its course in space and time is purposeless and must be brought to an end. The sensible attitude of man to the world is, therefore, to renounce the world and life.

Side by side with the kind of thought that is concerned with elemental issues, another kind has emerged, especially in European philosophy. I call it "secondary" because it does not focus on the relationship between man and the universe. It is concerned with the problem of the nature of knowledge, with logical speculation, with natural science, with psychology, with sociology, and with other things, as if philosophy were really concerned with the answers to all these questions for their own sake, or as if it consisted merely in sifting and systematizing the results of various sciences. Instead of urging man toward constant meditation about himself and his relationship to the world, this philosophy presents him with the results of epistemology, of logical deduction, of natural science, of psychology, or of sociology, as if it could, with the help of these disciplines, arrive at a concept of his relation with the universe.

On all these issues, this "secondary" philosophy discourses with him as if he were not a being who is in the world and lives his life in it but one who is stationed near it and contemplates it from the outside.

Because it approaches the problem of the relationship of man to the universe from some arbitrarily chosen standpoint, or perhaps bypasses it altogether, this non-elemental European philosophy lacks unity and cohesion. It appears more or less restless, artificial, eccentric, and fragmentary. At the same time, it is the richest and most universal. In its systems, half-systems, and non-systems, which succeed and interpenetrate each other, it is able to contemplate the problem of philosophy of civilization from every side and every possible perspective. It is also the most practical in that it deals with the natural sciences, history, and ethical questions more profoundly than the others do.

The world philosophy of the future will not result in efforts to reconcile European and non-European thought but rather in the confrontation between elemental and non-elemental thinking.

Mysticism is not part of intellectual life today. By its nature, it is a kind of elemental thought that attempts to establish a spiritual relationship between man and the universe. Mysticism does not believe that logical reasoning can achieve this unity, and it therefore retreats into intuition, where imagination has free reign. In a certain sense, then, mysticism goes back to a mode of thinking that takes roundabout routes.

Since we only accept knowledge that is based on truth attained through logical reasoning, the convictions on which mysticism is founded cannot become our own. Moreover, they are not satisfying in themselves. Of all the mysticism of the past, it must be said that its ethical content is slight. It puts men on the road of inwardness but not on that of a viable ethics. The truth of philosophy is not proved until it has led us to experience the relationship between our being and that of the universe, an experience that makes us genuine human beings, guided by an active ethics.

Against the spiritual void of our age, neither non-elemental thought, with its long-winded interpretations of the world, nor the intuition of mysticism can do anything effective.

The great German philosophical systems of the early nineteenth century were greeted with enthusiasm, yet they prepared the ground on which skepticism developed.

In order to become thinking beings again, people must rediscover their ability to think, so they can attain the knowledge and wisdom they need to truly live. The thinking that starts from reverence for life is a renewal of elemental thinking. The stream that has been flowing for a long distance underground resurfaces again.

The belief that elemental thought can lead us today to an affirmative ethics of life and the world, for which it has searched in the past in vain, is no illusion.

The world does not consist of phenomena only; it is also alive. I must establish a relationship with my life in this world, insofar as it is within my reach, one that is not only passive but active. In dedicating myself to the service of whatever lives, I find an activity that has meaning and purpose.

The idea of reverence for life offers itself as the realistic answer to the realistic question of how man and the universe are related to each other. Of the universe, man knows only that everything that exists is, like himself, a manifestation of the will to live. With this universe, he stands in both a passive and an active relationship. On the one hand he is subject to the flow of world events; on the other hand he is able to preserve and build, or to injure and destroy, the life that surrounds him.

The only possible way of giving meaning to his existence is to raise his physical relationship to the world to a spiritual one. If he remains a passive being, through resignation he enters into a spiritual relationship with the world. True resignation is this: that man, feeling his subordination to the course of world events, makes his way toward inward freedom from the fate that shapes his external existence. Inward freedom gives him the strength to triumph over the difficulties of everyday life and to become a deeper and more inward person, calm and peaceful. Resignation, therefore, is the spiritual and ethical affirmation of one's own existence. Only he who has gone through the trial of resignation is capable of accepting the world.

By playing an active role, man enters into a spiritual relationship with this world that is quite different: he does not see his existence in isolation. On the contrary, he is united with the lives that surround him; he experiences the destinies of others as his own. He helps as much as he can and realizes that there is no greater happiness than to participate in the development and protection of life.

Once man begins to think about the mystery of his life and the links connecting him with the life that fills the world, he cannot but accept, for his own life and all other life that surrounds him, the principle of reverence for life. He will act according to this principle of the ethical affirmation of life in everything he does. His life will become in every respect more difficult than if he lived for himself, but at the same time it will be richer, more beautiful, and happier. It will become, instead of mere living, a genuine experience of life.

Beginning to think about life and the world leads us directly and almost irresistibly to reverence for life. No other conclusions make any sense.

If the man who has begun to think wishes to persist in merely vegetating, he can do so only by submitting to a life devoid of thought. If he perseveres in his thinking, he will arrive at reverence for life.

Any thought that claims to lead to skepticism or life without ethical ideals is not genuine thought but thoughtlessness disguised as thinking. This is manifested by the absence of any interest in the mystery of life and the world.

Reverence for life in itself contains resignation, an affirmative attitude toward the world, and ethics. These are the three essential and inseparable elements of a worldview that is the result (or fruit) of thinking.

Because it has its origin in realistic thinking, the ethics of reverence for life is realistic and leads man to a realistic and clear confrontation with reality.

It may look, at first glance, as if reverence for life were something too general and too lifeless to provide the content for a living ethics. But thinking need not worry about whether its expressions sound lively, so long as they hit the mark and have life in them. Anyone who comes under the influence of the ethics of reverence for life will very soon be able to detect, thanks to what that ethics demands from him, the fire that glows in the seemingly abstract expression. The ethics of reverence for life is the ethics of love widened into universality. It is the ethics of Jesus, now recognized as a logical consequence of thought.

Some object that this ethics sets too high a value on natural life. To this, one can respond that the mistake made by all previous ethical systems has been the failure to recognize that life as such is the mysterious value with which they have to deal. Reverence for life, therefore, is applied to natural life, and the life of the mind alike. In the parable of Jesus, the shepherd saves not merely the soul of the lost sheep but the whole animal. The stronger the reverence for natural life, the stronger also that for spiritual life.

The ethics of reverence for life is judged particularly strange because it establishes no dividing line between higher and lower, between more valuable and less valuable life. It has its reasons for this omission.

To undertake to establish universally valid distinctions of value between different kinds of life will end in judging them by the greater or lesser distance at which they stand from us human beings. Our own judgment is, however, a purely subjective criterion. Who among us knows what significance any other kind of life has in itself, as a part of the universe?

From this distinction comes the view that there can be life that is worthless, which can be willfully destroyed. Then, in the category of worthless life, we may classify various kinds of insects, or primitive peoples, according to circumstances.

To the person who is truly ethical, all life is sacred, including that which from the human point of view seems lower. Man makes distinctions only as each case comes before him, and under the pressure of necessity, as, for example, when it falls to him to decide which of two lives he must sacrifice in order to preserve the other. But all through this series of decisions, he is conscious of acting on subjective grounds and arbitrarily, and he knows that he bears the responsibility for the life that is sacrificed.

I rejoice over the new remedies for sleeping sickness, which enable me to preserve life, where once I could witness only the progress of a painful disease. But every time I put the germs that cause the disease under the microscope, I cannot but reflect that I have to sacrifice this life in order to save another.

I bought from some villagers a young osprey they had caught on a sandbank, in order to rescue it from their cruel hands. But then I had to decide whether I should let it starve, or kill a number of small fishes every day in order to keep it alive. I decided on the latter course, but every day the responsibility to sacrifice one life for another caused me pain.

Standing, as all living beings are, before this dilemma of the will to live, man is constantly forced to preserve his own life, and life in general, only at the cost of other life. If he has been touched by the ethics of reverence for life, he injures and destroys life only under a necessity he cannot avoid and never from thoughtlessness.

Devoted as I was from boyhood to the cause of protecting animal life, it is a special joy to me that the universal ethics of reverence for life shows such sympathy with animals—so often represented as sentimentality—to be an obligation no thinking person can escape. Past ethics faced the problem of the relationship between man and animal either without sensitivity or as being incomprehensible. Even when there was sympathy with animal creation, it could not be brought within the scope of ethics because ethics focused solely on the behavior of man to man.

Will the time ever come when public opinion will no longer tolerate popular amusements that depend on the maltreatment of animals!

The ethics, then, that originates in thinking is not "rational" but irrational and enthusiastic. It does not draw a circle of well-defined tasks around me but charges each individual with responsibility for all life within his reach and forces him to devote himself to helping that life.

Any profound view of the universe is mystic in that it brings men into spiritual relationship with the Infinite. The concept of reverence for life is ethical mysticism. It allows union with the infinite to be realized by ethical action. This ethical mysticism originates in logical thinking. If our will to live begins to meditate about itself and the universe, we will become sensitive to life around us and will then, insofar as it is possible, dedicate through our actions our own will to live to that of the infinite will to live. Rational thinking, if it goes deep, ends of necessity in the irrational realm of mysticism. It has, of course, to deal with life and the world, both of which are non-rational entities.

In the universe the infinite will to live reveals itself to us as will to create, and this is filled with dark and painful riddles for us. It manifests itself in us as the will to love, which resolves the riddles through our actions. The concept of reverence for life, therefore, has a religious character. The person who adopts and acts upon this belief is motivated by a piety that is elemental.

With its active ethics of love, and through its spirituality, the concept of the world that is based on respect for life is in essence related to Christianity and to all religions that profess the ethics of love. Now we can establish a lively relationship between Christianity and thought that we never before had in our spiritual life.

In the eighteenth century, Christianity, in the time of rationalism, entered into an alliance with thought. It was able to do so because, at that time, it encountered an enthusiastic ethics that was religious in character. Thought itself had not produced this ethics, however, but had unwittingly taken it over from Christianity. When, later on, it had to depend solely upon its own ethics, this proved to have little life and so little religion that it had not much in common with Christian ethics. As a consequence, the bonds between Christianity and active thought were loosened. Today Christianity has withdrawn into itself and is occupied with the propagation of its own ideas in agreement with thought but prefers to regard them as something altogether outside of, and superior to, rational thought. Christianity thereby loses its connection with the elemental spirit of the times and the possibility of exercising any real influence over it.

The philosophy of reverence for life once again poses the question of whether Christianity will or will not join hands with a form of thought that is both ethical and religious in character.

To become aware of its real self, Christianity needs thought. For centuries it treasured the great commandments of love and mercy as traditional truths without opposing slavery, witch burning, torture, and all the other ancient and medieval forms of inhumanity committed in its name. Only when it experienced the influence of the thinking of the Enlightenment was Christianity stirred up to enter the struggle for humanitarian principles. This remembrance ought to keep it forever from assuming any air of arrogance vis-à-vis thought.

Many people find pleasure today in recalling how "superficial" Christianity became in the Enlightenment. It is, however, only fair to acknowledge to what degree this "superficial" character was balanced by the services Christianity rendered in this period.

Today torture has been reestablished. In many countries the system of justice quietly tolerates torture being applied before and simultaneously with the regular proceedings of police and prison officials in order to extract confessions from those accused. The amount of suffering thus caused every hour surpasses imagination. To this renewal of torture, Christianity today offers no opposition even in words, much less in deeds.

Because Christianity hardly acts on its spiritual or ethical principles, it deceives itself with the delusion that its position as a Church becomes stronger every year. It is accommodating itself to the spirit of the age by adopting a kind of modern worldliness. Like other organized bodies it tries to prove itself by becoming an ever stronger and more uniform organization, justified and recognized through its role in history and its institutions. But as it gains external power, it loses spiritual power.

Christianity cannot take the place of thinking, but it must be founded on it. In and by itself it is not capable of overcoming thoughtlessness and skepticism. Only an age that draws its strength from thought and from an elemental piety can recognize the imperishable character of Christianity.

Just as a stream is kept from gradually drying up because it flows along above underground water, so Christianity needs the underground water of elemental piety that issues from thinking. It can attain real spiritual power only when men no longer find the road from thought to religion barred.

I know that I myself owe it to thought that I was able to retain my faith in religion.

The thinking person stands up more freely in the face of traditional religious truth than the non-thinking person and feels the intrinsic, profound, and imperishable elements much more strongly.

Anyone who has recognized that the idea of love is the spiritual ray of light that reaches us from the infinite ceases to demand from religion that it offer him complete knowledge of the metaphysical. He ponders, indeed, the great questions: What is the meaning of evil in the world? How, in God, the source of being, are the will to create and the will to love one? In what relation do the spiritual life and the material life stand to one another? And in what way is our existence transitory and yet eternal? But he is able to leave these questions unanswered, however painful that may be. In the knowledge of his spiritual union with God through love, he possesses all that is necessary.

"Love never faileth: but whether there be knowledge it shall be done away," says Paul.

The deeper is piety, the humbler are its claims with regard to knowledge of the metaphysical. It is like a path that winds between the hills instead of running over them.

The fear that a Christianity that sees the origin of piety in thought will sink into pantheism is without foundation. All living Christianity is pantheistic, since it regards everything that exists as having its origin in the source of all being. But at the same time, all ethical piety is superior to any pantheistic mysticism, in that it does not find the God of love in nature but knows about him only from the fact that he announces himself in us as the will to love. The first cause of being, as he manifests himself in nature, is to us always impersonal. To the first cause of being that is revealed to us in the will to love, however, we relate as to an ethical personality.

The belief that the Christianity that has been influenced by rational thought has lost its ability to appeal to man's conscience, to his sinfulness, is unfounded. We cannot see that sin has diminished where it has been much talked about. There is not much about it in the Sermon on the Mount. But thanks to the longing for deliverance from sin and for purity of heart that Jesus has included in the Beatitudes, these form the great call to repentance that is unceasingly working on man.

If Christianity, for the sake of any tradition or for any considerations whatever, refuses to let itself be interpreted in terms of ethical religious thinking, it will be a misfortune for itself and for mankind. Christianity needs to be filled with the spirit of Jesus and, in the strength of that, shall spiritualize itself into the living religion of inwardness and love that is its destiny. Only then can it become the leaven in the spiritual life of mankind.

What has been presented as Christianity during these nineteen centuries is merely a beginning, full of mistakes, not a full-grown Christianity springing from the spirit of Jesus.

Because I am deeply devoted to Christianity, I am trying to serve it with loyalty and sincerity. I do not attempt to defend it with the fragile and ambiguous arguments of Christian apologetics. I demand from Christianity that it reform itself in the spirit of sincerity and with thoughtfulness, so it may become conscious of its true nature.

To the question of whether I am a pessimist or an optimist, I answer that my knowledge is pessimistic, but my willing and hoping are optimistic.

I am pessimistic because I feel the full weight of what we conceive to be the absence of purpose in the course of world events. Only at rare moments have I felt really glad to be alive. I cannot help but feel the suffering all around me, not only of humanity but of the whole creation.

I have never tried to withdraw myself from this community of suffering. It seemed to me a matter of course that we should all take our share of the burden of pain that lies upon the world. Even while I was a boy at school, it was clear to me that no explanation of the evil in the world could ever satisfy me; all explanations, I felt, ended in sophistries, and at the bottom had no other object than to minimize our sensitivity to the misery around us. That a thinker like Leibniz could reach the miserable conclusion that though this world is, indeed, not good, it is the best that is possible, I have never been able to understand.

But however concerned I was with the suffering in the world, I never let myself become lost in brooding over it. I always held firmly to the thought that each one of us can do a little to bring some portion of it to an end. Thus, I gradually came to the conclusion that all we can understand about the problem is that we must follow our own way as those who want to bring about deliverance.

I am also pessimistic about the current world situation. I cannot persuade myself that it is better than it appears to be. I feel that we are on a fatal road, that if we continue to follow it, it will bring us into a new "Dark Ages." I see before me, in all its dimensions, the spiritual and material misery to which mankind has surrendered because it has renounced thinking and the ideals that thought engenders.

And yet I remain optimistic. One belief from my childhood I have preserved with a certainty I can never lose: belief in truth. I am confident that the spirit generated by truth is stronger than the force of circumstances. In my view no other destiny awaits mankind than that which, through its mental and spiritual disposition, it prepares for itself. Therefore, I do not believe that it will have to tread the road to ruin right to the end.

If people can be found who revolt against the spirit of thoughtlessness and are sincere and profound enough to spread the ideals of ethical progress, we will witness the emergence of a new spiritual force strong enough to evoke a new spirit in mankind.

Because I have confidence in the power of truth and of the spirit, I believe in the future of mankind. Ethical acceptance of the world contains within itself an optimistic willing and hoping that can never be lost. It is, therefore, never afraid to face the somber reality as it really is.

In my own life, I had times in which anxiety, trouble, and sorrow were so overwhelming that, had my nerves not been so strong, I might have broken down under the weight. Heavy is the burden of fatigue and responsibility that has lain upon me without break for years. I have not had much of my life for myself. But I have had blessings, too: that I am allowed to work in the service of compassion; that my work has been successful; that I receive from other people affection and kindness in abundance; that I have loyal helpers who consider my work as their own; that I enjoy health that allows me to undertake the most exhausting work; that I have a well-balanced temperament, which varies little, and an energy that can be exerted with calm and deliberation; and that I can recognize whatever happiness I feel and accept it as a gift.

I am also deeply grateful that I can work in freedom at a time when an oppressive dependence is the fate of so many. Though my immediate work is practical, I also have opportunities to pursue my spiritual and intellectual interests.

That the circumstances of my life have provided such favorable conditions for my work, I accept as a blessing for which I hope to prove worthy.

How much of the work I have planned shall I be able to complete?

My hair is beginning to turn gray. My body is beginning to show signs of the exertions I have demanded of it and of the passage of the years.

I look back with gratitude to the time when, without having to manage my strength, I could pursue my physical and mental activities without interruption.

I look forward to the future with calmness and humility so that I may be prepared for renunciation if it be required of me. Whether we are active or suffering, we must find the courage of those who have struggled to achieve the peace that passeth all understanding.

Chronology

January 14, 1875. Albert Schweitzer born at Kayserberg, Alsace, to Adele Schillinger Schweitzer and the Lutheran pastor Louis Schweitzer. During his first year, family moved to Gunsbach.

1880–1884. First music instructions. Attended village school, Gunsbach.

1885–1893. Student at gymnasium, Mulhausen.

1893. Began studies of theology, philosophy, and musical theory at the University of Strasbourg. Studied organ with Widor.

April 1894–April 1895. Served required military service.

1896–1899. Studied at Sorbonne and University of Berlin; also studied organ in Paris and Berlin. Began giving concerts. First publication: *Eugene Munch, 1857–1898.*

1899. Received doctorate of philosophy, University of Strasbourg. Publication of the first book: *Kant's Religious Philosophy.*

1900. Received a licentiate degree in theology; ordained as curate. Pastor of the Church of St. Nicolas in Strasbourg.

1901. Provisional appointment at St. Thomas theological seminary in Strasbourg. Publication of *The Mystery of the Kingdom of God.*

1903. Principal of the theological seminary in Strasbourg.

1905. Age 30; made decision to study medicine and go to Africa. Publication of *J. S. Bach le musicien–poète.*

1906. Began medical studies, University of Strasbourg. Publication of *The Art of Organ-Building and Organ-Playing in Germany and France* and *The Quest of the Historical Jesus.*

1908. *J. S. Bach* published.

1911. Publication of *Paul and His Interpreters.*

1912. Married Hélène Bresslau (June 18). First two volumes of Bach's *Complete Organ Works* published with Widor.

1913. Completed internship and received medical degree. Publication of *The Psychiatric Study of Jesus* and volumes 3–5 of Bach's *Complete Organ Works.* Left for Africa with Hélène (March 26).

1914. Interned as enemy alien by French authorities but eventually allowed to continue medical practice.

September, 1915. Concept of Reverence for Life, which sums up his philosophy, came to him during Ogowe River journey.

1917. The Schweitzers transferred to France as civilian interns.

1918. Returned to Alsace in an exchange of prisoners. In poor health.

1919–1923. Daughter Rhena born (January 14, 1919), on his birthday. Recovered health, lectured widely, practiced medicine, gave organ concerts, preached, wrote, and published books.

1921. *On the Edge of the Primeval Forest* published.

1923. Published the two-volume *Philosophy of Civilization* (vol. 1: "The Decay and Restoration of Civilization," and vol. 2: "Civilization and Ethics") and *Christianity and the Religions of the World.*

1924. Publication of *Memoirs of Childhood and Youth.*

1924–1927. Returned to Africa; rebuilt hospital at new location.

1927–1939. Made several trips to and from Africa. Lectured widely and played organ throughout Europe.

1930. *The Mysticism of Paul the Apostle* published.

1931. *Out of My Life and Thought: An Autobiography* published.

1934. *Indian Thought and Its Development* published.

1938. *African Notebook* published.

1939–1948. Remained in Lambaréné during World War II. Mrs. Schweitzer joins him after hazardous escape from Europe.

1948. Published *The Forest Hospital in Lambaréné* and *Goethe: Two Addresses.*

1949. First and only trip to the United States. Attended Goethe Bicentennial Convocation in Aspen, Colorado. Visited Chicago, Boston, and New York.

1950. *The Story of My Pelican* published.

1954. Accepts in Oslo, Norway, the 1952 Nobel Peace Prize and gold
replica of the Albert Schweitzer Medal of the Animal Welfare Institute.

1957. First nuclear-test ban broadcast (April 23). Death of Hélène
Schweitzer in Switzerland (June 1).

1958. Worked for nuclear-test ban treaty. April 28, 29, 30, three addresses
over Norwegian radio about nuclear war. Publication of *Peace or Atomic
War?*

1963. Endorsed a U.S. Senate bill to reduce laboratory animal suffering.
The Teaching of Reverence for Life published.

1965. Celebrates his ninetieth birthday on January 14. Died at Lambaréné
on September 4.

Bibliography

SELECTED WRITINGS OF ALBERT SCHWEITZER

African Notebook, trans. Mrs. C. E. B. Russell. 1938. Reprint, Syracuse, N.Y.: Syracuse University Press, 2003.

The African Sermons, trans. Steven E. G. Melamed, Sr. Syracuse, N.Y.: Syracuse University Press, 2002.

Albert Schweitzer: An Anthology, ed. Charles R. Joy. Boston: Beacon Press, 1947.

Albert Schweitzer: Essential Writings, ed. James Brabazon. Maryknoll, N.Y.: Orbis Books, 2005.

Albert Schweitzer on Nuclear War and Peace, ed. Homer A. Jack. Elgin, Ill.: Brethren Press, 1988.

The Animal World of Albert Schweitzer, ed. Charles R. Joy. Boston: Beacon Press, 1950.

Christianity and the Religions of the World, trans. Johanna Powers. 1923. Reprint, London, Allan and Unwin, 1939.

"The Conception of the Kingdom of God in the Transformation of Eschatology." Appendix to E. N. Mozley, *The Theology of Albert Schweitzer*.

The Essence of Faith: Philosophy and Religion. New York: Philosophical Library, 1966.

"The Ethics of Reverence for Life," *Christendom*, vol. 1, No. 2. Winter 1936, 225–239.

The Forest Hospital in Lambaréné. New York: Henry Holt, 1931.

Gesammelte Werke in fünf Bänden, ed. R. Grabs. Zürich: Ex Libris, 1974.

Goethe: Five Studies, trans. C. R. Joy. Boston: Beacon Press, 1961.

Indian Thought and Its Development, trans. Mrs. Charles E. B. Russell. Boston: Beacon Press, 1936.

J. S. Bach, trans. Ernest Newman. 2 vols. 1938. Reprint, New York: Dover, 1996.

The Kingdom of God and Primitive Christianity, trans. L. A. Garrard. New York: Seabury Press, 1968.

Memoirs of Childhood and Youth, trans. C. T. Campion. 1924. Reprint, New York: Macmillan, 1949.

More from the Primeval Forest, trans. C. T. Campion. London: A. and C. Black, 1931.

Music in the Life of Albert Schweitzer, ed. and trans. Charles R. Joy. Boston: Beacon Press, 1951.

The Mystery of the Kingdom of God: The Secret of Jesus' Messiahship and Passion, trans. Walter Lowrie. 1914. Reprint, Amherst, N.Y.: Prometheus Books, 1985.

The Mysticism of Paul the Apostle, trans. William Montgomery. 1931. Reprint, Baltimore: Johns Hopkins University Press, 1998.

On the Edge of the Primeval Forest, trans. C. T. Campion. 1922. Reprint, New York: Macmillan, 1948.

Out of My Life and Thought: An Autobiography, trans. A. B. Lemke. Baltimore: Johns Hopkins University Press, 1998.

Paul and His Interpreters, trans. William Montgomery. London. A and C. Black, 1912.

Peace or Atomic War? New York: Henry Holt, 1958.

The Philosophy of Civilization, trans. C. T. Campion. 2 vols. in 1 (vol. 1: "The Decay and Restoration of Civilization"; vol. 2: "Civilization and Ethics"). 1949. Reprint, Amherst, N.Y.: Prometheus Books, 1987.

Pilgrimage to Humanity, trans. Walter E. Stuermann. New York: Philosophical Library, 1961.

A Place for Revelation: Sermons on Reverence for Life, trans. Reginald H. Fuller. New York: Macmillan, 1988.

"The Problem of Ethics in the Evolution of Human Thought." Appendix to Jacques Feschotte, *Albert Schweitzer: An Introduction*.

The Problem of Peace in the World of Today (Schweitzer's Nobel Peace Prize Address). New York: Harper and Brothers, 1954.

The Psychiatric Study of Jesus: Exposition and Criticism, trans. Charles R. Joy. 1948. Reprint, Gloucester, Mass: Peter Smith, 1975.

The Quest of the Historical Jesus: A Critical Study of Its Progress from Reimarus to Wrede, trans. William Montgomery. London: A and C. Black, 1910. Complete English edition, ed. John Bowden. Minneapolis: Fortress Press, 2001.

"The Relations of the White and Colored Races," *The Contemporary Review*, vol. 133, January 1928, 65–70.

"Religion in Modern Civilization," *The Christian Century*, vol. 51, November 21 and 28, 1934; 1483–1484, 1519–1521.

Reverence for Life: An Anthology of Selected Writings, ed. Thomas Kernan. New York: Philosophical Library, 1965.

Reverence for Life: Sermons 1900–1919, trans. Reginald H. Fuller. 1969. Reprint, New York: Irvington Publishers, 1980.

The Spiritual Life: Selected Writings of Albert Schweitzer, ed. and trans. Charles Joy. Boston: Beacon Press, 1947.

The Story of My Pelican, trans. Martha Wardenburg. London: Souvenir, 1964.
The Teaching of Reverence for Life, trans. R. and C. Winston. New York: Holt, Rinehart and Winston, 1965.
A Treasury of Albert Schweitzer, ed. Thomas Kiernan. New York: Citadel Press, 1965.
Die Weltanshauung der Ehrfurcht vor dem Leben, ed. Claus Günzler and Johann Zürcher. 2 vols. Vol. 1: Kulturphilosophie III: Erster und zweitzer Teil. Vol. 2: Kulturphilosophie III: Dritter und vierter Teil. München: C. H. Beck, 1999–2000.

SELECTED WRITINGS ABOUT ALBERT SCHWEITZER

Anderson, Erica. *Albert Schweitzer's Gift of Friendship*. New York: Harper and Row, 1964.
———. *The Schweitzer Album: A Portrait in Words and Pictures*. New York: Harper & Row, 1965.
Barsam, Ara Paul. *Reverence for Life: Albert Schweitzer's Great Contribution to Ethical Thought*. New York: Oxford University Press, 2008.
Bentley, James. *Albert Schweitzer—The Enigma*. New York: Harper Collins, 1992.
Berman, Edgar. *In Africa with Schweitzer*. Far Hills, N.J.: New Horizon Press, 1986.
Brabazon, James. *Albert Schweitzer: A Biography*. 1975. 2nd ed. Syracuse, N.Y.: Syracuse University Press, 2000.
Cameron, James. *Point of Departure*. London: Arthur Barker, 1967.
Clark, Henry. *The Ethical Mysticism of Albert Schweitzer*. Boston: Beacon Press, 1962.
Cousins, Norman. *Albert Schweitzer's Mission: Healing and Peace*. New York: W. W. Norton, 1985.
———. *Dr. Schweitzer of Lambaréné*. New York: Harper and Brothers, 1960.
Feschotte, Jacques. *Albert Schweitzer: An Introduction*, trans. John Russell. Boston: Beacon Press, 1955.
Franck, Frederick S. *Days with Albert Schweitzer: A Lambaréné Landscape*. New York: Holt, Rinehart and Winston, 1959.
Free, Ann Cottrell. *Animals, Nature and Albert Schweitzer*. Washington, DC.: Flying Fox Press, 1988.
Grässer, Erich. *Albert Schweitzer als Theologe*. Tübingen: J. C. B. Mohr, 1979.
Günzler, Claus. *Albert Schweitzer: Einführung in sein Denken*. München: C. H. Beck, 1996.
Ice, Jackson Lee. *Albert Schweitzer: Sketches for a Portrait*. Lanham, Md.: University Press of America, 1994.
———. *Schweitzer: Prophet of Radical Theology*. Philadelphia: Westminster Press, 1971.
Ives, David, and David A. Valone, ed. *Reverence for Life Revisited: Albert Schweitzer's Relevance Today*. Cambridge: Cambridge Scholars Publishing, 2007.
Jack, Homer A. ed. *To Dr. Albert Schweitzer: A Festschrift Commemorating His 80th Birthday*. Evanston, Ill.: Friends of Albert Schweitzer, 1955.
Jilek-Aall, Louise. *Working with Dr. Schweitzer: Sharing His Reverence for Life*. Blaine, Wash.: Hancock House, 1990.

Krauss, Oskar. *Albert Schweitzer: His Work and His Philosophy*, trans. E. G. McCalman. London: Adam and Charles Black, 1944.

Langfeldt, Gabriel. *Albert Schweitzer: A Study of His Philosophy of Life*, trans. Maurice Michael. London: George Allen and Unwin, 1960.

Marshall, George. *An Understanding of Albert Schweitzer*. New York: Philosophical Library, 1966.

Marshall, George, and David Poling. *Schweitzer: A Biography*. 1971. Reprint, New York: Albert Schweitzer Fellowship and Pillar Books, 1975.

Martin, Mike W. *Albert Schweitzer's Reverence for Life: Ethical Idealism and Self-Realization*. Burlington, Vt.: Ashgate, 2007.

McKnight, Gerald. *Verdict on Schweitzer: The Man behind the Legend of Lambaréné*. New York: John Day, 1964.

Meyer, Marvin, and Kurt Bergel, ed. *Reverence for Life: The Ethics of Albert Schweitzer for the Twenty-First Century*. Syracuse: University of Syracuse Press, 2002.

Miller, David C., and James Pouilliard, ed. *The Relevance of Albert Schweitzer at the Dawn of the 21ˢᵗ Century*. Lanham, Md.: University Press of America, 1992.

Mozley, E. N. *The Theology of Albert Schweitzer for Christian Inquirers*. New York: Macmillan, 1951.

Murry, John Middleton. *Love, Freedom and Society*. London: Jonathan Cape, 1957.

Payne, Robert. *The Three Worlds of Albert Schweitzer*. New York: Thomas Nelson and Sons, 1957.

Picht, Werner. *The Life and Thought of Albert Schweitzer*, trans. Edward Fitzgerald. New York: Harper and Row, 1964.

Pierhal, Jean. *Albert Schweitzer: The Life of a Great Man*. London: Lutterwroth, 1956.

Ratter, Magnus. *Albert Schweitzer: Life and Message*. Boston: Beacon Press. 1950.

Roback, A. A. ed. *The Albert Schweitzer Jubilee Book*. Cambridge, Mass.: Sci-Art, 1945.

Seaver, George. *Albert Schweitzer: The Man and His Mind*. New York: Harper and Brothers, 1947.

Steffahn, Harald. *Albert Schweitzer*. Reinbek bei Hamburg: Rowohlt, 1979.

Urquhart, Clara. *With Dr. Schweitzer in Lambaréné*. London: George C. Harrap, 1957.

The most complete bibliography of Schweitzer, covering the years of 1898 to 1979, and including 5003 items, was compiled by Nancy Shell Griffith and Laura Person, *Albert Schweitzer: An International Bibliography* (Boston: G. K. Hall, 1981).

Index